Get the eBooks FREE!
(PDF, ePub, Kindle, and liveBook all included)

We believe that once you buy a book from us, you should be able to read it in any format we have available. To get electronic versions of this book at no additional cost to you, purchase and then register this book at the Manning website.

Go to https://www.manning.com/freebook and follow the instructions to complete your pBook registration.

That's it!
Thanks from Manning!

The Little Elixir & OTP Guidebook

The Little Elixir & OTP Guidebook

BENJAMIN TAN WEI HAO

MANNING
SHELTER ISLAND

For online information and ordering of this and other Manning books, please visit
www.manning.com. The publisher offers discounts on this book when ordered in quantity.
For more information, please contact

> Special Sales Department
> Manning Publications Co.
> 20 Baldwin Road
> PO Box 761
> Shelter Island, NY 11964
> Email: orders@manning.com

♾ Recognizing the importance of preserving what has been written, it is Manning's policy to have
the books we publish printed on acid-free paper, and we exert our best efforts to that end.
Recognizing also our responsibility to conserve the resources of our planet, Manning books
are printed on paper that is at least 15 percent recycled and processed without the use of
elemental chlorine.

Manning Publications Co.   Development editor: Karen Miller
20 Baldwin Road   Technical development editors: John Guthrie, Michael Williams
PO Box 761   Technical proofreader: Riza Fahmi
Shelter Island, NY 11964   Copy editor: Tiffany Taylor
Proofreader: Melody Dolab
Typesetter: Dottie Marsico
Cover designer: Marija Tudor

ISBN 9781633430112
Printed in the United States of America
4 5 6 7 8 9 10 – SP – 21 20 19

brief contents

contents

preface

When I came up with this book's title, I thought it was pretty smart. Having the words *Little* and *Guidebook* hinted that the reader could expect a relatively thin volume. This meant I wouldn't be committed to coming up with a lot of content. That was just as well, because Elixir was a very new language, and there wasn't much of a community to speak of. It was 2014, Elixir was at version 0.13, and Phoenix was still a web socket library.

Two years and 300 pages later, much has changed. The language has experienced many updates, and the community has grown. The excitement over Elixir is undoubtable, judging by the number of blog posts and tweets. Companies are also starting to discover and fall in love with Elixir. There's even renewed interest in Erlang, which is a wonderful phenomenon, if you ask me!

This book is my humble attempt to spread the word. I learn best by examples, and I assume it's the same for you. I've tried my best to keep the examples interesting, relatable, and, most important, illuminating and useful.

Having spent more than two years writing this book, I'm thrilled to finally get it into your hands. I hope this book can bring you the same joy I experience when programming in Elixir. What are you waiting for?

acknowledgments

I wouldn't have anything to write about without José Valim and all the hard-working developers who are involved in creating Elixir and building its ecosystem. And without the hard work of Joe Armstrong, Robert Virding, Mike Williams, and all the brilliant people who were part of creating Erlang and OTP, there would be no Elixir.

I originally intended to self-publish this book, back in 2013. During the writing process, I needed reviewers to keep me honest. I reached out to the (very young) Elixir community and also to other developers via the book mailing list, fully expecting a dismal response. Instead, the response was incredible. So, to Chris Bailey, J. David Eisenberg, Jeff Smith, Johnny Winn, Julien Blanchard, Kristian Rasmussen, Low Kian Seong, Marcello Seri, Markus Mais, Matthew Margolis, Michael Simpson, Norberto Ortigoza, Paulo Alves Pereira, Solomon White, Takayuki Matsubara, and Tallak Tveide, a big "Thank you!" for sharing your time and energy. Thanks, too, to the reviewers for Manning, including Amit Lamba, Anthony Cramp, Bryce Darling, Dane Balia, Jeff Smith, Jim Amrhein, Joel Clermont, Joel Kotarski, Kosmas Chatzimichalis, Matthew Margolis, Nhu Nguyen, Philip White, Roberto Infante, Ryan Pulling, Sergio Arbeo, Thomas O'Rourke, Thomas Peklak, Todd Fine, and Unnikrishnan Kumar.

Thanks to Michael Stephens and Marjan Bace for giving me the opportunity to write for Manning. Michael probably has no idea how excited I was to receive that first email. This book is much better because of Karen Miller, my tireless editor. She has been with me on this project since day one. The rest of the Manning team has been an absolute pleasure to work with.

To the wonderful people at Pivotal Labs, whom I have the privilege to work with every day: you all are a constant source of inspiration.

To the two biggest joys in my life, my long-suffering wife and neglected daughter, thanks for putting up with me.

To my parents, thank you for everything.

about this book

Ohai, welcome! Elixir is a functional programming language built on the Erlang virtual machine. It combines the productivity and expressivity of Ruby with the concurrency and fault-tolerance of Erlang. Elixir makes full use of Erlang's powerful OTP library, which many developers consider the source of Erlang's greatness, so you can have mature, professional-quality functionality right out of the gate. Elixir's support for functional programming makes it a great choice for highly distributed, event-driven applications like internet of things (IoT) systems.

This book respects your time and is designed to get you up to speed with Elixir and OTP with minimum fuss. But it expects you to put in the required amount of work to grasp all the various concepts. Therefore, this book works best when you can try out the examples and experiment. If you ever get stuck, don't fret—the Elixir community is very welcoming!

Roadmap

This book has 3 parts, 11 chapters, and 1 appendix. Part 1 covers the fundamentals of Elixir and OTP:

- Chapter 1 introduces Elixir and how it's different from its parent language, Erlang; compares Elixir with other languages; and presents use cases for Elixir and OTP.
- Chapter 2 takes you on a whirlwind tour of Elixir. You'll write your first Elixir program and get acquainted with language fundamentals.
- Chapter 3 presents processes, the Elixir unit of concurrency. You'll learn about the Actor concurrency model and how to use processes to send and receive messages. You'll then put together an example program to see concurrent processes in action.

- Chapter 4 introduces OTP, one of Elixir's killer features that's inherited from Erlang. You'll learn the philosophy behind OTP and get to know some of the most important parts of OTP that you'll use as an Elixir programmer. You'll come to understand how OTP behaviors work, and you'll build your first Elixir/OTP application—a weather program that talks to a third-party service—using the GenServer behavior.

Part 2 covers the fault-tolerant and distribution aspects of Elixir and OTP:

- Chapter 5 looks at the primitives available to handle errors, especially in a concurrent setting. You'll learn about the unique approach that the Erlang VM takes with respect to processes crashing. You'll also build your own supervisor process (that resembles the Supervisor OTP behavior) before you get to use the real thing.
- Chapter 6 is all about the Supervisor OTP behavior and fault-tolerance. You'll learn about Erlang's "let it crash" philosophy. This chapter introduces a worker-pool application that uses the skills you've built up over the previous chapters.
- Chapter 7 continues with the worker-pool application: you'll add more features to make it more full-featured and realistic. In the process, you'll learn how to build nontrivial Supervisor hierarchies and how to dynamically create Supervisor and worker processes.
- Chapter 8 examines distribution and how it helps in load balancing. It walks you through building a distributed load balancer. Along the way, you'll learn how to build a command-line program in Elixir.
- Chapter 9 continues with distribution, but this time, we look at failovers and takeovers. This is absolutely critical in any nontrivial application that has to be resilient to faults. You'll build a Chuck Norris jokes service that is both fault-tolerant and distributed.

Part 3 (chapters 10 and 11) covers type specifications, property-based testing and concurrency testing in Elixir. We will look at three tools—Dialyzer, QuickCheck, and Concuerror—and examples in which these tools help you write better and more reliable Elixir code.

The appendix provides instructions to set up Erlang and Elixir on your machine.

Who should read this book

You don't have a lot of time available. You want to see what the fuss is all about regarding Elixir, and you want to get your hands on the good stuff as soon as possible.

I assume you know your way around a terminal and have some programming experience.

Although having prior knowledge of Elixir and Erlang would certainly be helpful, it's by no means mandatory. But this book isn't meant to serve as an Elixir reference; you should know how to look up documentation on your own.

I also assume that you're not averse to change. Elixir moves pretty fast. But then again, you're reading this book, so I expect this isn't a problem for you.

How to read this book

Read this book from front to back. It progresses linearly, and although the earlier chapters are more or less self-contained, later chapters build on the previous ones. Some of the chapters may require rereading, so don't think you should understand all the concepts on the first reading.

My favorite kind of programming books are those that encourage you to try out the code; the concepts always seem to sink in better that way. In this book, I do just that. Nothing beats hand-on experience. There are exercises at the end of some of the chapters: *do them!* This book will be most useful if you have a clear head, an open terminal, and a desire to learn something incredibly fun and worthwhile.

Getting the example code

This book is full of examples. The latest code for the book is hosted at the publisher's website, www.manning.com/books/the-little-elixir-and-otp-guidebook; and also in a GitHub repository, https://github.com/benjamintanweihao/the-little-elixir-otp-guidebook-code.

Author Online

Purchase of *The Little Elixir & OTP Guidebook* includes free access to a private web forum run by Manning Publications where you can make comments about the book, ask technical questions, and receive help from the author and from other users. To access the forum and subscribe to it, point your web browser to www.manning.com/books/the-little-elixir-and-otp-guidebook. This page provides information on how to get on the forum once you are registered, what kind of help is available, and the rules of conduct on the forum. It also provides links to the source code for the examples in the book, errata, and other downloads.

Manning's commitment to our readers is to provide a venue where a meaningful dialog between individual readers and between readers and the authors can take place. It is not a commitment to any specific amount of participation on the part of the authors, whose contribution to the Author Online forum remains voluntary (and unpaid). We suggest you try asking the author challenging questions lest his interest strays!

The Author Online forum and the archives of previous discussions will be accessible from the publisher's website as long as the book is in print.

About the author

Benjamin Tan Wei Hao is a software engineer at Pivotal Labs, Singapore. Deathly afraid of being irrelevant, he is always trying to catch up on his ever-growing reading list. He enjoys going to Ruby conferences and talking about Elixir.

He is the author of *The Ruby Closures Book*, soon to be published by the Pragmatic Bookshelf. He also writes for the Ruby column on SitePoint and tries to sneak in an Elixir article now and then. In his copious free time, he blogs at benjamintan.io.

Part 1

Getting started with Elixir and OTP

This book begins with the basics of Elixir. In chapter 1, I'll answer some existential questions about why we need Elixir and what it's good for. Then, in chapter 2, we'll dive into a series of examples that demonstrate the various language features.

Chapter 3 looks at processes, the fundamental unit of concurrency in Elixir. You'll see how processes in Elixir relate to the Actor concurrency model. If you've struggled with concurrency in other languages, Elixir will be like a breath of fresh air.

I'll conclude part 1 in chapter 4 with an introduction to OTP. You'll learn about the `GenServer` behavior, the most basic but most important of all the behaviors.

Introduction 1

This chapter covers

- What Elixir is
- How Elixir is different from Erlang
- Why Elixir is a good choice
- What Elixir/OTP is good for
- The road ahead

Just in case you bought this book for medicinal purposes—I'm sorry, wrong book. This book is about Elixir the programming language. No other language (other than Ruby) has made me so excited and happy to work with it. Even after spending more than two years of my life writing about Elixir, I still love programming in it. There's something special about being involved in a community that's so young and lively. I don't think any language has had at least *four* books written about it, a dedicated screencast series, and a conference—all before v1.0. I think we're on to something here.

Before I begin discussing Elixir, I want to talk about Erlang and its legendary virtual machine (VM), because Elixir is built on top of it. Erlang is a programming language that excels in building soft real-time, distributed, and concurrent systems. Its original use case was to program Ericsson's telephone switches. (Telephone switches are basically machines that connect calls between callers.)

3

These switches had to be concurrent, reliable, and scalable. They had to be able to handle multiple calls at the same time, and they also had to be extremely reliable—no one wants their call to be dropped halfway through. Additionally, a dropped call (due to a software or hardware fault) shouldn't affect the rest of the calls on the switch. The switches had to be massively scalable and work with a distributed network of switches. These production requirements shaped Erlang into what it is today; they're the exact requirements we have today with multicore and web-scale programming.

As you'll discover in later chapters, the Erlang VM's scheduler automatically distributes workloads across processors. This means you get an increase in speed *almost* for free if you run your program on a machine with more processors—*almost*, because you'll need to change the way you approach writing programs in Erlang and Elixir in order to reap the full benefits. Writing distributed programs—that is, programs that are running on different computers and that can communicate with each other—requires little ceremony.

1.1   *Elixir*

It's time to introduce Elixir. Elixir describes itself as *a functional, meta-programming-aware language built on top of the Erlang virtual machine.* Let's take this definition apart piece by piece.

Elixir is a *functional programming language.* This means it has all the usual features you expect, such as immutable state, higher-order functions, lazy evaluation, and pattern matching. You'll meet all of these features and more in later chapters.

Elixir is also a *meta-programmable language.* Meta-programming involves code that generates code (black magic, if you will). This is possible because code can be represented as data, and data can be represented as code. These facilities enable the programmer to add to the language new constructs (among other things) that other languages find difficult or even downright impossible.

This book is also about OTP, a framework to build fault-tolerant, scalable, distributed applications. It's important to recognize that Elixir essentially gains OTP for free because OTP comes as part of the Erlang distribution. Unlike most frameworks, OTP comes packaged with a lot of good stuff, including three kinds of databases, a set of debugging tools, profilers, a test framework, and much more. Although we only manage to play with a tiny subset, this book will give you a taste of the pure awesomeness of OTP.

NOTE   OTP used to be an acronym for *Open Telecom Platform*, which hints at Erlang's telecom heritage. It also demonstrates how naming is difficult in computer science: OTP is a general-purpose framework and has little to do with telecom. Nowadays, OTP is just plain OTP, just as *IBM* is just *IBM*.

1.2 *How is Elixir different from Erlang?*

Before I talk about how Elixir is different from Erlang, let's look at their similarities. Both Elixir and Erlang compile down to the same bytecode. This means both Elixir and Erlang programs, when compiled, emit instructions that run on the same VM.

Another wonderful feature of Elixir is that you can call Erlang code directly from Elixir, and vice versa! If, for example, you find that Elixir lacks a certain functionality that's present in Erlang, you can call the Erlang library function directly from your Elixir code.

Elixir follows most of Erlang's semantics, such as message passing. Most Erlang programmers would feel right at home with Elixir.

This interoperability also means a wealth of Erlang third-party libraries are at the disposal of the Elixir developer (that's you!). So why would you want to use Elixir instead of Erlang? There are at least two reasons: the tooling and ecosystem.

1.2.1 *Tooling*

Out of the box, Elixir comes with a few handy tools built in.

INTERACTIVE ELIXIR

The Interactive Elixir shell (`iex`) is a read-eval-print loop (REPL) that's similar to Ruby's `irb`. It comes with some pretty nifty features, such as syntax highlighting and a beautiful documentation system, as shown in figure 1.1.

```
iex(1)> h Enum.map

                       def map(collection, fun)

Returns a new collection, where each item is the result of
invoking fun on each corresponding item of collection.

For dicts, the function expects a key-value tuple.

Examples

  iex> Enum.map([1, 2, 3], fn(x) -> x * 2 end)
  [2, 4, 6]

  iex> Enum.map([a: 1, b: 2], fn({k, v}) -> {k, -v} end)
  [a: -1, b: -2]

iex(2)> []
```

Figure 1.1 Interactive Elixir has documentation built in.

There's more to `iex`: this tool allows you to connect to *nodes*, which you can think of as separate Erlang runtimes that can talk to each other. Each runtime can live on the same computer, the same LAN, or the same network.

`iex` has another superpower, inspired by the Ruby library Pry. If you've used Pry, you know that it's a debugger that allows you to pry into the state of your program. `iex` comes with a similarly named function called `IEx.pry`. You won't use this feature in the book, but it's an invaluable tool to be familiar with. Here's a brief overview of how to use it. Let's assume you have code like this:

```
require IEx

defmodule Greeter do
  def ohai(who, adjective) do
    greeting = "Ohai!, #{adjective} #{who}"
    IEx.pry
  end
end
```

The IEx.pry line will cause the interpreter to pause, allowing you to inspect the variables that have been passed in. First you run the function:

```
iex(1)> Greeter.ohai "leader", "glorious"
Request to pry #PID<0.62.0> at ohai.ex:6

      def ohai(who, adjective) do
        greeting = "Ohai!, #{adjective} #{who}"
        IEx.pry
      end
    end

Allow? [Yn] Y
```

Once you answer Yes, you're brought into iex, where you can inspect the variables that were passed in:

```
Interactive Elixir (1.2.4) - press Ctrl+C to exit (type h() ENTER for help)
pry(1)> who
"leader"
pry(2)> adjective
"glorious"
```

There are other nice features, like autocomplete, that you'll find handy when using iex. Almost every release of Elixir includes useful improvements and additional helper functions in iex, so it's worth keeping up with the changelog!

TESTING WITH EXUNIT

Testing aficionados will be pleased to know that Elixir has a built-in test framework called ExUnit. ExUnit has some useful features such as being able to run asynchronously and produce beautiful failure messages, as shown in figure 1.2. ExUnit can perform nifty tricks with error reporting mainly due to macros, which I won't cover in this book. Nonetheless, it's a fascinating topic that you may want to explore.[1]

MIX

mix is a build tool used for creating, compiling, and testing Elixir projects. It's also used to manage dependencies, among other things. Think of it like rake in Ruby and lein in Clojure. (Some of the first contributors to mix also wrote lein.) Projects such as the Phoenix web framework have used mix to great effect for things like building generators that reduce the need to write boilerplate.

---

[1] http://elixir-lang.org/getting-started/meta/macros.html.

```
% elixir foo_test.exs                                    1

  1) test beautiful failures (FooTest)

     match (=) failed
     code: [1, 2, 3] = {1, 2, 3}
     rhs:  {1, 2, 3}
     stacktrace:
       foo_test.exs:6



Finished in 0.1 seconds (0.09s on load, 0.01s on tests)
1 tests, 1 failures

Randomized with seed 780311
[ben@tan:~/Desktop]
%                                                        1
```

Figure 1.2 ExUnit comes with excellent error messages.

STANDARD LIBRARY

Elixir ships with an excellent standard library. Data structures such as ranges, strict and lazy enumeration APIs, and a sane way to manipulate strings are just some of the nice items that come packaged in it.

Although Elixir may not be the best language in which to write scripts, it includes familiar-sounding libraries such as Path and File. The documentation is also a joy to use. Explanations are clear and concise, with examples of how to use the various libraries and functions.

Elixir has modules that aren't in the standard Erlang library. My favorite of these is Stream. Streams are basically composable, lazy enumerables. They're often used to model potentially infinite streams of values.

Elixir has also added functionality to the OTP framework. For example, it's added a number of abstractions, such as Agent to handle state and Task to handle one-off asynchronous computation. Agent is built on GenServer (this stands for *generic server*), which comes with OTP by default.

METAPROGRAMMING

Elixir has LISP-like macros built into it, minus the parentheses. Macros are used to extend the Elixir language by giving it new constructs expressed in existing ones. The implementation employs the use of macros throughout the language. Library authors also use them extensively to cut down on boilerplate code.

1.2.2 Ecosystem

Elixir is a relatively new programming language, and being built on top of a solid, proven language definitely has its advantages.

THANK YOU, ERLANG!

I think the biggest benefit for Elixir is the years of experience and tooling available from the Erlang community. Almost any Erlang library can be used in Elixir with little effort. Elixir developers don't have to reinvent the wheel in order to build rock-solid applications. Instead, they can happily rely on OTP and can focus on building additional abstractions based on existing libraries.

LEARNING RESOURCES

The excitement around Elixir has led to a wellspring of learning resources (not to beat my own drum). There are already multiple sources for screencasts, as well as books and conferences. Once you've learned to translate from Elixir to Erlang, you can also benefit from the numerous well-written Erlang books, such as *Erlang and OTP in Action* by Martin Logan, Eric Merritt, and Richard Carlsson (Manning Publications, 2010); *Learn You Some Erlang for Great Good!* by Fred Hébert (No Starch Press, 2013); and *Designing for Scalability with Erlang/OTP* by Francesco Cesarini and Steve Vinoski (O'Reilly Media, 2016).

PHOENIX

Phoenix is a web framework written in Elixir that has gotten a lot of developers excited, and for good reason. For starters, response times in Phoenix can reach microseconds. Phoenix proves that you can have both high performance and a simple framework coupled with built-in support for WebSockets and backed by the awesome power of OTP.

IT'S STILL EVOLVING

Elixir is constantly evolving and exploring new ideas. One of the most interesting notions I've seen arise are the concurrency abstractions that are being worked on. Even better, the Elixir core team is always on the hunt for great ideas from other languages. There's already (at least!) Ruby, Clojure, and F# DNA in Elixir, if you know where to look.

1.3   *Why Elixir and not X?*

On many occasions, when I give a talk about Elixir or write about it, the same question pops up: "Should I learn Elixir instead of *X*?" *X* is usually Clojure, Scala, or Golang. This question usually stems from two other questions: "Is Elixir gaining traction?" and "Are jobs available in Elixir?" This section presents my responses.

Elixir is a young language (around five years old at the time of writing), so it will take time for the language, ecosystem, and community to mature. You can use this to your advantage. First, functional programming is on the rise, and certain principles remain more or less the same in most functional programming languages. Whether it's Scala, Clojure, or Erlang, these skills are portable.

Erlang seems to be gaining popularity. There's also a surge of interest in distributed systems and the internet of things (IoT), domains that are right up Elixir's alley.

I have a gut feeling that Elixir will take off soon. It's like Java in its early days: not many people bothered with it when it first came out, but the early adopters were hugely rewarded. The same went for Ruby. There's definitely an advantage to being ahead of the curve.

It would be selfish of me to keep everyone else from learning and experiencing this wonderful language. Cast your doubts aside, have a little faith, and enjoy the ride!

1.4 What is Elixir/OTP good for?

Everything that Erlang is great for also applies to Elixir. Elixir and OTP combined provide facilities to build concurrent, scalable, fault-tolerant, distributed programs. These include, but obviously aren't limited to, the following:

- Chat servers (WhatsApp, ejabberd)
- Game servers (Wooga)
- Web frameworks (Phoenix)
- Distributed databases (Riak and CouchDB)
- Real-time bidding servers
- Video-streaming services
- Long-running services/daemons
- Command-line applications

From this list, you probably gather that Elixir is ideal for building server-side software—and you're right! These software programs share similar characteristics. They have to

- Serve multiple users and clients, often numbering in the thousands or millions, while maintaining a decent level of responsiveness
- Stay up in the event of failure, or have graceful failover mechanisms
- Scale gracefully by adding either more CPU cores or additional machines

Elixir is no wonder drug (pun intended). You probably won't want to do any image processing, perform computationally intensive tasks, or build GUI applications on Elixir. And you wouldn't use Elixir to build hard real-time systems. For example, you shouldn't use Elixir to write software for an F-22 fighter jet.

But hey, don't let me tell you what you can or can't do with Elixir. Let your creativity flow. That's why programming is so awesome.

1.5 The road ahead

Now that I've given you some background on Elixir, Erlang, and the OTP framework, the following appetite-whetting sections provide a high-level overview of what's to come.

1.5.1 A sneak preview of OTP behaviors

Say you want to build a weather application. You decide to get some venture capital, and before you know it, you're funded.

After some thinking, you realize that what you're building essentially is a simple client-server application. Of course, you don't tell your investors this. Basically, clients (via HTTP, for example) will make requests, and your application will perform some computations and return the results to each client in a timely manner.

You implement your weather application, and it goes viral! But suddenly your users begin to encounter all sorts of issues: slow load times and, even worse, service disruptions. You attempt to do some performance profiling, you tweak settings here and there, and you try to add more concurrency.

Everything seems OK for a while, but that's just the calm before the storm. Eventually, users experience the same issues again, plus they see error messages, mysterious deadlocks occur, and other weird issues appear. In the end, you give up and write a long blog post about how your startup failed and why you should have built the application in Node.js or Golang. The post is #1 on Hacker News for a month. You then stumble upon OTP and learn that Elixir combined with OTP can be used to build concurrent, scalable, fault-tolerant, distributed programs.

Although this book won't explain how to get venture capital, it will show you how to build a weather service using OTP, among other fun things. The OTP framework is what gives BEAM languages (Erlang, Elixir, and so on) their superpowers, and it comes bundled with Elixir.

One of the most important concepts in OTP is the notion of *behaviors*. A behavior can be thought of as a contract between you and OTP.

When you use a behavior, OTP expects you to fill in certain functions. In exchange for that, OTP takes care of a slew of issues such as message handling (synchronous or asynchronous), concurrency errors (deadlocks and race conditions), fault tolerance, and failure handling. These issues are general—almost every respectable client/server program has to handle them somehow, but OTP steps in and handles all of these for you. Furthermore, these generic bits have been used in production and battle-tested for years.

In this book, you'll work with two of the most-used behaviors: GenServer and Supervisor. Once you're comfortable with them, learning to use other behaviors will be straightforward. You could roll your own Supervisor behavior, but there's no good reason to do so 99.999999999% of the time. The implementers have thought long and hard about the features that need to be included in most client-server programs, and they've also accounted for concurrency errors and all sorts of edge cases.

How do you use an OTP behavior? The following listing shows a minimal implementation of a weather service that uses GenServer.

Listing 1.1 Example GenServer

```
defmodule WeatherService do
  use GenServer # <- This brings in GenServer behavior
                                                    Synchronous
  def handle_call({:temperature, city}, _from, state) do   <-- request
    # ...
  end
                                                    Asynchronous
  def handle_cast({:email_weather_report, email}, state) do  <-- request
    # ...
  end

end
```

This implementation is obviously incomplete; the important thing to realize (and you'll see this as you work through the book) is how many things you *don't* need to do. For example, you don't have to implement how to handle a synchronous or an asynchronous request. I'll leave you in suspense for now (this is just a sneak preview), but in chapters 3 and 4 you'll build the same application without OTP and then with OTP.

OTP may look complicated or scary at first sight, but you'll see that this isn't the case as you work through the examples in the book. The best way to learn how something works is to implement it yourself. In that spirit, you'll learn how to implement the Supervisor behavior from scratch in chapter 5. The point is to demonstrate that there's little magic involved—the language provides the necessary tools to build out these useful abstractions.

You'll also implement a worker pool application from scratch and evolve it in stages in chapters 6 and 7. This will build on the discussion of GenServer and Supervisor.

1.5.2 *Distribution for load balancing and fault tolerance*

Elixir with OTP is an excellent candidate to build distributed systems. In this book, you'll build two distributed applications, highlighting two different uses of distribution.

One reason you might want to create a distributed application is to spread the load across multiple computers. In chapter 8, you'll create a load tester and see how you can exploit distribution to scale up the capabilities of your application. You'll see how Elixir's message-passing-oriented nature and the distribution primitives available make building distributed applications a much more pleasant experience compared to other languages and platforms.

Another reason you might require distribution is to provide fault tolerance. If one node fails, you want another node to stand in its place. In chapter 9, you'll see how to create an application that does this, too.

1.5.3 *Dialyzer and type specifications*

Because Elixir is a dynamic language, you need to be wary of introducing type errors in your programs. Therefore, one aspect of reliability is making sure your programs are type-safe.

Dialyzer is a tool in OTP that aims to detect some of these problems. You'll learn how to use Dialyzer in a series of examples in chapter 10. You'll also learn about Dialyzer's limitations and how to overcome some of them using type specifications. As you'll see, type specifications, in addition to helping Dialyzer, serve as documentation. For example, the following listing is taken from the List module.

> **Listing 1.2 Function that has been annotated with type specifications**

```
@spec foldl([elem], acc, (elem, acc -> acc)) :: acc when elem: var, acc: var
def foldl(list, acc, function) when is_list(list) and is_function(function)
    ➥do
  :lists.foldl(function, acc, list)
end
```

After reading chapter 10, you'll appreciate type specifications and how they can help make your programs clearer and safer.

1.5.4   *Property and concurrency testing*

Chapter 11 is dedicated to property-based and concurrency testing. In particular, you'll learn how to use QuickCheck and Concuerror. These tools don't come with Elixir or OTP by default, but they're extremely useful for revealing bugs that traditional unit-testing tools don't.

You'll learn about using QuickCheck for property-based testing and how property-based testing turns traditional unit testing on its head. Instead of thinking about specific examples, as in unit testing, property-based testing forces you to come up with general properties your tested code should hold. Once you've created a property, you can test it against hundreds or thousands of generated test inputs. Here's an example that says reversing a list twice gives you back the same list:

```
@tag numtests: 100
property "reverse is idempotent" do
  forall l <- list(char) do
    ensure l |> Enum.reverse |> Enum.reverse == l
  end
end
```

This code generates 100 lists and asserts that the property holds for each of those generated lists.

The other tool we'll explore in chapter 11 is Concuerror, which was born in academia but has seen real-world use. You'll learn how Concuerror reveals hard-to-detect concurrency bugs such as deadlocks and race conditions. Through a series of intentionally buggy examples, you'll use Concuerror to disclose the bugs.

1.6   *Summary*

In this chapter, I introduced Elixir and Erlang. In addition, you learned about the following:

- The motivations behind the creation of Erlang, and how it fits perfectly into the multi-core and web-scale phenomena we have today
- The motivations behind the creation of Elixir, and a few reasons Elixir is better than Erlang, such as Elixir's standard library and tool chain
- Examples for which Elixir and OTP are perfect use cases

A whirlwind tour

Instead of discussing each Elixir language feature in depth, I'm going to present them as a series of examples. I'll elaborate more when we come to concepts that may seem unfamiliar to, say, a Java or Ruby programmer. For certain concepts, you can probably draw parallels from whatever languages you already know. The examples will be progressively more fun and will highlight almost everything you need to understand the Elixir code in this book.

2.1   *Setting up your environment*

Elixir is supported by most of the major editors, such as Vim, Emacs, Spacemacs, Atom, IntelliJ, and Visual Studio, to name a few. The aptly named Alchemist (https://github.com/tonini/alchemist.el), the Elixir tooling integration that works with Emacs/Spacemacs, provides an excellent developer experience. It features things like documentation lookup, smart code completion, integration with `iex` and `mix`, and a ton of other useful features. It's by far the most supported and feature-rich of the editor integrations. Get your terminal and editor ready, because the whirlwind tour begins now.

2.2   *First steps*

Let's begin with something simple. Due to choices made by my former colonial masters (I'm from Singapore), I'm woefully unfamiliar with measurements in feet, inches, and so on. We're going to write a length converter to remedy that.

Here's how you can define the length converter in Elixir. Enter the code in the following listing into your favorite text editor and save the file as length_converter.ex.

Listing 2.1   Length converter program in Elixir (length_converter.ex)

```
defmodule MeterToFootConverter do
  def convert(m) do
    m * 3.28084
  end
end
```

`defmodule` defines a new module (`MeterToFootConverter`), and `def` defines a new function (`convert`).

2.2.1   *Running an Elixir program in Interactive Elixir*

Interactive Elixir (`iex` for short) is the equivalent of `irb` in Ruby or `node` in Node.js. In your terminal, launch `iex` with the filename as the argument:

```
% iex length_converter.ex
```

```
Interactive Elixir (0.13.0) - press Ctrl+C to exit (type h() ENTER for help)
iex(1)>
```

The record for the tallest man in the world is 2.72 m. What's that in feet? Let's find out:

```
iex> MeterToFeetConverter.convert(2.72)
```

The result is

```
8.9238848
```

2.2.2 Stopping an Elixir program

There are a few ways to stop an Elixir program or exit iex. The first way is to press Ctrl-C. The first time you do this, you'll see the following:

```
BREAK: (a)bort (c)ontinue (p)roc info (i)nfo (l)oaded
       (v)ersion (k)ill (D)b-tables (d)istribution
```

You can now either press A to abort or press Ctrl-C again. An alternative is to use System.halt, although personally I'm more of a Ctrl-C person.

2.2.3 Getting help

Because iex is your primary tool for interacting with Elixir, it pays to learn a bit more about it. In particular, iex features a sweet built-in documentation system. Fire up iex again. Let's say you want to learn about the Dict module. To do so, type h Dict in iex. The output will be similar to that shown in figure 2.1.

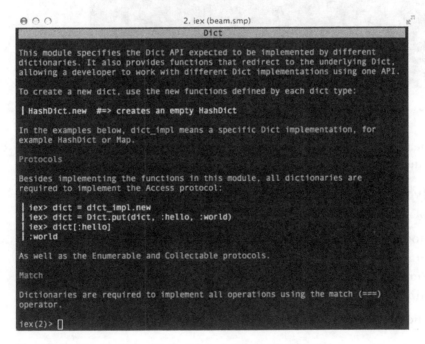

Figure 2.1 Documentation for the Dict module displayed in iex

Want to know the functions available in Dict? Type Dict. (the dot is important!), and then press the Tab key. You'll see a list of functions available in the Dict module, as shown in figure 2.2.

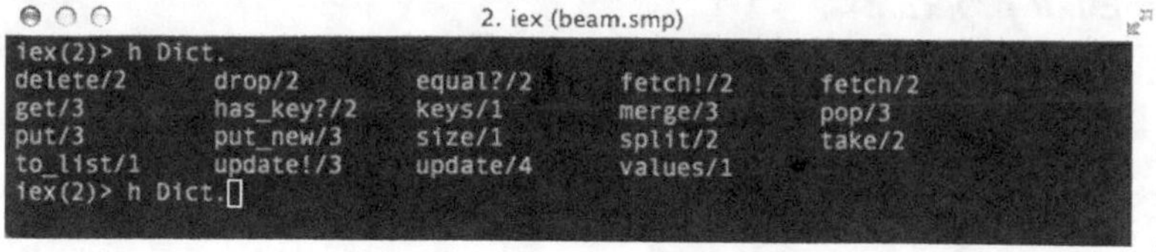

Figure 2.2 A list of functions available in the `Dict` module

Now, let's say you want to learn more about the `put/3` function. (I'll explain the `/3` in detail later. For now, it means this version of `put` accepts three arguments.) In `iex`, type `h Dict.put/3`. The output will look like figure 2.3.

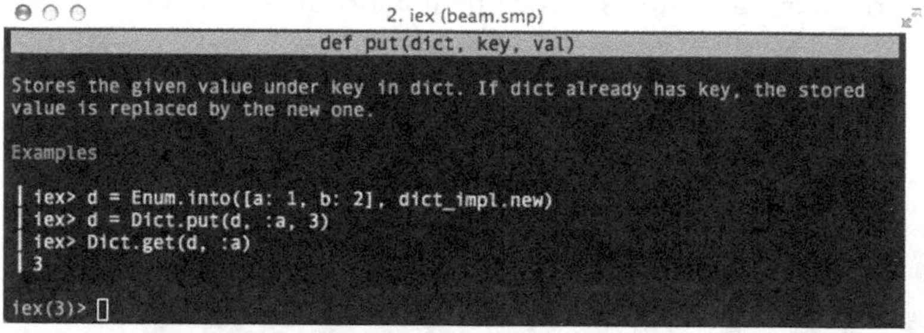

Figure 2.3 Documentation for `Dict.put/3`

Pretty neat, eh? What's even better is that the documentation is beautifully syntax-highlighted.

2.3 *Data types*

Here are the common data types we'll use in this book:

- Modules
- Functions
- Numbers
- Strings
- Atoms
- Tuples
- Maps

This section introduces each of them in more depth.

2.3.1 *Modules, functions, and function clauses*

Modules are Elixir's way of grouping functions together. Examples of modules are `List`, `String`, and, of course, `MeterToFootConverter`. You create a module using `defmodule`. Similarly, you create functions using `def`.

MODULES

Just for kicks, let's write a function to convert meters into inches. You need to make a few changes in the current implementation. First, the module name is too specific. Let's change that to something more general:

```
defmodule MeterToLengthConverter do
  # ...
end
```

More interestingly, how do you add a function that converts from meters to inches?
The next listing shows one possible approach.

Listing 2.2 Nesting `defmodules` to convert meters to inches

```
defmodule MeterToLengthConverter do
  defmodule Feet do
    def convert(m) do
      m * 3.28084
    end
  end

  defmodule Inch do
    def convert(m) do
      m * 39.3701
    end
  end
end
```

Now you can compute the height of the world's tallest man in inches:

```
iex> MeterToLengthConverter.Inch.convert(2.72)
```

Here's the result:

```
107.08667200000001
```

This example illustrates that modules can be nested. The modules `Feet` and `Inch` are
nested within `MeterToLengthConverter`. To access a function in a nested module, you
use *dot notation*. In general, to invoke functions in Elixir, the following format is used:

```
Module.function(arg1, arg2, ...)
```

> **NOTE** In mailing lists, this format is sometimes known as *MFA* (*M*odule, *F*unc-
> tion, and *A*rguments). Remember this format because you'll encounter it
> again in the book.

You can also flatten the module hierarchy, as shown in the next listing.

Listing 2.3 Flattening the module hierarchy (Interactive Elixir)

```
defmodule MeterToLengthConverter.Feet do      ◁┐
  def convert(m) do                                  Uses dot notation
    m * 3.28084                                      to specify a
  end                                                nested hierarchy
end

defmodule MeterToLengthConverter.Inch do      ◁┘
```

```
  def convert(m) do
    m * 39.3701
  end
end
```

You can call the function exactly the same way you did previously.

FUNCTIONS AND FUNCTION CLAUSES

There's a more idiomatic way to write the length converter: by using function clauses. Here's a revised version:

```
defmodule MeterToLengthConverter do
  def convert(:feet, m) do
    m * 3.28084
  end

  def convert(:inch, m) do
    m * 39.3701
  end
end
```

Defining a function is straightforward. Most functions are written like this:

```
def convert(:feet, m) do
  m * 3.28084
end
```

Single-lined functions are written like so:

```
def convert(:feet, m), do: m * 3.28084
```

While we're at it, let's add another function to convert meters to yards, this time using the single-line variety:

```
defmodule MeterToLengthConverter do
  def convert(:feet, m), do: m * 3.28084
  def convert(:inch, m), do: m * 39.3701
  def convert(:yard, m), do: m * 1.09361
end
```

Functions are referred to by their *arity*: the number of arguments they take. Therefore, we refer to the previous function as convert/2. This is an example of a *named function*. Elixir also has the notion of *anonymous functions*. Here's a common example of an anonymous function:

```
iex> Enum.map([1, 2, 3], fn x -> x*x end)
```

The result is as follows:

```
[1, 4, 9]
```

You can define a function with the same name multiple times, as in the example. The important thing to notice is that they must be grouped together. Therefore, this is bad form:

```
defmodule MeterToLengthConverter do
  def convert(:feet, m), do: m * 3.28084
  def convert(:inch, m), do: m * 39.3701
  def i_should_not_be_here, do: IO.puts "Oops"     ⟵——— Don't do this!
  def convert(:yard, m), do: m * 1.09361
end
```

Elixir will complain accordingly:

```
% iex length_converter.ex
length_converter.ex:5: warning: clauses for the same def
⮕should be grouped together,
def convert/2 was previously defined
```

Another important thing: order matters. Each function clause is matched in a top-down fashion. This means once Elixir finds a compatible function clause that matches (arity and/or arguments), it will stop searching and execute that function. For the current length converter, moving function clauses around won't affect anything. When we explore recursion later, you'll begin to appreciate why ordering of function clauses matters.

2.3.2 Numbers

Numbers in Elixir work much as you'd expect from traditional programming languages. Here's an example that operates on an integer, a hexadecimal, and a float:

```
iex> 1 + 0x2F / 3.0
16.666666666666664
```

And here are the division and remainder functions:

```
iex> div(10,3)
3

iex> rem(10,3)
1
```

2.3.3 Strings

Strings in Elixir lead two lives, as this section explains. On the surface, strings look pretty standard. Here's an example that demonstrates string interpolation:

```
iex(1)> "Strings are #{:great}!"
```

It gives you

```
"Strings are great!"
```

You can also perform various operations on strings:

```
iex(2)> "Strings are #{:great}!" |> String.upcase |> String.reverse
```

This returns

```
"!TAERG ERA SGNIRTS"
```

STRINGS ARE BINARIES

How do you test for a string? There isn't an is_string/1 function available. That's because a string in Elixir is a *binary*. A binary is a sequence of bytes:

```
iex(3)> "Strings are binaries" |> is_binary
```

This returns

```
true
```

One way to show the binary representation of a string is to use the binary concatenation operator <> to attach a null byte, <<0>>:

```
iex(4)> "ohai" <> <<0>>
```

This returns

```
<<111, 104, 97, 105, 0>>.
```

Each individual number represents a character:

```
iex(5)> ?o
111

iex(6)> ?h
104

iex(7)> ?a
97

iex(8)> ?i
105
```

To further convince yourself that the binary representation is equivalent, try this:
```
iex(44)> IO.puts <<111, 104, 97, 105>>
```
This gives you back the original string:
```
ohai
```

STRINGS AREN'T CHAR LISTS

A *char list*, as its name suggests, is a list of characters. It's an entirely different data type than strings, and this can be confusing. Whereas strings are always enclosed in double quotes, char lists are enclosed in single quotes. For example, this

```
iex(9)> 'ohai' == "ohai"
```

results in `false`. You usually won't use char lists in Elixir. But when talking to some Erlang libraries, you'll have to. For example, as you'll see in a later example, the Erlang HTTP client (`httpc`) accepts a char list as the URL:

```
:httpc.request 'http://www.elixir-lang.org'
```

What happens if you pass in a string (binary) instead? Try it:

```
iex(51)> :httpc.request "http://www.elixir-lang.org"
** (ArgumentError) argument error
         :erlang.tl("http://www.elixir-lang.org")
   (inets) inets_regexp.erl:80: :inets_regexp.first_match/3
   (inets) inets_regexp.erl:68: :inets_regexp.first_match/2
   (inets) http_uri.erl:186: :http_uri.split_uri/5
   (inets) http_uri.erl:136: :http_uri.parse_scheme/2
   (inets) http_uri.erl:88: :http_uri.parse/2
   (inets) httpc.erl:162: :httpc.request/5
```

We'll cover calling Erlang libraries later in the chapter, but this is something you need to keep in mind when you're dealing with certain Erlang libraries.

2.3.4 Atoms

Atoms serve as constants, akin to Ruby's symbols. Atoms always start with a colon. There are two different ways to create atoms. For example, both `:hello_atom` and `:"Hello Atom"` are valid atoms. Atoms are not the same as strings—they're completely separate data types:

```
iex> :hello_atom == "hello_atom"
false
```

On their own, atoms aren't very interesting. But when you place atoms into tuples and use them in the context of pattern matching, you'll begin to understand their role and how Elixir exploits them to write declarative code. We'll get to pattern matching in section 2.5. For now, let's turn our attention to tuples.

2.3.5 Tuples

A tuple can contain different types of data. For example, an HTTP client might return a successful request in the form of a tuple like this:

```
{200, "http://www.elixir-lang.org"}
```

Here's how the result of an unsuccessful request might look:

```
{404, "http://www.php-is-awesome.org"}
```

Tuples use zero-based access, just as you access array elements in most programming languages. Therefore, if you want the URL of the request result, you need to pass in 1 to `elem/2`

```
iex> elem({404, "http://www.php-is-awesome.org"}, 1)
```

which will return http://www.php-is-awesome.org.

You can update a tuple using put_elem/3

```
iex> put_elem({404, "http://www.php-is-awesome.org"}, 0, 503)
```

which returns

```
{503, "http://www.php-is-awesome.org"}
```

2.3.6   *Maps*

A map is essentially a key-value pair, like a hash or dictionary, depending on the language. All map operations are exposed with the Map module. Working with maps is straightforward, with a tiny caveat. (See the following sidebar on immutability.) See if you can spot it in the examples. Let's start with an empty map:

```
iex> programmers = Map.new
%{}
```

Now, let's add some smart people to the map:

```
iex> programmers = Map.put(programmers, :joe, "Erlang")
%{joe: "Erlang"}

iex> programmers = Map.put(programmers, :matz, "Ruby")
%{joe: "Erlang", matz: "Ruby"}

iex> programmers = Map.put(programmers, :rich, "Clojure")
%{joe: "Erlang", matz: "Ruby", rich: "Clojure"}
```

A very important aside: immutability

Notice that programmers is one of the arguments to Map.put/3, and it's re-bound to programmers. Why is that? Here's another example:

```
iex> Map.put(programmers, :rasmus, "PHP")
%{joe: "Erlang", matz: "Ruby", rasmus: "PHP", rich: "Clojure"}
```

The return value contains the new entry. Let's check the contents of programmers:

```
iex> programmers
%{joe: "Erlang", matz: "Ruby", rich: "Clojure"}
```

This property is called *immutability*.

All data structures in Elixir are immutable, which means you can't make any modifications to them. Any modifications you make always leave the original unchanged. A modified copy is returned. Therefore, in order to capture the result, you can either rebind it to the same variable name or bind the value to another variable.

2.4 Guards

Let's look at length_converter.ex once more. Suppose you want to ensure that the arguments are always numbers. You can modify the program by adding *guard clauses*:

```
defmodule MeterToLengthConverter do
  def convert(:feet, m) when is_number(m), do: m * 3.28084
  def convert(:inch, m) when is_number(m), do: m * 39.3701
  def convert(:yard, m) when is_number(m), do: m * 1.09361
end
```

Guards added to the function clause

Now, if you try something like MeterToLengthConverter.convert(:feet, "smelly"), none of the function clauses will match. Elixir will throw a FunctionClauseError:

```
iex(1)> MeterToLengthConverter.convert(:feet, "smelly")
(FunctionClauseError) no function clause matching in convert/2
```

Negative lengths make no sense. Let's make sure the arguments are non-negative. You can do this by adding another guard expression:

```
defmodule MeterToLengthConverter do
  def convert(:feet, m) when is_number(m) and m >= 0, do: m * 3.28084
  def convert(:inch, m) when is_number(m) and m >= 0, do: m * 39.3701
  def convert(:yard, m) when is_number(m) and m >= 0, do: m * 1.09361
end
```

Checks that m is a non-negative number.

In addition to is_number/1, other similar functions will come in handy when you need to differentiate between the various data types. To generate this list, fire up iex, and type is_ followed by pressing the Tab key:

```
iex(1)> is_
is_atom/1        is_binary/1      is_bitstring/1   is_boolean/1
is_float/1       is_function/1    is_function/2    is_integer/1
is_list/1        is_map/1         is_nil/1         is_number/1
is_pid/1         is_port/1        is_reference/1   is_tuple/1
```

The is_* functions should be self-explanatory, except for is_port/1 and is_reference/1. You won't use ports in this book, and you'll meet references in chapter 6 and see how they're useful in giving messages a unique identity. Guard clauses are especially useful for eliminating conditionals and, as you may have guessed, for making sure arguments are of the correct type.

2.5 Pattern matching

Pattern matching is one of the most powerful features in functional programming languages, and Elixir is no exception. In fact, pattern matching is one of my favorite features in Elixir. Once you see what pattern matching can do, you'll start to yearn for it in languages that don't support it.

Elixir uses the equals operator (=) to perform pattern matching. Unlike most languages, Elixir uses the = operator for more than variable assignment; = is called the *match operator*. From now on, when you see =, think *matches* instead of *equals*. What are you matching, exactly? In short, pattern matching is used to match both values and data structures. In this section, you'll learn to love pattern matching as a powerful tool you can use to produce beautiful code. First, let's learn the rules.

2.5.1   *Using = for assigning*

The first rule of the match operator is that variable assignments only happen when the variable is on the left side of the expression. For example:

```
iex> programmers = Map.put(programmers, :jose, "Elixir")
```

This is the result:

```
%{joe: "Erlang", jose: "Elixir", matz: "Ruby", rich: "Clojure"}
```

Here, you assign the result of `Map.put/2` to programmers. As expected, programmers contains the following:

```
iex> programmers
%{joe: "Erlang", jose: "Elixir", matz: "Ruby", rich: "Clojure"}
```

2.5.2   *Using = for matching*

Here's when things get slightly interesting. Let's swap the order of the previous expression:

```
iex> %{joe: "Erlang", jose: "Elixir", matz: "Ruby", rich: "Clojure"}
➥ = programmers
%{joe: "Erlang", jose: "Elixir", matz: "Ruby", rich: "Clojure"}
```

Notice that this is not an assignment. Instead, a *successful pattern match* has occurred, because the contents of both the left side and programmers are identical.

Next, let's see an *unsuccessful* pattern match:

```
iex> %{tolkien: "Elvish"} = programmers
** (MatchError) no match of right hand side value: %{joe: "Erlang", jose:
    ➥"Elixir", matz: "Ruby", rich: "Clojure"}
```

When an unsuccessful match occurs, a `MatchError` is raised. Let's look at destructuring next because you'll need this to perform some cool tricks with pattern matching.

2.5.3   *Destructuring*

Destructuring is where pattern matching shines. One of the nicest definitions of destructuring comes from *Common Lisp: The Language:*[1] "Destructuring allows you to

---

[1]   "Destructuring," in *Common Lisp: The Language*, 2nd ed., by Guy L. Steele Jr. (Digital Press, 1990).

bind a set of variables to a corresponding *set of values* anywhere that you can normally bind a value to a single variable." Here's what that means in code:

```
iex> %{joe: a, jose: b, matz: c, rich: d} =
        %{joe: "Erlang", jose: "Elixir", matz: "Ruby", rich: "Clojure"}
%{joe: "Erlang", jose: "Elixir", matz: "Ruby", rich: "Clojure"}
```

Here are the contents of each of the variables:

```
iex> a
"Erlang"

iex> b
"Elixir"

iex> c
"Ruby"

iex> d
"Clojure"
```

In this example, you bind a set of *variables* (a, b, c, and d) to a corresponding set of *values* ("Erlang", "Elixir", "Ruby", and "Clojure"). What if you're only interested in extracting some of the information? No problem, because you can do pattern matching without needing to specify the entire pattern:

```
iex> %{jose: most_awesome_language} = programmers
%{joe: "Erlang", jose: "Elixir", matz: "Ruby", rich: "Clojure"}
iex> most_awesome_language
"Elixir"
```

This will come in handy when you're only interesting in extracting a few pieces of information.

Here's another useful technique that's used often in Elixir programs. Notice the return values of these two expressions:

```
iex> Map.fetch(programmers, :rich)
{:ok, "Clojure"}
iex> Map.fetch(programmers, :rasmus)
:error
```

A tuple with the atom :ok and the value (the programming language) is returned when a key is found, or an :error atom otherwise. You can see how tuples and atoms are useful and how you can exploit this with pattern matching. By using the return values of both the happy ({:ok, language}) and exceptional paths (:error), you can express yourself as follows:

```
iex> case Map.fetch(programmers, :rich) do
...>    {:ok, language} ->
...>        IO.puts "#{language} is a legit language."
...>    :error ->
...>        IO.puts "No idea what language this is."
...> end
```

This returns

```
Clojure is a legit language.
```

EXAMPLE: READING A FILE

Destructuring is useful for declaring preconditions in your programs. What do I mean by that? Let's take reading a file as an example. If most of your logic depends on the file being readable, then it makes sense to find out as soon as possible whether an error occurs with file reading. It would also be helpful to know what kind of error occurred. Figure 2.4 shows a snippet from the `File.read/1` documentation.

---

read(path)

Specs:

> **read(Path.t) :: {:ok, binary} | {:error, posix}**

Returns `{:ok, binary}`, where binary is a binary data object that contains the contents of path, or `{:error, reason}` if an error occurs.

Typical error reasons:

- `:enoent` - the file does not exist
- `:eacces` - missing permission for reading the file,

  > or for searching one of the parent directories

- `:eisdir` - the named file is a directory
- `:enotdir` - a component of the file name is not a directory;

  > on some platforms, `` `:enoent` `` is returned instead

- `:enomem` - there is not enough memory for the contents of the file

---

Figure 2.4   Documentation for `File.read/1`

What can you learn from reading this documentation?

- For a successful read, `File.read/1` returns a `{:ok, binary}` tuple. Note that binary is the entire contents of the read file.
- Otherwise, a `{:error, posix}` tuple is returned. The variable posix contains the reason for the error, which is an atom such as `:enoent` or `:eaccess`.

Here's an example of the code to read a file:

```
case File.read("KISS - Beth.mp3") do
  {:ok, binary} ->
    IO.puts "KI♯♯ rocks!"
  {:error, reason} ->
    IO.puts "No Rock N Roll for anyone today because of #{reason}."
end
```

EXAMPLE: TIC-TAC-TOE BOARD

Listing 2.4 is an illustrative example of a Tic-Tac-Toe application. The check_board/1 function checks whether the tic-tac-toe's board configuration is a winning combination. The board is expressed using tuples. Notice how you "draw" the board using tuples and how easy the code is to understand.

Listing 2.4 Tic-tac-toe board that uses tuples to represent board configurations

```
def check_board(board) do
  case board do
    { :x, :x, :x,
      _ , _ , _ ,
      _ , _ , _ } -> :x_win

    { _ , _ , _ ,
      :x, :x, :x,
      _ , _ , _ } -> :x_win

    { _ , _ , _ ,
      _ , _ , _ ,
      :x, :x, :x} -> :x_win

    { :x, _ , _ ,
      :x, _ , _ ,
      :x, _ , _ } -> :x_win

    { _ , :x, _ ,
      _ , :x, _ ,
      _ , :x, _ } -> :x_win

    { _ , _ , :x,
      _ , _ , :x,
      _ , _ , :x} -> :x_win

    { :x, _ , _ ,
      _ , :x, _ ,
      _ , _ , :x} -> :x_win

    { _ , _ , :x,
      _ , :x, _ ,
      :x, _ , _ } -> :x_win

    # Player O board patterns omitted ...

    { a, b, c,
      d, e, f,
      g, h, i } when a and b and c and d and e and f and g and h and i ->
      :draw

    _ -> :in_progress
  end
end
```

Note that the underscore (_) is the "don't care" or "match everything" operator. You'll see quite a few examples of it in this book. And you'll see more pattern-matching in section 2.6 when we look at lists.

EXAMPLE: PARSING AN MP3 FILE

Elixir is brilliant for parsing binary data. In this example, you'll extract metadata from an MP3 file; it's also a good exercise to reinforce some of the concepts you've learned. Before you parse a binary, you must know the layout. The information you're interested in, the *ID3 tag*, is located in the last 128 bytes of the MP3 (see figure 2.5).

Figure 2.5   The ID3 tag is located in the last 128 bytes of the MP3.

You must somehow ignore the audio data portion and concentrate only on the ID3 tag. The diagram in figure 2.6 shows the ID3 tag's layout. The first three bytes are called the *header* and contain three characters: "T", "A", and "G". The next 30 bytes contain the *title*. The next 30 bytes are the *artist*, followed by another 30 bytes containing the *album*. The next four bytes are the *year* (such as "2", "0", "1", "4").

Try to imagine how you might extract this metadata in some other programming language. Listing 2.5 shows the Elixir version; save the file as id3.ex.

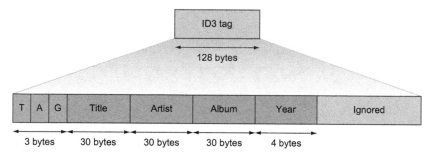

Figure 2.6   The layout of the ID3 tag

Listing 2.5   Full ID3-parsing program (id3.ex)

```
defmodule ID3Parser do
  def parse(file_name) do
    case File.read(file_name) do
      {:ok, mp3} ->
        mp3_byte_size = byte_size(mp3) - 128
        << _ :: binary-size(mp3_byte_size), id3_tag :: binary >> = mp3
        << "TAG", title  :: binary-size(30),
                 artist  :: binary-size(30),
                 album   :: binary-size(30),
                 year    :: binary-size(4),
                 _rest   :: binary >>         = id3_tag
```

Reads the MP3 binary

A successful file read returns a tuple that matches this pattern.

Calculates the audio portion of the MP3 in bytes

Pattern-matches the MP3 binary to capture the bytes of the ID3 tag

Pattern-matches the ID3 tag to capture the ID3 fields

```
        IO.puts "#{artist} - #{title} (#{album}, #{year})"
    _ ->
        IO.puts "Couldn't open #{file_name}"
    end
  end
end
```

⟵ **A failed file read is matched with anything else.**

Here's an example run of the program:

```
% iex id3.ex

iex(1)> ID3Parser.parse "sample.mp3"
```

And here's an example result:

```
Lana Del Rey - Ultraviolence (Ultraviolence, 2014)
:ok
```

Let's walk through the program. First the program reads the MP3. A happy path will return a tuple that matches {:ok, mp3}, where mp3 contains the binary contents of the file. Otherwise, the catch-all _ operator will match a failed file read.

Because you're only interested in the ID3 tag, you need a way to skip ahead. You first compute the size in bytes of the audio portion of the binary. Once you have this information, you can use the size of the audio portion to tell Elixir how to destructure the binary. You pattern-match the MP3 by declaring a pattern on the left and the mp3 variable on the right. Recall that variable assignment takes place when the variable is on the left side of an expression, and pattern matching is attempted otherwise (see figure 2.7).

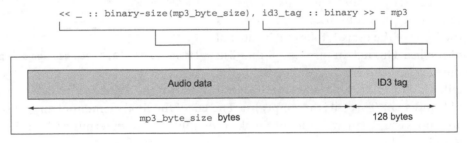

Figure 2.7 How the MP3 is destructured

You may recognize the << >>: it's used to represent an Elixir binary. You then declare that you aren't interested in the audio part. How? By specifying the binary size you computed previously. What remains is the ID3 tag, which is captured in the id3_tag variable. Now you're free to extract the information from the ID3 tag!

To do that, you perform another pattern match with the declared pattern on the left and id3_tag on the right. By declaring the appropriate number of bytes, you can capture the title, the artist, and other information in the respective variables (see figure 2.8).

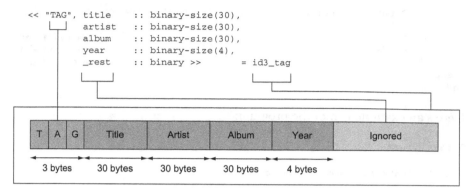

Figure 2.8   Destructuring the ID3 binary

2.6   *Lists*

Lists are another data type in Elixir. You can do quite a few interesting things with lists, and they therefore deserve their own section.

Lists are somewhat similar to *linked lists*[2] in that random access is essentially a O(n) (linear) operation. Here's the recursive definition of a list: a non-empty list consists of a head and a tail. The tail is also a list. Here it is, translated to code:

```
iex> [1, 2, 3] == [1 | [2 | [3 | []]]]
true
```

A diagram illustrates this better, as shown in figure 2.9.

Let's try to understand this picture by starting at the outermost box. This says the head of the list is 1, followed by the tail of the list. This tail, in turn, is another list: the head of this list is 2, followed by the

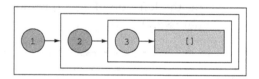

Figure 2.9   [1,2,3] represented as a picture

tail, which (again) is another list. Finally, this list (in the third box) consists of a head of 3 and a tail. This tail is an empty list. The tail of the final element of any list is always an empty list. Recursive functions make use of this fact to determine when the end of a list is reached.

You can also use the pattern-matching operator to prove that [1, 2, 3] and [1 | [2 | [3 | []]]] are the same thing:

```
iex> [1, 2, 3] = [1 | [2 | [3 | []]]]
[1, 2, 3]
```

---

[2] http://en.wikipedia.org/wiki/Linked_list.

Because no `MatchError` occurs, you can be certain that both representations of the list are equivalent. Of course, you won't be typing `[1|[2|[3|[]]]]` in your day-to-day code; this is just to emphasize that a list is a recursive data structure.

I haven't explained what the `|` is. This is commonly called the *cons* operator.[3] When applied to lists, it separates the head and tail. That is, the list is destructured. This is another instance of pattern matching in action:

```
iex> [head | tail] = [1, 2, 3]
[1, 2, 3]
```

Let's check the contents of head and tail:

```
iex> head
1
iex> tail          <——— Also a list
[2, 3]
```

Notice that `tail` is also a list, which is in line with the definition. You can also use the cons operator to add (or append) to the beginning of a list:

```
iex(1)> list = [1, 2, 3]
[1, 2, 3]
iex(2)> [0 | list ]
[0, 1, 2, 3]
```

You can use the ++ operator to concatenate lists:

```
iex(3)> [0] ++ [1, 2, 3]
[0, 1, 2, 3]
```

What about a list with a single element? If you understood figure 2.9, then this is a piece of cake:

```
iex(1)> [ head | tail ] = [:lonely]
[:lonely]
iex(2)> head
:lonely
iex(3)> tail
[]
```

This list contains a single atom. Notice that `tail` is an empty list; this may seem strange at first, but if you think about it, it fits the definition. It's precisely this definition that allows you to do interesting things with lists and recursion, which we examine next.

2.6.1 *Example: flattening a list*

Now that you know how lists work, let's build a `flatten/1` function. `flatten/1` takes in a possibly nested list and returns a flattened version. Flattening a list can be useful,

---

[3] Short for *construct*. See http://en.wikipedia.org/wiki/Cons for more information.

especially if the list is used to represent a tree data structure;[4] flattening the tree returns all the elements contained in the tree. Let's see an example:

```
List.flatten [1, [:two], ["three", []]]
```

This returns

```
[1, :two, "three"]
```

Here's one possible implementation of `flatten/1`:

```
defmodule MyList do
  def flatten([]), do: []          ◄──────── ❶ Base case: an empty list

  def flatten([ head | tail ]) do           ❷ Non-empty list with more
    flatten(head) ++ flatten(tail)             than one element
  end

  def flatten(head), do: [ head ]  ◄──────── ❸ Single-element list
end
```

Take a moment to digest the code, because there's more to it than meets the eye. There are three cases to consider.

You begin with the base case (or *degenerate case*, if you've taken a computer science course): an empty list ❶. If you get an empty list, you return an empty list.

For a non-empty list ❷, you use the cons operator to split the list into `head` and `tail`. You then recursively call `flatten/1` on both `head` and `tail`. Next, the result is concatenated using the `++` operator. Note that `head` can also be a nested list; for example, `[[1], 2]` means `head` is `[1]`.

If you get a non-list argument, you turn it into a list. Now, consider what happens to a list such as `[[1], 2]`. It helps to trace the execution on paper:

1 The first function clause ❶ doesn't match.
2 The second function clause ❷ matches. In this case, you pattern-match the list: `head` is `[1]`, and `tail` is 2. Now, `flatten([1])` and `flatten(2)` are called recursively.
3 Handle `flatten([1])`. Again it doesn't match the first clause ❶. The second one ❷ matches. `head` is 1, and `tail` is `[]`.
4 `flatten(1)` is called. The third function clause ❸ matches, and it returns `[1]`. `flatten([])` matches the first clause and returns `[]`. A previous call to `flatten(2)` (see step 2) returns `[2]`. `[1] ++ [] ++ [2]` yields the flattened list.

Don't despair if you don't get that the first time through. As with most things, practice will go a long way in helping your understanding. Also, you'll see numerous examples in the upcoming chapters.

---

4 http://mng.bz/cj87.

2.6.2   *Ordering of function clauses*

I previously mentioned that the order of function clauses matters. This is a perfect place to explain why. Consider this example:

```
defmodule MyList do

  def flatten([ head | tail ]) do
    flatten(head) ++ flatten(tail)
  end

  def flatten(head), do: [ head ]

  def flatten([]), do: []       ◁————❶ This line never runs!

end
```

The base case is the last clause. What will happen if you try `MyList.flatten([])`? You'd expect the result to be `[]`, but in fact you'd get back `[[]]`. If you give it a little thought, you'll realize that ❶ never runs. The reason is that the second function clause will match `[]`, and therefore the third function clause will be ignored.

   Let's try running this for real:

```
% iex length_converter.ex
warning: this clause cannot match because a previous clause at
line 7 always matches
```

Elixir has your back! Take heed of warnings like this because they can save you hours of debugging headaches. An unmatched clause can mean dead code or, in the worst case, an infinite loop.

2.7   *Meet |>, the pipe operator*

I'd like to introduce one of the most useful operators ever invented in programming-language history: the pipe operator, `|>`.[5] It takes the result of the expression on the left and inserts it as the first parameter of the function call on the right. Let's look at a code snippet from an Elixir program I wrote recently. Without the pipe operator, this is how I would have written it:

```
defmodule URLWorker do
  def start(url) do
    do_request(HTTPoison.get(url))
  end
  # ...
end
```

`HTTPoison` is a HTTP client. It takes `url` and returns the HTML page. The page is then passed to the `do_request` function to perform some parsing. Notice that in this version, you have to look for the innermost brackets to locate `url` and then move outward as you mentally trace the successive function calls.

---

[5] Here's a little trivia: the `|>` operator is inspired by F#.

Now, I present you with the version that uses pipe operators:

```
defmodule URLWorker do
  def start(url) do
    result = url |> HTTPoison.get |> do_request
  end
  # ...
end
```

No contest, right? Many of the examples in this book make extensive use of |>. The more you use it, the more you'll start to see data as being transformed from one form to another, something like an assembly line. When you use it often enough, you'll begin to miss it when you program in other languages.

2.7.1   *Example: filtering files in a directory by filename*

Let's say you have a directory filled with e-books, and this directory could potentially have folders nested within it. You want to get the filenames of only the Java-related EPUBs—that is, you only want books that have filenames that end with *.epub and that include "Java". Here's how to do it:

String representation of the directory

```
      "/Users/Ben/Books"
        |> Path.join("**/*.epub")
        |> Path.wildcard
        |> Enum.filter(fn fname ->
             String.contains?(Path.basename(fname), "Java")
           end)
```

Constructs a path using wildcards and specifies that you're only interested in EPUBs

Reads the path and returns a list of matched filenames

Selects only filenames containing "Java"

Here's some example output:

```
["/Users/Ben/Books/Java/Java_Concurrency_In_Practice.epub",
 "/Users/Ben/Books/Javascript/JavaScript Patterns.epub",
 "/Users/Ben/Books/Javascript/Functional_JavaScript.epub",
 "/Users/Ben/Books/Ruby/Using_JRuby_Bringing_Ruby_to_Java.epub"]
```

It's nice to read code in which the steps are so explicit and obvious.

2.8   *Erlang interoperability*

Because both Elixir and Erlang share the same bytecode, calling Erlang code doesn't affect performance in any way. More important, this means you're free to use any Erlang library with your Elixir code.

2.8.1   *Calling Erlang functions from Elixir*

The only difference is how the code is called. For example, you can generate a random number in Erlang like so:

```
1> random:uniform(123)
55
```

This function comes as part of the standard Erlang distribution. You can invoke the same Erlang function in Elixir with some syntactical tweaks:

```
iex> :random.uniform(123)
55
```

Notice the positions of the colon and dot in the two snippets. Those are the only differences!

There's a minor caveat in Elixir when working with native Erlang functions—you can't access documentation for Erlang functions from `iex`:

```
iex(3)> h :random
:random is an Erlang module and, as such, it does not have Elixir-style docs
```

Calling Erlang functions can be useful when Elixir doesn't have an implementation available in the standard library. If you compare the Erlang standard library and that of Elixir, you may conclude that Erlang's library has many more features. But if you think about it, Elixir gets everything for free!

2.8.2 Calling the Erlang HTTP client in Elixir

When Elixir is missing a feature I want, I usually check whether there's an Erlang standard library function I can use before I search for third-party libraries. For example, I once wanted to build a web crawler in Elixir. One of the first steps in building a web crawler is having the ability to download a web page. This requires an HTTP client. Elixir doesn't come with a built-in HTTP client—it doesn't need to, because Erlang comes with one, aptly named `httpc`.[6]

Let's say you want to download the web page for a certain programming language. You can go to the Erlang documentation[7] and find exactly what you need, as shown in figure 2.10.

```
EXPORTS

request(Url) ->
request(Url, Profile) -> {ok, Result} | {error, Reason}

    Types:

        Url = url()
        Result = {status_line(), headers(), Body} | {status_code(), Body} |
        request_id()
        Body = string() | binary()
        Profile = profile() | pid() (when started stand_alone)
        Reason = term()

    Equivalent to httpc:request(get, {Url, []}, [], []).
```

Figure 2.10   The `httpc:request/1` Erlang documentation

---

[6] http://erlang.org/doc/man/httpc.html#request-1.

[7] Who am I kidding? In reality, I'd probably go to Stack Overflow first.

First you need to start the `inets` application (it's in the documentation), and then you make the actual request:

```
iex(1)> :inets.start
:ok
iex(2)> {:ok, {status, headers, body}} = :httpc.request 'http://www.elixir-
    ➥lang.org'
{:ok,
 {{'HTTP/1.1', 200, 'OK'},
  [{'cache-control', 'max-age=600'}, {'date', 'Tue, 28 Oct 2014 16:17:24 GMT'},
   {'accept-ranges', 'bytes'}, {'server', 'GitHub.com'},
   {'vary', 'Accept-Encoding'}, {'content-length', '17251'},
   {'content-type', 'text/html; charset=utf-8'},
   {'expires', 'Tue, 28 Oct 2014 16:27:24 GMT'},
   {'last-modified', 'Tue, 21 Oct 2014 23:38:22 GMT'}],
  [60, 33, 68, 79, 67, 84, 89, 80, 69, 32, 104, 116, 109, 108, 62, 10, 60, 104,
   116, 109, 108, 32, 120, 109, 108, 110, 115, 61, 34, 104, 116, 116, 112, 58,
   47, 47, 119, 119, 119, 46, 119, 51, 46, 111, 114, 103, 47, 49, 57, 57, ...]}}
```

2.8.3   One more thing...

Erlang has also a neat GUI front end called *Observer* that lets you inspect the Erlang virtual machine, among other things. Invoking it is simple:

```
iex(1)> :observer.start
```

Because you aren't running any computationally intensive processes, you won't see much action for now. Figure 2.11 will whet your appetite.

Figure 2.11   Screenshots from Observer *(continued on next page)*

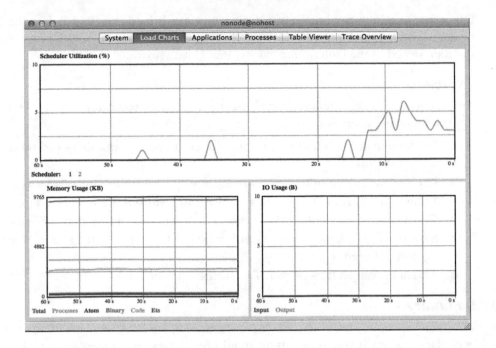

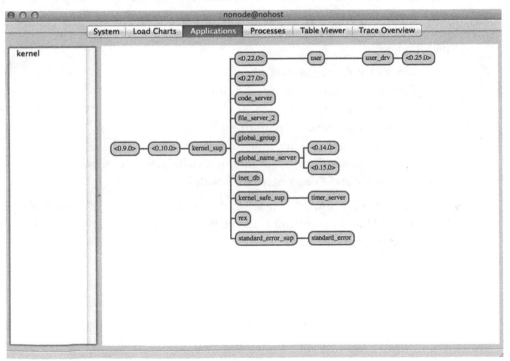

Figure 2.11 Screenshots from Observer *(continued from previous page)*

Observer is useful when it comes to seeing how much load the VM is taking and the layout of your supervision trees (you'll learn about that in chapter 6). You can also see the data stored in the built-in database(s) that Erlang provides.

2.9   *Exercises*

This was a pretty long chapter. Now it's time to make sure you understood everything! Try the following exercises:

1 Implement sum/1. This function should take in a list of numbers and return the sum of the list.
2 Explore the Enum module and familiarize yourself with the various functions.
3 Transform [1,[[2],3]] to [9, 4, 1] with and without the pipe operator.
4 Translate crypto:md5("Tales from the Crypt"). from Erlang to Elixir.
5 Explore the official Elixir "Getting Started" guide (http://elixir-lang.org /getting_started/1.html).
6 Take a look at an IPV4 packet. Try writing a parser for it.

2.10   *Summary*

This concludes our whirlwind tour. If you've made it this far, give yourself a pat on the back. Don't worry if you didn't understand everything; the concepts will make more sense as you continue to read, and many of the programming constructs will be obvious once you see their applications. As a quick recap, here's what you learned about in this chapter:

- Elixir's fundamental data types.
- Guards and how they work with function clauses.
- Pattern matching and how it leads to declarative code. We also looked at a few real-world examples of pattern matching.
- Lists, which are another fundamental data structure. You saw how lists are represented internally in Elixir and how that facilitates recursion.
- How Elixir and Erlang play nicely with each other.

In the next chapter, you'll learn about the fundamental unit of concurrency in Elixir: the process. This is one of the features that makes Elixir vastly different from traditional programming languages.

Processes 101

3

This chapter covers

- The Actor concurrency model
- Creating processes
- How to send and receive messages using processes
- Achieving concurrency using processes
- How to make processes communicate with each other

The concept of Elixir *processes* is one of the most important to understand, and it rightly deserves its own chapter. Processes are the fundamental units of concurrency in Elixir. In fact, the Erlang VM supports up to 134 million (!) processes,[1] which would cause all of your CPUs to happily light up. (I always get a warm, fuzzy feeling when I know I'm getting my money's worth from my hardware.) The processes created by the Erlang VM are independent of the operating system; they're lighter weight and take mere microseconds to create.[2]

---

[1] www.erlang.org/doc/man/erl.html#max_processes.
[2] Joe Armstrong, "Concurrency Oriented Programming in Erlang," Feb. 17, 2003, http://mng.bz/uT4q.

We're going to embark on a fun project. In this chapter, you'll build a simple program that reports the temperature of a given city/state/country. But first, let's learn about the Actor concurrency model.

3.1   *Actor concurrency model*

Erlang (and therefore Elixir) uses the Actor concurrency model. This means the following:

- Each *actor* is a *process.*
- Each process performs a *specific task.*
- To tell a process to do something, you need to *send it a message.* The process can reply by *sending back another message.*
- The kinds of messages the process can act on are specific to the process itself. In other words, messages are *pattern-matched.*
- Other than that, processes *don't share any information* with other processes.

If all this seems fuzzy, fret not. If you've done any object-oriented programming, you'll find that processes resemble objects in many ways. You could even argue that this is a purer form of object-orientation.

Here's one way to think about actors. Actors are like people. We communicate with each other by talking. For example, suppose my wife tells me to do the dishes. Of course, I respond by doing the dishes—I'm a good husband. But if my wife tells me to eat my vegetables, she'll be ignored—I won't respond to that. In effect, I'm choosing to respond only to certain kinds of messages. In addition, I don't know what goes on inside her head, and she doesn't know what goes on inside my head. As you'll soon see, the actor concurrency model acts the same way: it responds only to certain kinds of messages.

3.2   *Building a weather application*

Conceptually, the application you'll create in this chapter is simple (see figure 3.1). The first version accepts a single argument containing a location, and it reports the temperature in degrees Celsius. That involves making a HTTP request to an external weather service and parsing the JSON response to extract the temperature.

Making a single request is trivial. But what happens if you want to find out the temperatures in 100 cities simultaneously? Assuming that each request takes 1 second, are you going to wait 100 seconds? Obviously not! You'll see how to make concurrent requests so you can get the results as soon as possible.

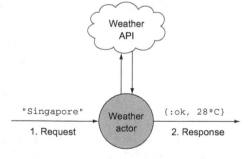

Figure 3.1   Weather actor handling a single request

One of the properties of concurrency is that you never know the order of the responses. For example, imagine that you pass in a list of cities in alphabetical order. The responses you get back are in no way guaranteed to be in the same order.

How can you ensure that the responses are in the correct order? Read on, dear reader—you begin your meteorological adventures in Elixir next.

3.2.1 *The naïve version*

Let's start with a naïve version of the weather application. It will contain all the logic needed to make a request, parse the response, and return the result, but no concurrency will be involved. By the end of this iteration, you'll know how to do the following:

- Install and use third-party libraries using `mix`
- Make a HTTP request to a third-party API
- Parse a JSON response using pattern matching
- Use pipes to facilitate data transformation

This is the first nontrivial program you'll work through in this book. But no worries: I'll guide you every step of the way.

CREATING A NEW PROJECT

The first order of business is to create a new project and, more important, give it a great name. Because I'm the author, I get to choose the name: Metex. Use `mix new <project name>` to create the new project:

```
% mix new metex
* creating README.md
* creating .gitignore
* creating mix.exs
* creating config
* creating config/config.exs
* creating lib
* creating lib/metex.ex
* creating test
* creating test/test_helper.exs
* creating test/metex_test.exs
Your mix project was created successfully.
You can use mix to compile it, test it, and more:

    cd metex
    mix test

% cd metex
```

Follow the instructions and `cd` into the metex directory.

INSTALLING THE DEPENDENCIES

Now open mix.exs. This is what you'll see:

```
defmodule Metex.Mixfile do
  use Mix.Project

  def project do
```

```
    [app: :metex,
     version: "0.0.1",
     elixir: "~> 1.0",
     deps: deps]
  end

  def application do
    [applications: [:logger]]
  end

  defp deps do
    []
  end
end
```

Every project generated by mix contains this file. It consists of two public functions: project and application. The project function basically sets up the project. More important, it sets up the project's dependencies by invoking the deps private function. deps is an empty list—for now. The application function is used to generate an application resource file. Certain dependencies in Elixir must be started in a specific way; such dependencies are declared in the application function. For example, before the application starts, the logger application is started first.

Let's add two dependencies by modifying the deps function to look like this:

```
defp deps do
  [
    {:httpoison, "~> 0.9.0"},     │ Declares dependencies and specifies
    {:json,     "~> 0.3.0"}       │ the respective version numbers
  ]
end
```

Next, add an entry to the application function:

```
def application do
  [applications: [:logger, :httpoison]]
end
```

Dependency version numbers are important!
Pay attention to the version numbers of your dependencies. Using the wrong version number can result in puzzling errors. Also note that many of these libraries specify the minimum version of Elixir they're compatible with.

How did I know to include :httpoison and not, say, :json? The truth is, I didn't—but I always read the manual. Each time I install a library, I first take a look at the README. In :httpoison's case, the README is as shown in figure 3.2.

Make sure you're in the metex directory and install the dependencies using the mix deps.get command:

```
% mix deps.get
```

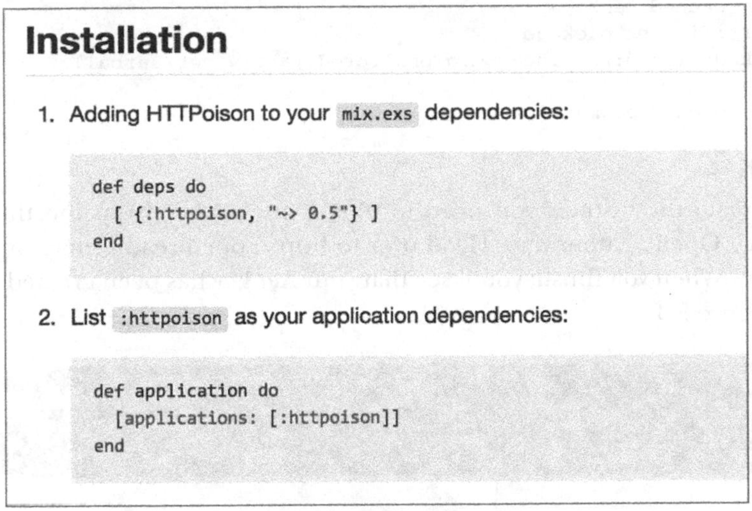

Installation

1. Adding HTTPoison to your `mix.exs` dependencies:

```
def deps do
  [ {:httpoison, "~> 0.5"} ]
end
```

2. List `:httpoison` as your application dependencies:

```
def application do
  [applications: [:httpoison]]
end
```

Figure 3.2   It's always helpful to look at the README for third-party libraries to check for important installation instructions.

Notice that `mix` helpfully resolves dependencies, too. In this case, it brings in two other libraries, `hackney` and `idna`:

```
Running dependency resolution
* Getting httpoison (Hex package)
Checking package (http://s3.hex.pm.global.prod.fastly.net/tarballs/httpoison-
    0.9.0.tar)
➥Using locally cached package
* Getting json (Hex package)
Checking package (http://s3.hex.pm.global.prod.fastly.net/tarballs/
➥json-0.3.2.tar)
Using locally cached package
* Getting hackney (Hex package)
Checking package (http://s3.hex.pm.global.prod.fastly.net/tarballs/
➥hackney-1.5.7.tar)
Using locally cached package
* Getting ssl_verify_fun (Hex package)
Checking package (http://s3.hex.pm.global.prod.fastly.net/tarballs/
➥ssl_verify_fun-1.1.0.tar)
Using locally cached package
* Getting mimerl (Hex package)
Checking package (http://s3.hex.pm.global.prod.fastly.net/tarballs/
➥mimerl-1.0.2.tar)
Using locally cached package
* Getting metrics (Hex package)
Checking package (http://s3.hex.pm.global.prod.fastly.net/tarballs/
➥metrics-1.0.1.tar)
Using locally cached package
* Getting idna (Hex package)
Checking package (http://s3.hex.pm.global.prod.fastly.net/tarballs/
➥idna-1.2.0.tar)
```

```
Using locally cached package
* Getting certifi (Hex package)
Checking package (http://s3.hex.pm.global.prod.fastly.net/tarballs/
➥certifi-0.4.0.tar)
Using locally cached package
```

3.3   *The worker*

Before you create the worker, you need to obtain an API key from the third-party weather service OpenWeatherMap. Head over to http://openweathermap.org to create an account. When you finish, you'll see that your API key has been created for you, as shown in figure 3.3.

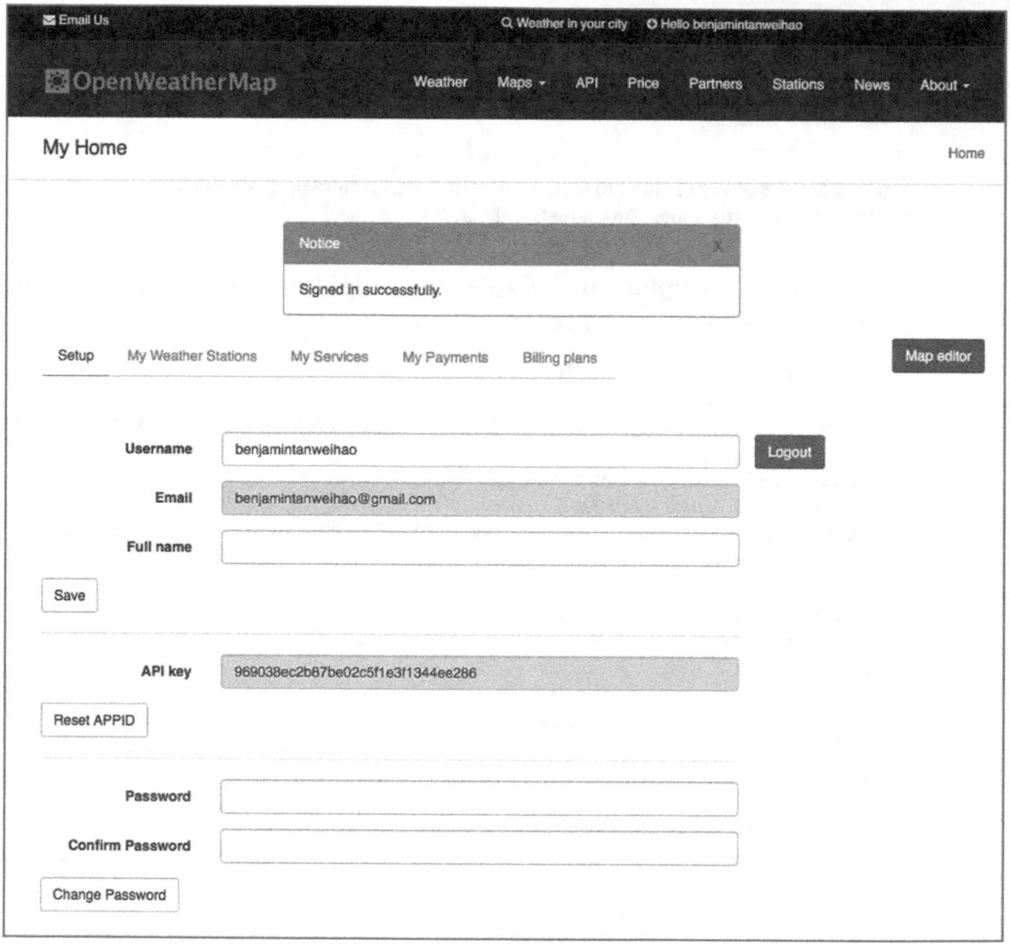

Figure 3.3   Creating an account and getting an API key from OpenWeatherMap

Now you can get into the implementation details of the worker. The worker's job is to fetch the temperature of a given location from OpenWeatherMap and parse the results. Create a worker.ex file in the lib directory, and enter the code in the following listing in it.

Listing 3.1 Full source of lib/worker.ex

```elixir
defmodule Metex.Worker do

  def temperature_of(location) do
    result = url_for(location) |> HTTPoison.get |> parse_response
    case result do
      {:ok, temp} ->
        "#{location}: #{temp}°C"
      :error ->
        "#{location} not found"
    end
  end

  defp url_for(location) do
    location = URI.encode(location)
    "http://api.openweathermap.org/data/2.5/weather?q=#{location}&appid=
#{apikey}"
  end

  defp parse_response({:ok, %HTTPoison.Response{body: body, status_code:
200}}) do
    body |> JSON.decode! |> compute_temperature
  end

  defp parse_response(_) do
    :error
  end

  defp compute_temperature(json) do
    try do
      temp = (json["main"]["temp"] - 273.15) |> Float.round(1)
      {:ok, temp}
    rescue
      _ -> :error
    end
  end

  defp apikey do
    "APIKEY-GOES-HERE"
  end

end
```

3.3.1 *Taking the worker for a spin*

Don't be alarmed if you don't entirely understand what's going on; we'll go through the program bit by bit. First, let's see how to run this program from iex. From the project root directory, launch iex like so:

```
% iex -S mix
```

If this is the first time you've run that command, you'll notice a list of dependencies being compiled. You won't see this the next time you run iex unless you modify the dependencies.

Now, let's find out the temperature of one of the coldest places in the world:

```
iex(1)> Metex.Worker.temperature_of "Verkhoyansk, Russia"
"Verkhoyansk, Russia: -37.3°C"
```

Just for kicks, let's try another:

```
iex(2)> Metex.Worker.temperature_of "Snag, Yukon, Canada"
"Snag, Yukon, Canada: -27.6°C"
```

What happens when you give a nonsensical location?

```
iex(3)> Metex.Worker.temperature_of "Omicron Persei 8"
"Omicron Persei 8 not found"
```

Now that you've seen the worker in action, let's take a closer look at how it works, beginning with the temperature_of/1 function:

```
defmodule Metex.Worker do

  def temperature_of(location) do
    result = url_for(location) |> HTTPoison.get |>  parse_response
    case result do
      {:ok, temp} ->
        "#{location}: #{temp}°C"
      :error ->
        "#{location} not found"
    end
  end

  # ...
end
```

Data transformation: from URL to HTTP response to parsing that response

A successfully parsed response returns the temperature and location.

Otherwise, an error message is returned.

The most important line in the function is

```
result = location |> url_for |> HTTPoison.get |> parse_response
```

Without using the pipe operator, you'd have to write the function like so:

```
result = parse_response(HTTPoison.get(url_for(location)))
```

location |> url_for constructs the URL that's used to call the weather API. For example, the URL for Singapore is as follows (substitute your own API key for <APIKEY>):

```
http://api.openweathermap.org/data/2.5/weather?q=Singapore&appid=<APIKEY>
```

Once you have the URL, you can use httpoison, an HTTP client, to make a GET request:

```
location |> url_for |> HTTPoison.get
```

If you try that URL in your browser, you'll get something like this (I've trimmed the JSON for brevity):

```
{
  ...
  "main": {
    "temp": 299.86,
    "temp_min": 299.86,
    "temp_max": 299.86,
    "pressure": 1028.96,
    "sea_level": 1029.64,
    "grnd_level": 1028.96,
    "humidity": 100
  },
  ...
}
```

Let's take a closer look at the response from the HTTP client. Try this in iex, too. (If you exited iex, remember to use iex -S mix so that the dependencies—such as httpoison—are loaded properly.) Use the URL for Singapore's temperature:

```
iex(1)> HTTPoison.get
➡ "http://api.openweathermap.org/data/2.5/weather?q=Singapore&appid=<APIKEY>"
```

Take a look at the results:

```
{:ok,
 %HTTPoison.Response{body:
➡ "{\"coord\":{\"lon\":103.85,\"lat\":1.29},\"sys\":{\"message\":0.098,
➡ \"country\":\"SG\",\"sunrise\":1421795647,\"sunset\":1421839059},
➡ \"weather\":[{\"id\":802,\"main\":\"Clouds\",\"description\":
➡ \"scattered clouds\",\"icon\":\"03n\"}],\"base\":\"cmc stations\",
➡ \"main\":{\"temp\":299.86,\"temp_min\":299.86,\"temp_max\":299.86,
➡ \"pressure\":1028.96,\"sea_level\":1029.64,\"grnd_level\":1028.96,
➡ \"humidity\":100},\"wind\":{\"speed\":6.6,\"deg\":29.0007},
➡ \"clouds\":{\"all\":36},\"dt\":1421852665,\"id\":1880252,
➡ \"name\":\"Singapore\",\"cod\":200}\n",
   headers: %{"Access-Control-Allow-Credentials" => "true",
     "Access-Control-Allow-Methods" => "GET, POST",
     "Access-Control-Allow-Origin" => "*",
     "Connection" => "keep-alive",
     "Content-Type" => "application/json; charset=utf-8",
     "Date" => "Wed, 21 Jan 2015 15:59:14 GMT", "Server" => "nginx",
     "Transfer-Encoding" => "chunked", "X-Source" => "redis"},
   status_code: 200}}
```

What about passing in a URL to a missing page?

```
iex(2)> HTTPoison.get "http://en.wikipedia.org/phpisawesome"
```

This returns something like the following:

```
{:ok,
 %HTTPoison.Response{body: "<html>Opps</html>",
```

```
headers: %{"Accept-Ranges" => "bytes", "Age" => "12",
  "Cache-Control" => "s-maxage=2678400, max-age=2678400",
  "Connection" => "keep-alive", "Content-Length" => "2830",
  "Content-Type" => "text/html; charset=utf-8",
  "Date" => "Wed, 21 Jan 2015 16:04:48 GMT",
  "Refresh" => "5; url=http://en.wikipedia.org/wiki/phpisawesome",
  "Server" => "Apache",
  "Set-Cookie" => "GeoIP=SG:Singapore:1.2931:103.8558:v4; Path=/;
➥Domain=.wikipedia.org",
  "Via" => "1.1 varnish, 1.1 varnish, 1.1 varnish",
  "X-Cache" => "cp1053 miss (0), cp4016 hit (1), cp4018 frontend miss (0)",
  "X-Powered-By" => "HHVM/3.3.1",
  "X-Varnish" => "2581642697, 646845726 646839971, 2421023671",
  "X-Wikimedia-Debug" => "prot=http:// serv=en.wikipedia.org
➥loc=/phpisawesome"},
  status_code: 404}}
```

And finally, a ridiculous URL yields this error:

```
iex(3)> HTTPoison.get "phpisawesome"
{:error, %HTTPoison.Error{id: nil, reason: :nxdomain}}
```

You've just seen several variations of what `HTTPoison.get(url)` can return. The happy path returns a pattern that resembles this:

```
{:ok, %HTTPoison.Response{status_code: 200, body: content}}}
```

This pattern conveys the following information:

- This is a two-element tuple.
- The first element of the tuple is an `:ok` atom, followed by a structure that represents the response.
- The response is of type `HTTPoison.Response` and contains at least two fields.
- The value of `status_code` is 200, which represents a successful HTTP GET request.
- The value of `body` is captured in `content`.

As you can see, pattern matching is incredibly succinct and is a beautiful way to express what you want.

Similarly, an error tuple has the following pattern:

```
{:error, %HTTPoison.Error{reason: reason}}
```

Let's do the same analysis here:

- This is a two-element tuple.
- The first element of the tuple is an `:error` atom, followed by a structure that represents the error.
- The response is of type `HTTPoison.Error` and contains at least one field, `reason`.
- The reason for the error is captured in `reason`.

With all that in mind, let's take a look at the `parse_response/1` function:

```
defp parse_response({:ok, %HTTPoison.Response{body: body, status_code:
➥200}}) do
  body |> JSON.decode! |> compute_temperature
end

defp parse_response(_) do
  :error
end
```

This specifies two versions of `parse_response/1`. The first version matches a successful GET request because you're matching a response of type `HTTPoison.Response` and also making sure `status_code` is 200. You treat any other kind of response as an error.

Let's take a closer look now at the first version of `parse_response/1`:

```
defp parse_response({:ok, %HTTPoison.Response{body: body, status_code: 200}})
    ➥do
  # ...
end
```

On a successful pattern match, the string representation of the JSON is captured in the `body` variable. To turn it into real JSON, you need to decode it:

```
body |> JSON.decode!
```

You then pass this JSON into the `compute_temperature/1` function. Here's the function again:

```
defp compute_temperature(json) do
  try do
    temp = (json["main"]["temp"] - 273.15) |> Float.round(1)
    {:ok, temp}
  rescue
    _ -> :error
  end
end
```

You wrap the computation in a `try ... rescue ... end` block, where you attempt to retrieve the temperature from the given JSON and then perform some arithmetic: you subtract 273.15 because the API provides the results in kelvins. You also round off the temperature to one decimal place.

At any of these points, an error may occur. If it does, you want the return result to be an `:error` atom. Otherwise, a two-element tuple containing `:ok` as the first element and the temperature is returned. Having return values of different shapes is useful because code that calls this function can, for example, easily pattern-match on both success and failure cases. You'll see many more examples that take advantage of pattern matching in the following chapters.

What happens if the HTTP GET response doesn't match the first pattern? That's the job of the second `parse_response/1` function:

```
defp parse_response(_) do
  :error
end
```

Here, any response other than a successful one is treated as an error. That's basically it!

You should now have a better understanding of how the worker works. Let's look at how processes are created in Elixir.

3.4   *Creating processes for concurrency*

Let's imagine you have a list of cities for which you want to get temperatures:

```
iex> cities = ["Singapore", "Monaco", "Vatican City", "Hong Kong", "Macau"]
```

You send the requests to the worker, one at a time:

```
iex(2)> cities |> Enum.map(fn city ->
  Metex.Worker.temperature_of(city)
end)
```

This results in the following:

```
["Singapore: 27.5°C", "Monaco: 7.3°C", "Vatican City: 10.9°C", "Hong Kong:
    ⮕18.1°C", "Macau: 19.5°C"]
```

The problem with this approach is that it's wasteful. As the size of the list grows, so will the time you have to wait for all the responses to complete. The next request will be processed only when the previous one has completed (see figure 3.4). You can do better.

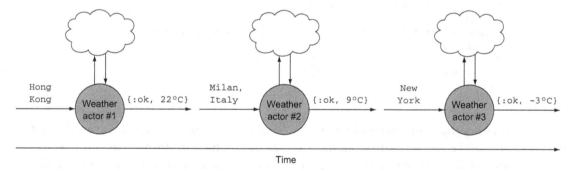

Figure 3.4   **Without concurrency, the next request has to wait for the previous one to complete. This is inefficient.**

It's important to realize that requests don't depend on each other. In other words, you can package each call to Metex.Worker.temperature_of/1 into a process. Let's teach the worker how to respond to messages. First, add the loop/0 function to lib/worker.ex in the next listing.

Listing 3.2 Adding `loop/0` to the worker so it can respond to messages

```
defmodule Metex.Worker do

  def loop do
    receive do
      {sender_pid, location} ->
        send(sender_pid, {:ok, temperature_of(location)})
      _ ->
        IO.puts "don't know how to process this message"
    end
    loop
  end

  defp temperature_of(location) do
    # ...
  end

  # ...
end
```

Before we go into the details, let's play around with this. If you already have iex open, you can reload the module:

```
iex> r(Metex.Worker)
```

Otherwise, run iex -S mix again. Create a process that runs the worker's loop function:

```
iex> pid = spawn(Metex.Worker, :loop, [])
```

The built-in spawn function creates a process. There are two variations of spawn. The first version takes a single function as a parameter; the second takes a module, a symbol representing the function name, and a list of arguments. Both versions return a process id (pid).

3.4.1 Receiving messages

A pid is a *reference* to a process, much as in object-oriented programming the result of initializing an object is a *reference* to that object. With the pid, you can send the process *messages*. The kinds of messages the process can receive are defined in the receive block:

```
receive do
  {sender_pid, location} ->
    send(sender_pid, {:ok, temperature_of(location)})
  _ ->
    IO.puts "don't know how to process this message"
end
```

Messages are pattern-matched from top to bottom. In this case, if the incoming message is a two-element tuple, then the body will be executed. Any other message will be pattern-matched in the second pattern.

What would happen if you wrote the previous code with the function clauses swapped?

```
receive do
  _ ->                                           <──── Matches any message!
    IO.puts "don't know how to process this message"
  {sender_pid, location} ->
    send(sender_pid, {:ok, temperature_of(location)})
end
```

If you try to run this, Elixir helpfully warns you:

```
lib/worker.ex:7: warning: this clause cannot match because a previous
➥clause at line 5 always matches
```

In other words, {sender_pid, location} will never be matched because the match-all operator (_), as it name suggests, will greedily match every single message that comes its way.

In general, it's good practice to have the match-all case as the last message to be matched. This is because unmatched messages are kept in the mailbox. Therefore, it's possible to make the VM run out of memory by repeatedly sending messages to a process that doesn't handle unmatched messages.

3.4.2 *Sending messages*

Messages are sent using the built-in send/2 function. The first argument is the pid of the process you want to send the message to. The second argument is the actual message:

```
receive do                                  │ The incoming message contains
  {sender_pid, location} ->                 │ the sender pid and location.
    send(sender_pid, {:ok, temperature_of(location)})  ◁──┘
end
```

Here, you're sending the result of the request to sender_pid. Where do you get sender_pid? From the incoming message, of course! You expect the incoming message to consist of the sender's pid and the location. Putting in the sender's pid (or any process id, for that matter) is like putting a return address on an envelope: it gives the recipient a place to reply to.

Let's send the process you created earlier a message:

```
iex> send(pid, {self, "Singapore"})
```

Here's the result:

```
{#PID<0.125.0>, "Singapore"}
```

Wait—other than the return result, nothing else happened! Let's break it down. The first thing to note is that the result of send/2 is always the message. The second thing is that `send/2` always returns immediately. In order words, `send/2` is like fire-and-forget. That explains how you got the result, because again, the result of `send/2` is the message. But what about *why* you aren't getting back any temperatures?

What did you pass into the message payload as the sender pid? `self`! What is `self`, exactly? `self` is the pid of the calling process. In this case, it's the pid of the `iex` shell session. You're effectively telling the worker to send all replies to the shell session. To get back responses from the shell session, you can use the built-in `flush/0` function:

```
iex> flush
"Singapore: 27.5°C"
:ok
```

`flush/0` clears out all the messages that were sent to the shell and prints them out. Therefore, the next time you do a `flush`, you'll only get the `:ok` atom. Let's see this in action. Once again, you have a list of cities:

```
iex> cities = ["Singapore", "Monaco", "Vatican City", "Hong Kong", "Macau"]
```

You iterate through each city, and in each iteration, you spawn a new worker. Using the pid of the new worker, you send the worker process a two-element tuple as a message containing the return address (the `iex` shell session) and the city:

```
iex> cities |> Enum.each(fn city ->
        pid = spawn(Metex.Worker, :loop, [])
        send(pid, {self, city})
     end)
```

Now, let's flush the messages:

```
iex> flush
{:ok, "Hong Kong: 17.8°C"}
{:ok, "Singapore: 27.5°C"}
{:ok, "Macau: 18.6°C"}
{:ok, "Monaco: 6.7°C"}
{:ok, "Vatican City: 11.8°C"}
:ok
```

Awesome! You finally got back results. Notice that they aren't in any particular order. That's because the response that completed first sent its reply back to the sender as soon as it was finished (see figure 3.5). If you run the iteration again, you'll probably get the results in a different order.

Look at the `loop` function again. Notice that it's *recursive*—it calls itself after a message has been processed:

```
def loop do
  receive do
    {sender_pid, location} ->
      send(sender_pid, {:ok, temperature_of(location)})
    _ ->
```

```
        send(sender_pid, "Unknown message")
      end
      loop                          <——  Recursive call to loop
    end
```

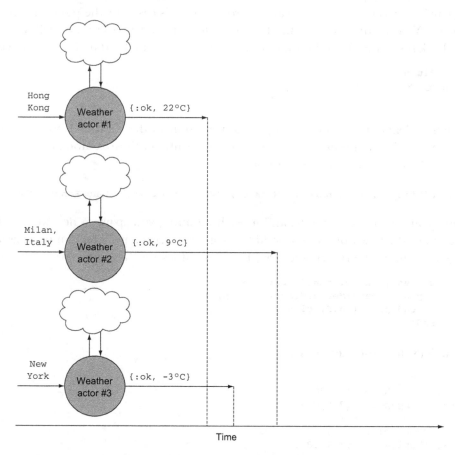

Figure 3.5 **The order of sent messages isn't guaranteed when processes
don't have to wait for each other.**

You may wonder why you need the loop in the first place. In general, the process
should be able to handle more than one message. If you left out the recursive call,
then the moment the process handled that first (and only) message, it would exit and
be garbage-collected. You usually want processes to be able to handle more than one
message! Therefore, you need a recursive call to the message-handling logic.

3.5   *Collecting and manipulating results with another actor*

Sending results to the shell session is great for seeing what messages are sent by workers, but nothing more. If you want to manipulate the results—say, by sorting them—

you need to find another way. Instead of using the shell session as the sender, you can create another actor to collect the results.

This actor must keep track of how many messages are expected. In other words, the actor must keep state. How can you do that?

Let's set up the actor first. Create a file called lib/coordinator.ex, and fill it as shown in the next listing.

Listing 3.3   Full source of lib/coordinator.ex

```
defmodule Metex.Coordinator do
  def loop(results \\ [], results_expected) do
    receive do
      {:ok, result} ->
        new_results = [result|results]
        if results_expected == Enum.count(new_results) do
          send self, :exit
        end
        loop(new_results, results_expected)
      :exit ->
        IO.puts(results |> Enum.sort |> Enum.join(", "))
      _ ->
        loop(results, results_expected)
    end
  end
end
```

Let's see how you can use the coordinator together with the workers. Open lib/metex.ex, and enter the code in the next listing.

Listing 3.4   Function to spawn a coordinator process and worker processes

```
defmodule Metex do
  def temperatures_of(cities) do
    coordinator_pid =
      spawn(Metex.Coordinator, :loop, [[], Enum.count(cities)])

    cities |> Enum.each(fn city ->
      worker_pid = spawn(Metex.Worker, :loop, [])
      send worker_pid, {coordinator_pid, city}
    end)
  end
end
```

Creates a coordinator process

Iterates through each city

Creates a worker process and executes its loop function

Sends the worker a message containing the coordinator process's pid and city

---

You can now determine the temperatures of cities by creating a list of cities

```
iex> cities = ["Singapore", "Monaco", "Vatican City", "Hong Kong", "Macau"]
```

and then calling `Metex.temperatures_of/1`:

```
iex> Metex.temperatures_of(cities)
```

The result is as expected:

```
Hong Kong: 17.8°C, Macau: 18.4°C, Monaco: 8.8°C, Singapore: 28.6°C, Vatican
➥City: 8.5°C
```

Here's how `Metex.temperatures_of/1` works. First you create a coordinator process. The `loop` function of the coordinator process expects two arguments: the current collected results and the total expected number of results. Therefore, when you create the coordinator, you initialize it with an empty result list and the number of cities:

```
iex> coordinator_pid = spawn(Metex.Coordinator, :loop, [[],
➥Enum.count(cities)])
```

Now the coordinator process is waiting for messages from the worker. Given a list of cities, you iterate through each city, create a worker, and then send the worker a message containing the coordinator pid and the city:

```
iex> cities |> Enum.each(fn city ->
        worker_pid = spawn(Metex.Worker, :loop, [])
        send worker_pid, {coordinator_pid, city}
    end)
```

Once all five workers have completed their requests, the coordinator dutifully reports the results:

```
Hong Kong: 16.6°C, Macau: 18.3°C, Monaco: 8.1°C, Singapore: 26.7°C, Vatican
➥City: 9.9°C
```

Success! Notice that the results are sorted in lexicographical order.

What kinds of messages can the coordinator receive from the worker? Inspecting the `receive do ... end` block, you can conclude that there are at least two kinds you're especially interested in:

- `{:ok, result}`
- `:exit`

Other kinds of messages are ignored. Let's examine each kind of message in closer detail.

3.5.1   *{:ok, result}—the happy path message*

If nothing goes wrong, you expect to receive a "happy path" message from a worker:

```
def loop(results \\ [], results_expected) do
  receive do
    {:ok, result} ->
      new_results = [result|results]          ◄─── Adds result to current
                                                    list of results
```

Checks if all results have been collected →
```
    if results_expected == Enum.count(new_results) do
      send self, :exit
    end
    loop(new_results, results_expected)

    # ... other patterns omitted ...

  end
end
```

Sends the coordinator the exit message

Loops with new results. Notice that results_expected remains unchanged.

When the coordinator receives a message that fits the `{:ok, result}` pattern, it adds the result to the current list of results (see figure 3.6). Next, you check whether the coordinator has received the expected number of results. Let's assume it hasn't. In this case, the `loop` function calls itself again. Notice the arguments to the recursive call to `loop`: this time you pass in `new_results`, and `results_expected` remains unchanged (see figure 3.7).

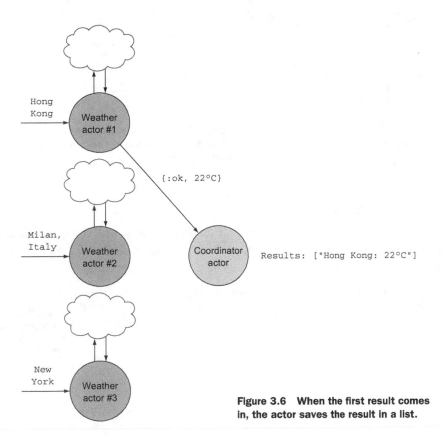

Figure 3.6   **When the first result comes in, the actor saves the result in a list.**

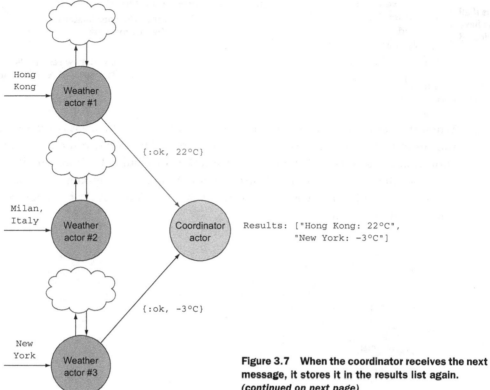

Figure 3.7 **When the coordinator receives the next message, it stores it in the results list again.** *(continued on next page)*

3.5.2 *:exit—the poison-pill message*

When the coordinator has received all the messages, it must find a way to tell itself to stop and to report the results if necessary. A simple way to do this is via a poison-pill message:

```
def loop(results \\ [], results_expected) do
  receive do
    # ... other pattern omitted ...

    :exit ->
      IO.puts(results |> Enum.sort |> Enum.join(", "))

    # ... other pattern omitted ...
  end
end
```

Prints the results lexicographically, separated by commas

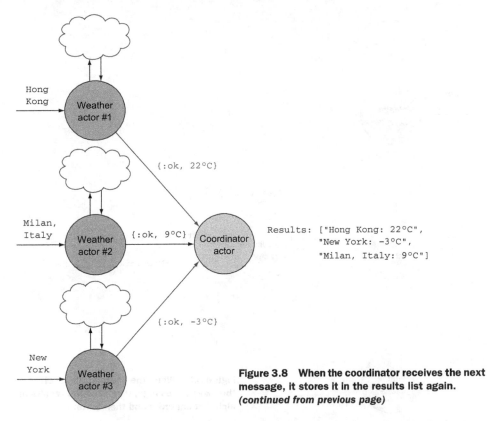

Figure 3.8   **When the coordinator receives the next message, it stores it in the results list again.** *(continued from previous page)*

When the coordinator receives an :exit message, it prints out the results lexicographically, separated by commas (see figure 3.8). Because you want the coordinator to exit, you don't have to call the loop function. Note that the :exit message isn't special; you can call it :kill, :self_destruct, or :kaboom.

3.5.3   *Other messages*

Finally, you must take care of any other types of messages the coordinator may receive. You capture these unwanted messages with the _ operator. Remember to loop again, but leave the arguments unmodified:

```
def loop(results \\ [], results_expected) do
  receive do
    # ... other patterns omitted ...
    _ ->
      loop(results, results_expected)
  end
end
```

Matches every other kind of message

Loops again, leaving the arguments unmodified

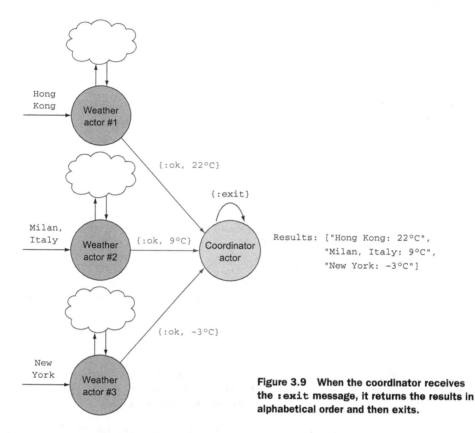

Figure 3.9 When the coordinator receives the :exit message, it returns the results in alphabetical order and then exits.

3.5.4 *The bigger picture*

Congratulations—you've just written you first concurrent program in Elixir! You used multiple processes to perform computations concurrently. The processes didn't have to wait for each other while performing computations (except the coordinator process).

It's important to remember that there's no shared memory. The only way a change of state can occur within a process is when a message is sent to it. This is different from threads, because threads share memory. This means multiple threads can modify the same memory—an endless source of concurrency bugs (and headaches).

When designing your own concurrent programs, you must decide which types of messages the processes should receive and send, along with the interactions between processes. In the example program, I decided to use {:ok, result} and :exit for the coordinator process and {sender_pid, location} for the worker process. I personally find it helpful to sketch out the interactions between the various processes along with the messages that are being sent and received. Resist the temptation to dive right into coding, and spend a few minutes sketching. Doing this will save you hours of head scratching and cursing!

3.6 *Exercises*

Processes are fundamental to Elixir. You'll gain a better understanding only by running and experimenting with the code. Try these exercises:

1 Read the documentation for send and receive. For send, figure out the valid destinations to which you can send messages. For receive, study the example that the documentation provides.

2 Read the documentation for Process.

3 Write a program that spawns two processes. The first process, on receiving a ping message, should reply to the sender with a pong message. The second process, on receiving a pong message, should reply with a ping message.

3.7 *Summary*

This chapter covered the all-important topic of processes. You were introduced to the Actor concurrency model. Through the example application, you've learned how to do the following:

- Create processes
- Send and receive messages using processes
- Achieve concurrency using multiple processes
- Collect and manipulate messages from worker processes using a coordinator process

You've now had a taste of concurrent programming in Elixir! Be sure to give your brain a little break. See you in the next chapter, where you'll learn about Elixir's secret sauce: OTP!

Writing server applications with GenServer

4

In this chapter, you begin by learning about OTP. OTP originally stood for Open Tele-com Platform and was coined by the marketing geniuses over at Ericsson (I hope they don't read this!). It's now only referred to by its acronym. Part of the reason is that the naming is myopic—the tools provided by OTP are in no way specific to the telecommunications domain. Nonetheless, the name has stuck, for better or worse. (Naming is said to be one of the most difficult problems in computer science.)

In this chapter, you'll learn exactly what OTP is. Then we'll look at some of the motivations that drove its creation. You'll also see how OTP behaviors can help you build applications that reduce boilerplate code, drastically reduce potential concurrency bugs, and take advantage of code that has benefited from decades of hard-earned experience.

Once you understand the core principles of OTP, you'll learn about one of the most important and common OTP behaviors: GenServer. Short for Generic Server, the Gen-Server behavior is an abstraction of client/server functionality. You'll take Metex, the temperature-reporting application that you built in chapter 3, and turn it into a GenServer. By then, you'll have a firm grasp of how to implement your own GenServers.

4.1 What is OTP?

OTP is sometimes referred to as a framework, but that doesn't give it due credit. Instead, think of OTP as a complete development environment for concurrent programming. To prove my point, here's a non-exhaustive laundry list of the features that come with OTP:

- The Erlang interpreter and compiler
- Erlang standard libraries
- Dialyzer, a static analysis tool
- Mnesia, a distributed database
- Erlang Term Storage (ETS), an in-memory database
- A debugger
- An event tracer
- A release-management tool

You'll encounter various pieces of OTP as you progress through the book. For now, let's turn our attention to OTP behaviors.

4.2 OTP behaviors

Think of OTP behaviors as design patterns for processes. These behaviors emerged from battle-tested production code and have been refined continuously ever since. Using OTP behaviors in your code helps you by providing the generic pieces of your code for free, leaving you to implement the specific pieces of business logic.

Take GenServer, for example. GenServer provides client/server functionality out of the box. In particular, it provides the following functionality that's common to all servers:

- Spawning the server process
- Maintaining state within the server
- Handling requests and sending responses
- Stopping the server process

GenServer has the generic side covered. You, on the other hand, have to provide the following business logic:

- The state with which you want to initialize the server
- The kinds of messages the server handles
- When to reply to the client
- What message to use to reply to the client
- What resources to clean up after termination

There are also other benefits to using a GenServer behavior. When you're building a server application, for example, how do you know you've covered all the necessary edge cases and concurrency issues that may crop up? The truth is you probably won't, even with all your tests. GenServer (and the other behaviors, for that matter) are production-tested and battle-hardened.

It also wouldn't be fun to have to understand multiple different implementations of server logic. Consider worker.ex in the Metex example. In my programs that don't use the GenServer behavior, I usually name the main loop, well, loop. But nothing is stopping me from naming it await, recur, or something ridiculous like while_1_true. Using the GenServer behavior releases me (and naming-challenged developers) from the burden of having to think about these trivialities by enforcing standard naming conventions via its callbacks.

4.2.1   The different OTP behaviors

Table 4.1 lists the common OTP behaviors provided out of the box. OTP doesn't limit you to these four; you can implement your own behaviors. But it's imperative to understand how to use the default behaviors well because they cover most of the use cases you'll encounter.

Table 4.1   OTP behaviors and their functionality

Behavior	Used for...
GenServer	Implementing the server of a client-server relationship
GenEvent	Implementing event-handling functionality
Supervisor	Implementing supervision functionality
Application	Working with applications and defining application callbacks

To make things more concrete, let's look at how these behaviors fit together. For this, you need the Observer tool, which is provided by OTP. Fire up iex, and start Observer:

```
% iex
iex(1)> :observer.start
:ok
```

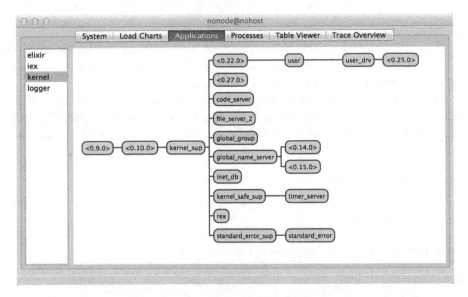

Figure 4.1   The Observer tool displaying the supervisor tree of the `kernel` application

When the window pops up, click the Applications tab. You should see something like figure 4.1.

The left column shows a list of OTP applications that were started when `iex` was started. The next chapter covers applications; for now, you can think of them as self-contained programs. Clicking each option in the left column reveals the *supervisor* hierarchy for that application. For example, figure 4.1 shows the supervisor hierarchy for the `kernel` application, which is the first application started, even before the `elixir` application starts.

If you look closely, you'll notice that the supervisors have `sup` appended to their names. `kernel_sup`, for example, supervises 10 other processes. These processes could be GenServers (`code_server` and `file_server`, for example) or even other supervisors (`kernel_safe_sup` and `standard_error_sup`).

Behaviors like `GenServer` and `GenEvent` are the *workers*—they contain most of the business logic and do much of the heavy lifting. You'll learn more about them as you progress. Supervisors are exactly what they sound like: they manage processes under them and take action when something bad happens. Let's examine the most frequently used OTP behavior: `GenServer`.

4.3   *Hands-on OTP: revisiting Metex*

Using `GenServer` as an example, let's implement an OTP behavior. You'll re-implement Metex, the weather application in chapter 3. But this time, you'll implement it using `GenServer`.

In case you need a refresher, Metex reports the temperature in degrees Celsius, given a location such as the name of a city. This is done through a HTTP call to a third-party weather service. You'll add other bells and whistles to illustrate various Gen-Server concepts such as keeping state and process registration. For example, you'll track the frequency of valid locations requested.

Pieces of functionality discussed in chapter 3 will be skipped here, so if all this sounds new to you, now would be the perfect time to read chapter 3! Once you've completed the application, we'll take a step back and compare the approaches in chapter 3 and chapter 4. Let's get started!

4.3.1   Creating a new project

As usual, create a new project. Remember to place your old version of Metex in another directory first:

```
% mix new metex
```

In mix.exs, enter application and deps as shown in the next listing.

Listing 4.1   Project setup

```
defmodule Metex.Mixfile do
  use Mix.Project

  # ...

  def application do
    [applications: [:logger, :httpoison]]
  end

  defp deps do
    [
      {:httpoison, "~> 0.9.0"},
      {:json,      "~> 0.3.0"}
    ]
  end

end
```

You now need to get your dependencies. In the terminal, use the mix deps.get command to do just that.

4.3.2   Making the worker GenServer compliant

You begin with the workhorse of the application: the worker. In lib/worker.ex, declare a new module and specify that you want to use the GenServer behavior, as shown in the following listing.

Listing 4.2   Using the GenServer behavior

```
defmodule Metex.Worker do
  use GenServer                          Defines the callbacks
                                         required for GenServer
end
```

Before we go any further, it helps to be reminded why you're bothering to make the worker a GenServer, especially because (as you'll soon see) you need to learn about the various callback functions and proper return values.

The biggest benefits of using OTP are all the things you don't have to worry about when you write your own client-server programs and supervisors. For example, how would you write a function that makes an asynchronous request? What about a synchronous one? The GenServer behavior provides handle_cast/2 and handle_call/3 for those exact use cases.

Your process has to handle different kinds of messages. As the number of kinds of messages increases, a hand-rolled process can grow unwieldy. GenServer's various handle_* functions provide a neat way to specify the kinds of messages you want to handle. And receiving messages is only half the equation; you also need a way to handle replies. As expected, the callbacks have your back (pun intended!) by making it convenient to access the pid of the sender process.

Next, let's think about state management. Every process needs a way to initialize state. It also needs a way to potentially perform some cleanup before the process is terminated. GenServer's init/1 and terminate/2 are just the callbacks you need. Recall that in chapter 3, you managed state by using a recursive loop and passing the (potentially) modified state into the next invocation of that loop. The return values of the various callbacks will affect the state. Hand-rolling this is a nontrivial process that results in clumsy-looking code.

Using GenServer also makes it easy to be plugged into, say, a supervisor. A nice thing about writing programs that conform to OTP behaviors is that they tend to look similar. This means that if you were to look at someone else's GenServer, you could probably easily tell which messages it could handle and what replies it could give, and whether the replies were synchronous or asynchronous.

Now you know some of the benefits of including use GenServer. In addition, Elixir automatically defines all the callbacks needed by the GenServer. In Erlang, you'd have to specify quite a bit of boilerplate. This means you get to pick and choose which callbacks you want to implement. What exactly are these callbacks? Glad you asked.

4.3.3 *Callbacks*

Six callbacks are automatically defined for you. Each callback expects a return value that conforms to what GenServer expects. Table 4.2 summarizes the callbacks, the functions that call them, and the expected return values. You'll find the table especially helpful when you need to figure out the exact return values that each callback expects. I find myself referring to this table constantly.

Table 4.2   `GenServer` callbacks and their expected return values

Callback	Expected return values

`init(args)`	`{:ok, state}`
	`{:ok, state, timeout}`
	`:ignore`
	`{:stop, reason}`

`handle_call(msg, {from, ref},state)`	`{:reply, reply, state}`
	`{:reply, reply, state, timeout}`
	`{:reply, reply, state, :hibernate}`
	`{:noreply, state}`
	`{:noreply, state, timeout}`
	`{:noreply, state, hibernate}`
	`{:stop, reason, reply, state}`
	`{:stop, reason, state}`

`handle_cast(msg, state)`	`{:noreply, state}`
	`{:noreply, state, timeout}`
	`{:noreply, state, :hibernate}`
	`{:stop, reason, state}`

`handle_info(msg, state)`	`{:noreply, state}`
	`{:noreply, state, timeout}`
	`{:stop, reason, state}`

`terminate(reason, state)`	`:ok`
`code_change(old_vsn, state, extra)`	`{:ok, new_state}` `{:error, reason}`

Table 4.3 maps the `GenServer` functions to their corresponding callbacks. For instance, if `GenServer.call/3` is invoked, `Metex.handle_call/3` will be invoked, too.

Table 4.3   Callback functions defined in `Metex.Worker` that are called by `GenServer` functions

GenServer module calls...	Callback module (Implemented in Metex.Worker)
`GenServer.start_link/3`	`Metex.init/1`
`GenServer.call/3`	`Metex.handle_call/3`
`GenServer.cast/2`	`Metex.handle_cast/2`

START_LINK/3 AND INIT/1

`init(args)` is invoked when `GenServer.start_link/3` is called. The following listing shows that in code.

Listing 4.3   Structuring the code

```elixir
defmodule Metex.Worker do
  use GenServer

  ## Client API

  def start_link(opts \\ []) do
    GenServer.start_link(__MODULE__, :ok, opts)
  end

  ## Server Callbacks

  def init(:ok) do
    {:ok, %{}}
  end

  ## Helper Functions

end
```

Here, I've demarcated the different sections of code using comments. You'll usually find that Elixir/Erlang programs in the wild follow a similar convention. Because you haven't introduced any helper functions yet, the Helper Functions section has been left unfilled.

`GenServer.start_link/3` takes the module name of the `GenServer` implementation where the `init/1` callback is defined. It starts the process and also links the server process to the parent process. This means if the server process fails for some reason, the parent process is notified.

The second argument is for arguments to be passed to `init/1`. Because you don't require any, `:ok` suffices.

The final argument is a list of options to be passed to `GenServer.start_link/3`. These options include defining a name with which to register the process and enable extra debugging information. For now, you can pass in an empty list.

When `GenServer.start_link/3` is called, it invokes `Metex.init/1`. It waits until `Metex.init/1` has returned, before returning. What are valid return values for `Metex.init/1`? Consulting table 4.2, you get the following four values:

- `{:ok, state}`
- `{:ok, state, timeout}`
- `:ignore`
- `{:stop, reason}`

For now, you use the simplest: `{:ok state}`. Looking at the implementation, `state` in this case is initialized to an empty Map, `%{}`. You need this map to keep the frequency of requested locations.

Let's give this a spin! Open your console, and launch `iex` like so:

```
% iex -S mix
```

Now, let's start a server process and link it to the calling process. In this case, it's the shell process:

```
iex(1)> {:ok, pid} = Metex.Worker.start_link
{:ok, #PID<0.134.0>}
```

The result is a two-element tuple: :ok and the pid of the new server process.

HANDLING SYNCHRONOUS REQUESTS WITH HANDLE_CALL/3

You want to have the server process handle requests, which is the whole point of having a server process. Let's start from the client API and work downward, as shown in the next listing.

> **Listing 4.4   Implementing a synchronous request with GenServer.call/3**

```
defmodule Metex.Worker do
  use GenServer

  ## Client API

  # ...

  def get_temperature(pid, location) do
    GenServer.call(pid, {:location, location})
  end

  ## Server API

  # ...

end
```

Here's how a client might retrieve the temperature of Singapore:

```
Metex.Worker.get_temperature(pid, "Singapore").
```

This function wraps a call to GenServer.call/3, passing in the pid, a tuple that is tagged :location, and the actual location. In turn, GenServer.call/3 expects a handle_call/3 defined in the Metex.Worker module and invokes it accordingly.

GenServer.call/3 makes a *synchronous* request to the server. This means a reply from the server is expected. The sibling to GenServer.call/3 is GenServer.cast/2, which makes an *asynchronous* request to the server. We'll take a look at that shortly. For now, the following listing shows the implementation of handle_call/3 for the {:location, location} message.

> **Listing 4.5   Implementing the handle_call callback**

```
defmodule Metex.Worker do
  use GenServer

  ## Client API

  # ...
```

```
def get_temperature(pid, location) do
  GenServer.call(pid, {:location, location})
end

## Server API

# ...

def handle_call({:location, location}, _from, stats) do
  case temperature_of(location) do
    {:ok, temp} ->
      new_stats = update_stats(stats, location)
      {:reply, "#{temp}°C", new_stats}

    _ ->

      {:reply, :error, stats}
  end
end

end
```

Let's first take a closer look at the function signature:

```
def handle_call({:location, location}, _from, stats) do
  # ...
end
```

The first argument declares the expected request to be handled. The second argument returns a tuple in the form of {pid, tag}, where the pid is the pid of the client and tag is a unique reference to the message. The third argument, state, represents the *internal state* of the server. In this case, it's the current frequency counts of valid locations.

Now, let's turn out attention to the body of handle_call({:location, location}, ...}):

```
def handle_call({:location, location}, _from, stats) do       Makes a request to the
  case temperature_of(location) do            <----------------| API for the location's
    {:ok, temp} ->                                               temperature
      new_stats = update_stats(stats, location)   <-------- Updates the stats Map with
      {:reply, "#{temp}°C", new_stats}          <--------   the location frequency

    _ ->                                          Returns a three-element
      {:reply, :error, stats}   <------------     tuple as a response
  end
end                             Returns a three-element
                                tuple that has an :error tag
```

Metex.Worker.temperature_of/1 makes a request to the third-party API to get the location's temperature. If it succeeds, Metex.Worker.update_stats/2 is invoked to return a new Map with the updated frequency of location. Finally, it returns a three-element tuple that any handle_call/3 is expected to return. In particular, this tuple begins with :reply, followed by the actual computed responses, followed by the updated state, which in this case is new_stats. If the request to the third-party API fails for some reason, then {:reply, :error, stats} is returned.

Here are the valid responses for handle_call/3:

- {:reply, reply, state}
- {:reply, reply, state, timeout}
- {:reply, reply, state, :hibernate}
- {:noreply, state}
- {:noreply, state, timeout}
- {:noreply, state, hibernate}
- {:stop, reason, reply, state}
- {:stop, reason, state}

Let's fill in the missing pieces to get Metex.Worker.get_temperature/2 to work in the next listing.

Listing 4.6   Implementing the helper functions

```elixir
defmodule Metex.Worker do
  use GenServer

  ## Client API and Server API

  ## previously implemented code

  ## Helper Functions

  defp temperature_of(location) do
    url_for(location) |> HTTPoison.get |> parse_response
  end

  defp url_for(location) do
    "http://api.openweathermbap.org/data/2.5/weather?q=#{location}&APPID=
➥#{apikey}"
  end

  defp parse_response({:ok, %HTTPoison.Response{body: body, status_code:
➥200}}) do
    body |> JSON.decode! |> compute_temperature
  end

  defp parse_response(_) do
    :error
  end

  defp compute_temperature(json) do
    try do
      temp = (json["main"]["temp"] - 273.15) |> Float.round(1)
      {:ok, temp}
    rescue
      _ -> :error
    end
  end
end
```

```
def apikey do
  "APIKEY-GOES-HERE"
end

defp update_stats(old_stats, location) do
  case Map.has_key?(old_stats, location) do
    true ->
      Map.update!(old_stats, location, &(&1 + 1))
    false ->
      Map.put_new(old_stats, location, 1)
  end
end

end
```

Most of the implementation is the same as in chapter 3, except for minor changes to `Metex.Worker.temperature_of/1` and `Metex.Worker.update_stats/2`, which are new. The implementation of `Metex.Worker.update_stats/2` is simple. See the following listing.

Listing 4.7   Updating the frequency of a requested location

```
defp update_stats(old_stats, location) do
  case Map.has_key?(old_stats, location) do
    true ->
      Map.update!(old_stats, location, &(&1 + 1))
    false ->
      Map.put_new(old_stats, location, 1)
  end
end
```

This function takes `old_stats` and the `location` requested. You first check whether `old_stats` contains the location of the key. If so, you can fetch the value and increment the counter. Otherwise, you put in a new key called `location` and set it to 1. If `&(&1 + 1)` seems confusing, you can do a syntactical "unsugaring" in your head:

```
Map.update!(old_stats, location, fn(val) -> val + 1 end)
```

Let's take `Metex.Worker` out for another spin. Once again, fire up `iex`, and then start the server with `Metex.Worker.start_link/1`:

```
% iex -S mix
iex(1)> {:ok, pid} = Metex.Worker.start_link
{:ok, #PID<0.125.0>}]
```

Now, let's get the temperatures from a few famous locations:

```
iex(2)> Metex.Worker.get_temperature(pid, "Babylon")
"12.7°C"
iex(3)> Metex.Worker.get_temperature(pid, "Amarillo")
"5.3°C"
iex(4)> Metex.Worker.get_temperature(pid, "Memphis")
"7.3°C"
```

```
iex(5)> Metex.Worker.get_temperature(pid, "Rio")
"23.5°C"
iex(6)> Metex.Worker.get_temperature(pid, "Philadelphia")
"12.5°C"
```

Success! But wait—how do you see the contents of stat? In other words, how do you access the *server state*? Turns out it isn't difficult.

ACCESSING THE SERVER STATE

Let's implement the client-facing API first, as shown in the following listing.

> **Listing 4.8   Client-facing API**

```
def get_stats(pid) do
  GenServer.call(pid, :get_stats)
end
```

You expect a synchronous reply from the server. Therefore, you should invoke Gen-Server.call/3. Here, you're saying that the server should handle a synchronous :get_stats message. Notice that messages can come in the form of any valid Elixir term. This means tuples, lists, and atoms are all fair game. The next listing shows the callback function.

> **Listing 4.9   handle_call callback**

```
def handle_call(:get_stats, _from, stats) do
  {:reply, stats, stats}
end
```

Because you're interested in stats, you can return stats in the second argument as the reply. Because you're accessing stats, as opposed to modifying it, you pass it along unchanged as the third argument.

Grouping handle_calls

Here's a gentle reminder to *group* all your handle_calls (and, later, handle_casts) together! Doing so is important because the Erlang virtual machine relies on this for pattern matching. For example, suppose you "misplace" handle_calls like this:

```
defmodule Metex.Worker do
  use GenServer

  ## Client API

  # ...

  ## Server Callbacks

  def handle_call(:get_stats, _from, stats) do      ◁─┐ handle_calls and
    # ...                                              handle_casts should
  end                                                  be grouped together.
```

```
def init(:ok) do
  # ...
end

def handle_call({:location, location}, _from, stats) do
  # ...
end

## Helper Functions

# ...
end
```

The compiler will issue a friendly warning:

```
% iex -S mix

lib/worker.ex:29: warning: clauses for the same def should be grouped
together, def handle_call/3 was previously defined (lib/worker.ex:20)
```

HANDLING ASYNCHRONOUS REQUESTS WITH HANDLE_CAST/2

Asynchronous requests don't require a reply from the server. This also means a Gen-Server.cast/2 returns immediately. What's a good use case for GenServer.cast/2? A fine example is a command that's issued to a server and that causes a side effect in the server's state. In that case, the client issuing the command shouldn't care about a reply.

Let's construct such a command in the next listing. This command, reset_stats, will reinitialize stats back to an empty Map.

Listing 4.10 Handling the resetting of stats

```
# Client API

# ...

def reset_stats(pid) do
  GenServer.cast(pid, :reset_stats)
end

# Server Callbacks

# handle_calls go here

def handle_cast(:reset_stats, _stats) do
  {:noreply, %{}}
end
```

Metex.Worker.stats/1 makes a call to GenServer.cast/2. This in turn invokes the handle_cast(:reset_stats, _stats) callback. Because you don't care about the current state of the server (after all, you're resetting it), you prepend an underscore to stats.

The return value is a two-element tuple with `:noreply` as the first element and an empty Map, the response, as the second argument. Again, notice that the response is one of the valid `handle_cast/2` responses.

Let's see your handiwork! Fire up `iex -S mix` again, and try a few locations:

```
iex(1)> {:ok, pid} = Metex.Worker.start_link
{:ok, #PID<0.134.0>}
iex(2)> Metex.Worker.get_temperature pid, "Singapore"
"29.0°C"
iex(3)> Metex.Worker.get_temperature pid, "Malaysia"
"22.7°C"
iex(4)> Metex.Worker.get_temperature pid, "Brunei"
"24.2°C"
iex(5)> Metex.Worker.get_temperature pid, "Singapore"
"29.0°C"
iex(6)> Metex.Worker.get_temperature pid, "Cambodia"
"27.7°C"
iex(7)> Metex.Worker.get_temperature pid, "Brunei"
"24.2°C"
iex(8)> Metex.Worker.get_temperature pid, "Singapore"
"29.0°C"
```

Now you can try the `get_stats/1` function:

```
iex(9)> Metex.Worker.get_stats pid
%{"Brunei" => 2, "Cambodia" => 1, "Malaysia" => 1, "Singapore" => 3}
```

It works! You can clearly see the frequency of the requested locations represented by the Map. Next, try to reset stats:

```
iex(10)> Metex.Worker.reset_stats pid
:ok
iex(11)> Metex.Worker.get_stats pid
%{}
```

Perfect! It works as expected.

STOPPING THE SERVER AND CLEANING UP

Sometimes you need to free up resources or perform other cleanup tasks before the server stops. That's where `GenServer.terminate/2` comes in.

How do you stop the server? If you look at table 4.2, in the `handle_call`/`handle_cast` rows you'll find two valid responses that begin with `:stop`:

- `{:stop, reason, new_state}`
- `{:stop, reason, reply, new_state}`

This is a signal to the `GenServer` that the server will be terminated. Therefore, all you need to do is to provide a `handle_call/3`/`handle_cast/2` callback that returns either of these two responses, and include any cleanup logic in the `GenServer.terminate/2` callback. First write the `stop/1` function in the Client API section, as shown in the next listing.

Listing 4.11   `stop/1` function

```
def stop(pid) do
  GenServer.cast(pid, :stop)
end
```

Again, you use `GenServer.cast/2` because you don't care about a return value. Another reason could be that the server takes time to properly clean up all resources, and you don't want to wait. The corresponding callback is simple, as shown in the following listing.

Listing 4.12   `handle_cast` callback

```
def handle_cast(:stop, stats) do
  {:stop, :normal, stats}
end
```

You don't have any resources to speak of, but you can imagine that you might, for example, write `stats` to a file or database. In this example, let's print the current state in the next listing before you stop the server.

Listing 4.13   Calling the `terminate` callback

```
def terminate(reason, stats) do
  # We could write to a file, database etc
  IO.puts "server terminated because of #{inspect reason}"
    inspect stats
  :ok
end
```

`GenServer.terminate/2` has two arguments. The first provides a reason why the server terminated. In a normal termination, `reason` is `:normal`, which comes from the response from `handle_cast/2`, defined earlier. For errors—for example, arising from caught exceptions—you could include other reasons. Finally, `GenServer.terminate/2` must always return `:ok`. Let's see how to terminate a server in `iex`:

```
% iex -S mix
iex(1)> {:ok, pid} = Metex.Worker.start_link
{:ok, #PID<0.152.0>}
iex(2)> Process.alive? pid
true
iex(3)> Metex.Worker.stop pid
server terminated because of :normal
:ok
iex(4)> Process.alive? pid
false
```

WHAT HAPPENS WHEN A CALLBACK RETURNS AN INVALID RESPONSE?

Let's modify the `handle_cast(:stop, stats)` return value slightly:

```
def handle_cast(:stop, stats) do
  {:stop, :normal, :ok, stats}
end
```

If you look at table 4.2 again, this corresponds to a valid `handle_call/3` response, not a `handle_cast/2` response! The extraneous `:ok` is for a reply to the client. Because `handle_cast/2` isn't meant for replying to the client (at least, not directly), this is obviously wrong. Let's see what happens when you repeat the same process of stopping the server:

```
% iex -S mix
iex(1)> {:ok, pid} = Metex.Worker.start_link
{:ok, #PID<0.152.0>}
iex(2)> Metex.Worker.stop pid
iex(2)>
10:59:15.906 [error] GenServer #PID<0.134.0> terminating
Last message: {:"$gen_cast", :stop}
State: %{}
** (exit) bad return value: {:stop, :normal, :ok, %{}}
```

> **GenServer reports an error when it receives an invalid response from a callback handler.**

First, notice that there's no compile-time error. The error only surfaces when you try to stop the server: GenServer freaks out by throwing `bad return value: {:stop, :normal, :ok, %{}}`. Whenever you see something like that, your first instinct should be to double-check the return values of your callback handlers. It's easy to miss a minor detail, and the error messages may not be obvious at first glance.

RECEIVING OTHER KINDS OF MESSAGES

Messages may arrive from processes that aren't defined in `handle_call/3`/`handle_cast/2`. That's where `handle_info/2` comes in. It's invoked to handle any other messages that are received by the process, sometimes referred to as *out-of-band* messages. You don't need to supply a client API counterpart for `handle_info/2`. This callback takes two arguments, the message received and the current state, as the next listing shows.

> **Listing 4.14   `handle_info` callback**

```
def handle_info(msg, stats) do
  IO.puts "received #{inspect msg}"
  {:noreply, stats}
end
```

Let's see this in action:

```
iex(1)> {:ok, pid} = Metex.Worker.start_link
{:ok, #PID<0.134.0>}
iex(2)> send pid, "It's raining men"
received "It's raining men"
```

You'll see much more interesting uses for handle_info/2 in later chapters. The main thing to remember is that handle_info/2 is used for any message that isn't covered by handle_call/3/handle_cast/2.

PROCESS REGISTRATION

Having to constantly reference the GenServer via the pid can be a pain. Fortunately, there's another way to do it. GenServer.start_link/3 takes a list of options as its third argument.

There are two common ways to register a GenServer with a name. The difference lies in whether the name should be visible locally or globally. If the name is registered globally, then it's unique across a cluster of connected nodes. (You'll learn more about distribution soon.) On the other hand, a locally registered name is visible only from within the local node.

Having a registered name is great for a singleton GenServer (that is, only one exists in a node or cluster). You'll let Metex.Worker be registered under Metex.Worker. When you choose to register a name for the GenServer, you no longer have to reference the process using its pid. Fortunately, the only places you have to make changes are the invocations to GenServer.call/3 and GenServer.cast/2 in the client API.

Listing 4.15 Registering the GenServer with an explicit name

```elixir
defmodule Metex.Worker do
  use GenServer

  @name MW                    ←── Stores the name

  ## Client API

  def start_link(opts \\ []) do
    GenServer.start_link(__MODULE__, :ok, opts ++ [name: MW])    ←┘ Initializes the server with a registered name
  end

  def get_temperature(location) do
    GenServer.call(@name, {:location, location})    ←
  end

  def get_stats do
    GenServer.call(@name, :get_stats)    ←
  end

  def reset_stats do
    GenServer.cast(@name, :reset_stats)    ←
  end

  def stop do
    GenServer.cast(@name, :stop)    ←
  end

  # The rest of the code remains unchanged.
  # ...
end
```

Notice that you pass @name instead of the pid.

Fire up iex -S mix again. This time, you don't have to explicitly capture the pid. But it's a good idea because you usually want to know whether the server started correctly, and therefore you need to make sure the :ok is pattern-matched.

Here's how you interact with Metex.Worker now:

```
% iex -S mix
iex(1)> Metex.Worker.start_link
{:ok, #PID<0.134.0>}
iex(2)> Metex.Worker.get_temperature "Singapore"
"29.3°C"
iex(3)> Metex.Worker.get_temperature "London"
"2.0°C"
iex(4)> Metex.Worker.get_temperature "Hong Kong"
"24.0°C"
iex(5)> Metex.Worker.get_temperature "Singapore"
"29.3°C"
iex(6)> Metex.Worker.get_stats
%{"Hong Kong" => 1, "London" => 1, "Singapore" => 2}
iex(7)> Metex.Worker.stop
server terminated because of :normal
:ok
```

4.3.4   *Reflecting on chapter 3's Metex*

Look again at the Metex you built in chapter 3. Try to imagine what you'd need to add to obtain the same functionality as the Metex you built in this chapter. Also try to figure out where you'd put all that functionality.

You may realize that some features aren't as straightforward to implement. For instance, how would you implement synchronous and asynchronous calls? What about stopping the server? In that case, you'd have to specially handle the stop message and not run the loop. Where would you then put the logic for cleaning up resources?

In the earlier version of Metex.Worker, you had to handle unexpected messages explicitly with the catchall operator (the underscore) in loop. With OTP, this is handled with the handle_info/2 callback. Stopping the server also wasn't handled.

Given all these issues, the loop function would soon balloon in size. Of course, you could always abstract everything out in nice little functions, but that approach can only go so far.

I hope you're beginning to see the benefits of OTP. Using OTP behaviors helps you attain a consistent structure in your code. It makes it easy to eyeball exactly where the client API is, where the server callbacks are defined, and where the helper methods are located.

In addition to providing consistency, OTP provides many helpful features that are common to all server-like programs. For example, managing state using GenServer is a breeze; you no longer have to put your state in a loop. Being able to decide when your state should change in the callbacks is also extremely useful.

4.4   Exercise

Write a `GenServer` that can store any valid Elixir term, given a key. Here are a few operations to get you started:

- `Cache.write(:stooges, ["Larry", "Curly", "Moe"])`
- `Cache.read(:stooges)`
- `Cache.delete(:stooges)`
- `Cache.clear`
- `Cache.exist?(:stooges)`

Structure your program similar to how you did in this chapter. In particular, pay attention to which of these operations should be `handle_calls` or `handle_casts`.

4.5   Summary

When I first learned about `GenServer`, it was a lot to take in—and that's putting it mildly. You'll find table 4.4 useful because it groups all the related functions. In addition to some of the function names, I've abbreviated `Metex.Worker` as `MW` and `GenServer` as `GS`. `state` is shortened to `st`, and `from` is shortened to `fr`. Finally, `pid` is `p`.

Table 4.4   Summary of the relationships between the client API, `GenServer`, and callback functions

Metex.Worker client API		GenServer		Metex.Worker callback
`MW.start_link(:ok)`	→	`GS.start_link`	→	`MW.init(:ok)`
`MW.get_temp(p, "NY")`	→	`GS.call(p,{:loc, "NY"})`	→	`MW.handle_call(` `{:loc, "NY"}, fr, st)`
`MW.reset(p)`	→	`GS.cast(p, :reset)`	→	`MW.handle_cast(:reset, st)`

`MW.stop(p)`	→	`GS.cast(p, :stop)`	→	`MW.handle_cast(:stop, st)`
				If this returns
				`{:stop, :normal, st}`
				then
				`MW.terminate(:normal, st)`
				is called

Let's go through the last row. Say you want to stop the worker process, and you call `Metex.Worker.stop/1`. This will in turn invoke `GenServer.cast/2`, passing in `pid` and `:stop` as arguments. The callback that's triggered is `Metex.Worker.handle_cast` `(:stop, state)`. If the callback returns a tuple of the form `{:stop, :normal, state}`, then `Metex.Worker.terminate/2` is invoked.

We covered a lot of ground in this chapter. Here's a recap of what you learned:

- What OTP is, and the principles and motivations behind it
- The different kinds of OTP behaviors available
- Converting Metex to use `GenServer`

- The various callbacks provided by GenServer
- Managing state in GenServer
- Structuring your code according to convention
- Process registration

There's one other benefit of OTP that I've intentionally kept from you until now: using the GenServer behavior lets you stick GenServers into a supervision tree. What happens if your GenServer crashes? How will it affect the rest of the parts of your system, and how can you ensure that your system stays functional? Read on, because supervisors—one of my favorite features of OTP—are up next!

Part 2

Fault tolerance, supervision, and distribution

We've come to the area where most languages and platforms struggle to do well: fault tolerance and distribution. In chapter 5, you'll learn about the primitives that the Erlang VM provides to detect when processes crash.

Then you'll learn about the second OTP behavior, Supervisor, and how to manage hierarchies of processes and automatically take action when a process crashes. Chapters 6 and 7 are dedicated to building a full-featured worker-pool application that uses GenServers and Supervisors.

Chapters 8 and 9 explore distribution through the lens of load balancing and fault tolerance. By the end of those two chapters, you'll have built a distributed load tester: a distributed, fault-tolerant Chuck Norris jokes service. More important, you'll have a firm grasp of how to use OTP effectively.

Concurrent error-handling and fault tolerance with links, monitors, and processes

5

This chapter covers

- Handling errors, Elixir style
- Links, monitors, and trapping exits
- Implementing a supervisor

Ever watched *The Terminator*, the movie about an assassin cyborg from the future (played by Arnold Schwarzenegger)? Even when the Terminator is shot multiple times, it just keeps coming back unfazed, over and over again. Once you're acquainted with Elixir's fault-tolerance features, you'll be able to build programs that can handle errors gracefully and take corrective actions to fix the problems. (You won't be able to build Skynet, though—at least, not yet.)

In sequential programs, there's typically only one main process doing all the hard work. What happens if this process crashes? Usually, this means the entire program crashes. The normal approach is to program defensively, which means lacing the program with `try`, `catch`, and `if err != nil`.

The story is different when it comes to building concurrent programs. Because more than one process is running, it's possible for another process to detect the crash and subsequently handle the error. Let that sink in, because it's a liberating notion.

You may have heard or read about the unofficial motto that Erlang programmers are so fond of saying: "Let it crash!" That's the way things are done in the Erlang VM, but this unique way of handling errors can cause programmers who are used to defensive programming to twitch involuntarily. As it turns out, there are several good reasons for this approach, as you'll soon learn.

In this chapter, you'll first learn about *links, monitors, trapping exits*, and *processes*, and how they come together as the fundamental building blocks of fault-tolerant systems. You'll then embark on building a simple version of a supervisor, whose only job is to manage worker processes. This will be a perfect segue to chapter 6, where you'll come to fully appreciate the convenience and additional features the OTP Supervisor behavior provides.

5.1 Links: 'til death do us part

When a process links to another, it creates a bidirectional relationship. A linked process has a *link set*, which contains a set of all the processes it's linked to. If either process terminates for whatever reason, an *exit signal* is propagated to all the processes it's linked to (see figure 5.1). Furthermore, if any of these processes is linked to a different set of processes, then the same exit signal is propagated along, too.

If you're scratching your head and wondering why this is a good thing, consider an example of a bunch of processes working on a MapReduce job. If any of these processes crashes and dies, it doesn't make sense for the rest of the processes to keep working. In fact, having the processes linked will make it easier to clean up the remaining processes, because a failure in one of the processes will automatically bring down the rest of the linked processes.

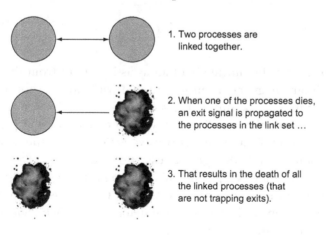

1. Two processes are linked together.

2. When one of the processes dies, an exit signal is propagated to the processes in the link set ...

3. That results in the death of all the linked processes (that are not trapping exits).

Figure 5.1   When a process dies, all other processes linked to it will die, too (assuming they aren't trapping exits).

5.1.1   *Linking processes together*

To make sense of this, an example is in order. A link is created using `Process.link/1`, the sole argument being the process id (pid) of the process to link to. This means `Process.link/1` must be called from within an existing process.

> **NOTE**   `Process.link/1` must be called from an existing process because there's no such thing as `Process.link(link_from, link_to)`. The same is true for `Process.monitor/1`.

Open an `iex` session. You're going to create a process that's linked to the `iex` shell process. Because you're in the context of the shell process, whenever you invoke `Process.link/1`, you'll link the shell process to whatever process you point to.

The process you'll create will crash when you send it a `:crash` message. Observe what happens when it does. First, let's make a note of the pid of the current shell process:

```
iex> self
#PID<0.119.0>
```

You can inspect the current link set of the shell process:

```
iex> Process.info(self, :links)
{:links, []}
```

`Process.info/1` contains other useful information about a process. This example uses `Process.info(self, :links)` because you're only interested in the link set for now. Other interesting information includes the total number of messages in the mailbox, heap size, and the arguments with which the process was spawned.

As expected, the link set is empty because you haven't linked any processes yet. Next, let's make a process that only responds to a `:crash` message:

```
iex> pid = spawn(fn -> receive do :crash -> 1/0 end end)
#PID<0.133.0>
```

Now, link the shell process to the process you just created:

```
iex> Process.link(pid)
```

`<0.133.0>` is now in `self`'s link set:

```
iex> Process.info(self, :links)
{:links, [#PID<0.133.0>]}
```

Conversely, `self` (`<0.119.0>`) is also in `<0.133.0>`'s link set:

```
iex> Process.info(pid, :links)
{:links, [#PID<0.119.0>]}
```

It should be clear that calling `Process.link/1` from within the shell process creates a bidirectional link between the shell process and process you just spawned.

Now, the moment you've been waiting for—let's crash the process and see what happens:

```
iex> send(pid, :crash)

11:39:40.961 [error] Error in process <0.133.0> with exit value:
➥{badarith,[{erlang,'/',[1,0],[]}]}

** (EXIT from #PID<0.119.0>) an exception was raised:
    ** (ArithmeticError) bad argument in arithmetic expression
        :erlang./(1, 0)
```

The result says that you performed a shoddy math calculation in <0.133.0> that caused the `ArithmeticError`. In addition, notice that the same error also brought down the shell process, <0.119.0>. To convince yourself that the previous shell process is really gone, try this:

```
iex> self
#PID<0.145.0>
```

The pid of `self` is no longer <0.119.0>.

5.1.2   *Chain reaction of exit signals*

In the previous example, you set up a link between two processes. In this example, you'll create a ring of linked processes so that you can see for yourself the error being propagated and re-propagated to all the links. In a terminal, create a new project:

```
% mix new ring
```

Open lib/ring.ex, and add the code in the following listing.

Listing 5.1   Creating a ring of linked processes (ring.ex)

```
defmodule Ring do

  def create_processes(n) do
    1..n |> Enum.map(fn _ -> spawn(fn -> loop end) end)
  end

  def loop do
    receive do
      {:link, link_to} when is_pid(link_to) ->
        Process.link(link_to)
        loop

      :crash ->
        1/0
    end
  end

end
```

This is straightforward. `Ring.create_processes/1` creates n processes, each of which runs the `loop` function defined previously. The return value of `Ring.create _processes/1` is a list of spawned pids.

The `loop` function defines two types of messages that the process can receive:

- `{:link, link_to}`—To link to a process specified by `link_to`.
- `:crash`—To purposely crash the process

5.1.3 Setting up the ring

Setting up a ring of links is interesting. In particular, pay attention to how you use pattern matching and recursion to set up the ring in the next listing.

Listing 5.2   Setting up the ring of links using recursion (ring.ex)

```elixir
defmodule Ring do

  # ...

  def link_processes(procs) do
    link_processes(procs, [])
  end

  def link_processes([proc_1, proc_2|rest], linked_processes) do
    send(proc_1, {:link, proc_2})
    link_processes([proc_2|rest], [proc_1|linked_processes])
  end

  def link_processes([proc|[]], linked_processes) do
    first_process = linked_processes |> List.last
    send(proc, {:link, first_process})
    :ok
  end

  # ...

end
```

The first function clause, `link_processes/1`, is the entry point to `link_processes/2`. The `link_processes/2` function initializes the second argument to the empty list. The first argument of `link_processes/2` is a list of processes (initially unlinked). See the following listing.

Listing 5.3   Linking the first two processes using pattern matching (ring.ex)

```elixir
def link_processes([proc_1, proc_2|rest], linked_processes) do
  send(proc_1, {:link, proc_2})
  link_processes([proc_2|rest], [proc_1|linked_processes])
end
```

You can use pattern matching to get the first two processes in the list. You then tell the first process to link to the second process by sending it a `{:link, link_to}` message.

Next, `link_processes/2` is recursively called. This time, the input processes do not include the first process. Instead, it's added to the second argument, signifying that this process has been sent the `{:link, link_to}` message.

Soon there will be only one process left in the input process list. It shouldn't be hard to see why: each time you recursively call `link_processes/2`, the size of the input list decreases by one. You can detect this condition by pattern-matching `[proc|[]]`, as shown in the following listing.

Listing 5.4   Terminating condition with only one process left (ring.ex)

```elixir
def link_processes([proc|[]], linked_processes) do
  first_process = linked_processes |> List.last
  send(proc, {:link, first_process})
  :ok
end
```

Finally, to complete the ring, you need to link `proc` to the first process. Because processes are added to the `linked_processes` list in *last in, first out* (LIFO) order, the first process is the last element. Once you've created the link from the last process to the first, you've completed the ring. Let's take this for a spin:

```
% iex -S mix
```

Create five processes:

```
iex(1)> pids = Ring.create_processes(5)
[#PID<0.84.0>, #PID<0.85.0>, #PID<0.86.0>, #PID<0.87.0>, #PID<0.88.0>]
```

Next, link all of them up:

```
iex(2)> Ring.link_processes(pids)
:ok
```

What's the link set of each of these processes? Let's find out:

```
iex> pids |> Enum.map(fn pid -> "#{inspect pid}:
  #{inspect Process.info(pid, :links)}" end)
```

This gives you the following result (see figure 5.2):

```
["#PID<0.84.0>: {:links, [#PID<0.85.0>, #PID<0.88.0>]}",
 "#PID<0.85.0>: {:links, [#PID<0.84.0>, #PID<0.86.0>]}",
 "#PID<0.86.0>: {:links, [#PID<0.85.0>, #PID<0.87.0>]}",
 "#PID<0.87.0>: {:links, [#PID<0.86.0>, #PID<0.88.0>]}",
 "#PID<0.88.0>: {:links, [#PID<0.87.0>, #PID<0.84.0>]}"]
```

Let's crash a random process! Pick a random pid from the list of `pids` and send it the `:crash` message:

```
iex(6)> pids |> Enum.shuffle |> List.first |> send(:crash)
:crash
```

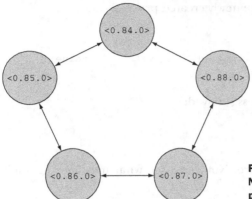

Figure 5.2 A ring of linked processes.
Notice that each process has two other
processes in its link set.

You can now check that none of the processes survived:

```
iex(8)> pids |> Enum.map(fn pid -> Process.alive?(pid) end)
[false, false, false, false, false]
```

5.1.4 *Trapping exits*

So far, all you've done is see the links bring down all the linked processes. What if you didn't want the process to die when it received an error signal? You need to make the process *trap exit signals*. To do so, the process needs to call Process.flag(:trap_exit, true). Calling this turns the process from a normal process to a system process.

What's the difference between a normal process and a system process? When a system process receives an error signal, instead of crashing like a normal process, it can turn the signal into a regular message that looks like {:EXIT, pid, reason}, where pid is the process that was terminated and reason is the reason for the termination. This way, the system process can take corrective action on the terminated process. Let's see how this works with two processes, similar to the first example in this section.

You first note the current shell process:

```
iex> self
#PID<0.58.0>
```

Next, turn the shell process into a system process by making it trap exits:

```
iex> Process.flag(:trap_exit, true)
false
```

Note that like Process.link/1, this must be called from within the calling process. Once again, you create a process that you're going to crash:

```
iex> pid = spawn(fn -> receive do :crash -> 1/0 end end)
#PID<0.62.0>
```

Then link the newly created process to the shell process:

```
iex> Process.link(pid)
true
```

What happens if you try to crash the newly created process?

```
iex> send(pid, :crash)
:crash
14:37:10.995 [error] Error in process <0.62.0> with exit value:
➥{badarith,[{erlang,'/',[1,0],[]}]}
```

Let's check whether the shell process survived:

```
iex> self
#PID<0.58.0>
```

Yup! It's the same process as before. Now, let's see what message the shell process receives:

```
iex> flush
{:EXIT, #PID<0.62.0>, {:badarith, [{:erlang, :/, [1, 0], []}]}}
```

As expected, the shell process receives a message in the form of {:EXIT, pid, reason}. You'll exploit this later when you learn how to create your own supervisor process.

5.1.5   *Linking a terminated/nonexistent process*

Let's try to link a dead process to see what happens. First, make sure that you are starting from a fresh shell session. Then, create a process that exits quickly:

```
iex> pid = spawn(fn -> IO.puts "Bye, cruel world." end)
Bye, cruel world.

#PID<0.80.0>
```

Make sure the process is really dead:

```
iex> Process.alive? pid
false
```

Then, attempt to link to the dead process:

```
iex> Process.link(pid)
** (ErlangError) erlang error: :noproc
    :erlang.link(#PID<0.62.0>)
```

Process.link/1 makes sure you're linking to a non-terminated process; it errors out if you try to link to a terminated or nonexistent process.

5.1.6   *spawn_link/3: spawning and linking in one atomic step*

Most of the time, when spawning a process, you'll use spawn_link/3. Is spawn_link/3 like a glorified wrapper for spawn/3 and link/1? In other words, is spawn_link (Worker, :loop, []) the same as doing the following?

```
pid = spawn(Worker, :loop, [])
Process.link(pid)
```

Turns out, the story is slightly more complicated than that. spawn_link/3 does the spawning and linking in one atomic operation. Why is this important? Because when link/1 is given a process that has terminated or doesn't exist, it throws an error. spawn/3 and link/1 are two separate steps, so spawn/3 could fail, causing the subsequent call to link/1 to raise an exception.

5.1.7　Exit messages

There are three flavors of :EXIT messages. You've seen the first one, where the reason for termination describes the exception, such as {:EXIT, #PID<0.62.0>, {:badarith, [{:erlang, :/, [1, 0], []}]}}.

NORMAL TERMINATION

Processes send :EXIT messages when the process terminates normally. This means the process doesn't have any more code to run. For example, consider this process, whose only job is to receive an :ok message and then exit:

```
iex> pid = spawn(fn -> receive do :ok -> :ok end end)
#PID<0.73.0>
```

Remember to link the process:

```
iex> Process.link(pid)
true
```

You then send the process the :ok message, causing it to exit normally:

```
iex> send(pid, :ok)
:ok
```

Now, let's reveal the message that the shell process received:

```
iex> flush
{:EXIT, #PID<0.73.0>, :normal}
```

Note that if a normal process is linked to a process that just exited normally (with :normal as the reason), the former process is not terminated.

FORCEFULLY KILLING A PROCESS

There's one more way a process can die: using Process.exit(pid, :kill). This sends an *un-trappable* exit signal to the targeted process. Even though the process may be trapping exits, this is one signal it can't trap. Let's set up the shell process to trap exits:

```
iex> self
#PID<0.91.0>

iex> Process.flag(:trap_exit, true)
false
```

Now, try to kill the process using Process.exit/2 with a reason other than :kill:

```
iex> Process.exit(self, :whoops)
true
```

```
iex> self
#PID<0.91.0>

iex> flush
{:EXIT, #PID<0.91.0>, :whoops}

iex> self
#PID<0.91.0>
```

Here, you can see that the shell process successfully trapped the signal, because it receives the {:EXIT, pid, reason} message in its mailbox. Next, try Process.exit (self, :kill):

```
iex> Process.exit(self, :kill)
** (EXIT from #PID<0.91.0>) killed

iex> self
#PID<0.103.0>
```

This time, the shell process restarts, and the process id is no longer the one you had before.

5.1.8 Ring, revisited

Let's again consider a ring of processes, as shown in figure 5.3, with only two processes trapping exits. Open lib/ring.ex again, and add messages that let the process trap exits and handle {:EXIT, pid, reason}, as shown in the next listing.

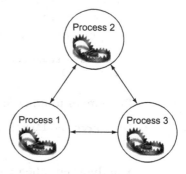

Figure 5.3 What happens when process 2 is killed?

Listing 5.5 Letting the process handle :EXIT and :DOWN messages (ring.ex)

```
defmodule Ring do
  # ...

  def loop do
    receive do
      {:link, link_to} when is_pid(link_to) ->
        Process.link(link_to)
        loop

      :trap_exit ->                                    ⟵ Handles a message
        Process.flag(:trap_exit, true)                    to trap exits
        loop

      :crash ->
        1/0                                            ⟵ Handles a message to
                                                          detect :EXIT messages
      {:EXIT, pid, reason} ->
        IO.puts "#{inspect self} received {:EXIT, #{inspect pid}, #{reason}}"
        loop

    end
  end

end
```

Process 1 and process 2 are trapping exits. All processes are linked to each other. Now, what happens when process 2 is killed? Create three processes to find out:

```
iex> [p1, p2, p3]  = Ring.create_processes(3)
[#PID<0.97.0>, #PID<0.98.0>, #PID<0.99.0>]
```

Link all of them together:

```
iex> [p1, p2, p3]  |> Ring.link_processes
```

Set the first two processes to trap exits:

```
iex> send(p1, :trap_exit)
iex> send(p2, :trap_exit)
```

Observe what happens when you kill p2:

```
iex> Process.exit(p2, :kill)
#PID<0.97.0> received {:EXIT, #PID<0.98.0>, killed}
#PID<0.97.0> received {:EXIT, #PID<0.99.0>, killed}
```

As a final check, make sure only p1 survives:

```
iex> [p1, p2, p3]  |> Enum.map(fn p -> Process.alive?(p) end)
[true, false, false]
```

Here's the lesson: if a process is trapping exits, and it's targeted to be killed using `Process.exit(pid, :kill)`, it will be killed anyway. When it dies, it propagates an `{:EXIT, #PID<0.98.0>, :killed}` message to the processes in its link set, which can be trapped. Table 5.1 summarizes all the different scenarios.

Table 5.1   The different scenarios that can happen when a process in a link set exits

When a process in its link set...	Trapping exits?	What happens then?
Exits normally	Yes	Receives {:EXIT, pid, :normal}
	No	Nothing
Killed using `Process.exit(pid, :kill)`	Yes	Receives {:EXIT, pid, :normal}
	No	Terminates with ':killed'
Killed using `Process.exit(pid, other)`	Yes	Receives {:EXIT, pid, other }
	No	Terminates with `other`

5.2   *Monitors*

Sometimes you don't need a bidirectional link. You just want the process to know if some other process has gone down, and not affect anything about the monitoring process. For example, in a client-server architecture, if the client goes down for some reason, the server shouldn't go down.

That's what *monitors* are for. They set up a unidirectional link between the monitoring process and the process to be monitored. Let's do some monitoring! Create your favorite crashable process:

```
iex> pid = spawn(fn -> receive do :crash -> 1/0 end end)
#PID<0.60.0>
```

Then, tell the shell to monitor this process:

```
iex> Process.monitor(pid)
#Reference<0.0.0.80>
```

Notice that the return value is a *reference* to the monitor.

> **NOTE**   A reference is unique, and can be used to identify where the message comes from, although that's a topic for a chapter later on.

Now, crash the process and see what happens:

```
iex> send(pid, :crash)
:crash

iex>
18:55:20.381 [error] Error in process <0.60.0> with exit value:
⮩{badarith,[{erlang,'/',[1,0],[]}]}
nil
```

Let's inspect the shell processes' mailbox:

```
iex> flush
{:DOWN, #Reference<0.0.0.80>, :process, #PID<0.60.0>,
 {:badarith, [{:erlang, :/, [1, 0], []}]}}
```

Notice that the reference matches the reference returned from `Process.monitor/1`.

5.2.1   *Monitoring a terminated/nonexistent process*

What happens when you try to monitor a terminated/nonexistent process? Continuing from the previous example, first convince yourself that the `pid` is indeed dead:

```
iex> Process.alive?(pid)
false
```

Then try monitoring again:

```
iex(11)> Process.monitor(pid)
#Reference<0.0.0.114>
```

`Process.monitor/1` processes without incident, unlike `Process.link/1`, which throws a `:noproc` error. What message does the shell process get?

```
iex(12)> flush
{:DOWN, #Reference<0.0.0.114>, :process, #PID<0.60.0>, :noproc}
```

You get a similar-looking :noproc message, except that it isn't an error but a plain old message in the mailbox. Therefore, this message can be pattern-matched from the mailbox.

5.3 Implementing a supervisor

A *supervisor* is a process whose only job is to monitor one or more processes. These processes can be worker processes or even other supervisors.

Supervisors and workers are arranged in a supervision tree (see figure 5.4). If a worker dies, the supervisor can restart the dead worker and, potentially, other workers in the supervision tree based on certain *restart strategies*. What are worker processes? They're usually processes that have implemented the GenServer, GenFSM, or GenEvent behaviors.

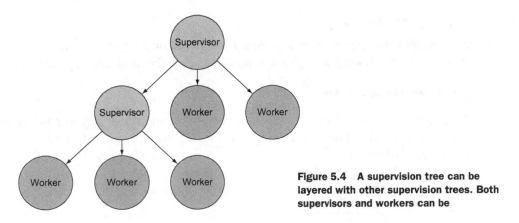

Figure 5.4 A supervision tree can be layered with other supervision trees. Both supervisors and workers can be

At this point, you have all the building blocks needed to build your own supervisor. Once you're finished with this section, supervisors won't seem magical anymore, although that doesn't make them any less awesome.

5.3.1 Supervisor API

Table 5.2 lists the API of the Supervisor along with brief descriptions. Implementing this API will give you a pretty good grasp of how the actual OTP Supervisor works under the hood.

Table 5.2 A summary of the Supervisor API that you'll implement

API	Description
start_link(child_spec_list)	Given a list of child specifications (possibly empty), start the supervisor process and corresponding children.
start_child(supervisor, child_spec)	Given a supervisor pid and a child specification, start the child process and link it to the supervisor.

Table 5.2 A summary of the Supervisor API that you'll implement (continued)

API	Description
terminate_child(supervisor, pid)	Given a supervisor pid and a child pid, terminate the child.
restart_child(supervisor, pid, child_spec)	Given a supervisor pid, a child pid, and a child specification, restart the child process and initialize it with the child specification.
count_children(supervisor)	Given the supervisor pid, return the number of child processes.
which_children(supervisor)	Given the supervisor pid, return the state of the supervisor.

5.3.2 Building your own supervisor

As usual, you start with a new mix project. Because calling it Supervisor is unoriginal, and MySupervisor is boring, let's give it some Old English flair and call it ThySupervisor:

```
% mix new thy_supervisor
```

As a form of revision, you'll build your supervisor using the GenServer behavior. You may be surprised to know that the Supervisor behavior does, in fact, implement the GenServer behavior:

```
defmodule ThySupervisor do
  use GenServer

end
```

5.3.3 start_link(child_spec_list)

The first step is to implement start_link/1:

```
defmodule ThySupervisor do
  use GenServer

  def start_link(child_spec_list) do
    GenServer.start_link(__MODULE__, [child_spec_list])
  end

end
```

This is the main entry point to creating a supervisor process. Here, you call Gen-Server.start_link/2 with the name of the module and pass in a list with a single element of child_spec_list. child_spec_list specifies a (potentially empty) list of *child specifications.*

This is a fancy way of telling the supervisor what kinds of processes it should manage. A child specification for two (similar) workers could look like this: [{ThyWorker, :start_link, []}, {ThyWorker, :start_link, []}].

Recall that `GenServer.start_link/2` expects the `ThySupervisor.init/1` callback to be implemented. It passes the second argument (the list) into `:init/1`. See the following listing.

Listing 5.6 `start_link/1` and `init callback/1` (thy_supervisor.ex)

```elixir
defmodule ThySupervisor do
  use GenServer

  #######
  # API #
  #######

  def start_link(child_spec_list) do
    GenServer.start_link(__MODULE__, [child_spec_list])
  end

  #######################
  # Callback Functions #
  #######################

  def init([child_spec_list]) do
    Process.flag(:trap_exit, true)           # Makes the supervisor
    state = child_spec_list                  # process trap exits
              |> start_children
              |> Enum.into(HashDict.new)

    {:ok, state}
  end

end
```

The first thing you do here is let the supervisor process trap exits. This is so it can receive exit signals from its children as normal messages.

There's quite a bit going on in the lines that follow. `child_spec_list` is fed into `start_children/1`. This function, as you'll soon see, spawns the child processes and returns a list of tuples. Each tuple is a pair that contains the pid of the newly spawned child and the child specification. For example:

```elixir
[{<0.82.0>, {ThyWorker, :init, []}}, {<0.84.0>, {ThyWorker, :init, []}}]
```

This list is then fed into `Enum.into/2`. By passing in `HashDict.new` as the second argument, you're effectively transforming the list of tuples into a `HashDict`, with the pids of the child processes as the keys and the child specifications as the values.

Transforming an enumerable to a collectable with enum.into

`Enum.into/2` (and `Enum.into/3`, which takes an additional transformation function) takes an enumerable (such as a `List`) and inserts it into a `Collectable` (such as a `HashDict`). This is helpful because `HashDict` knows that if it gets a tuple, the first element becomes the key and the second element becomes the value:

```elixir
iex> h = [{:pid1, {:mod1, :fun1, :arg1}}, {:pid2, {:mod2, :fun2, :arg2}}]
     |> Enum.into(HashDict.new)
```

(continued)

This returns a `HashDict`:

```
#HashDict<[pid2: {:mod2, :fun2, :arg2}, pid1: {:mod1, :fun1, :arg1}]>
```

The value can be retrieved like so:

```
iex> HashDict.fetch(h, :pid2)
{:ok, {:mod2, :fun2, :arg2}}
```

The resulting `HashDict` of pid and child-specification mappings forms the state of the supervisor process, which you return in an `{:ok, state}` tuple, as expected from `init/1`.

START_CHILD(SUPERVISOR, CHILD_SPEC)

I haven't described what goes on in the private function `start_children/1` that's used in `init/1`. Let's skip ahead a little and look at `start_child/2` first. This function takes the supervisor pid and child specification and attaches the child to the supervisor, as shown in the next listing.

Listing 5.7   Starting a single child process (thy_supervisor.ex)

```elixir
defmodule ThySupervisor do
  use GenServer

  #######
  # API #
  #######

  def start_child(supervisor, child_spec) do
    GenServer.call(supervisor, {:start_child, child_spec})
  end


  ######################
  # Callback Functions #
  ######################

  def handle_call({:start_child, child_spec}, _from, state) do
    case start_child(child_spec) do
      {:ok, pid} ->
        new_state = state |> HashDict.put(pid, child_spec)
        {:reply, {:ok, pid}, new_state}
      :error ->
        {:reply, {:error, "error starting child"}, state}
    end
  end

  #####################
  # Private Functions #
  #####################

  defp start_child({mod, fun, args}) do
```

```
      case apply(mod, fun, args) do
        pid when is_pid(pid) ->
          Process.link(pid)
          {:ok, pid}
        _ ->
          :error
      end
    end
  end

end
```

The `start_child/2` API call makes a synchronous call request to the supervisor. The request contains a tuple containing the `:start_child` atom and the child specification. The request is handled by the `handle_call({:start_child, child_spec}, _, _)` call-back. It attempts to start a new child process using the `start_child/1` private function.

On success, the caller process receives `{:ok, pid}` and the state of the supervisor is updated to `new_state`. Otherwise, the caller process receives a tuple tagged with `:error` and is provided a reason.

> ## Supervisors and spawning child processes with spawn_link
> Here's an important point: you're making a large assumption here. You assume that the created process links to the supervisor process. What does this mean? That you assume the process is spawned using `spawn_link`. In fact, the OTP `Supervisor` behavior assumes that processes are created using `spawn_link`.

STARTING CHILD PROCESSES

Now let's look at the `start_children/1` function, which is used in `init/1`, as shown in the following listing.

Listing 5.8 Starting children processes (thy_supervisor.ex)

```
defmodule ThySupervisor do
  # ...

  #####################
  # Private Functions #
  #####################

    defp start_children([child_spec|rest]) do
      case start_child(child_spec) do
        {:ok, pid} ->
          [{pid, child_spec}|start_children(rest)]
        :error ->
          :error
      end
    end

    defp start_children([]), do: []
end
```

The `start_children/1` function takes a list of child specifications and hands `start_child/1` a child specification, all the while accumulating a list of tuples. As you saw previously, each tuple is a pair that contains the `pid` and the child specification.

How does `start_child/1` do its work? Turns out there isn't a lot of sophisticated machinery involved. Whenever you see a `pid`, you'll link it to the supervisor process:

```
defp start_child({mod, fun, args}) do
  case apply(mod, fun, args) do
    pid when is_pid(pid) ->
      Process.link(pid)
      {:ok, pid}
    _ ->
      :error
  end
end
```

TERMINATE_CHILD(SUPERVISOR, PID)

The supervisor needs a way to terminate its children. The next listing shows the API, callback, and private function implementations.

Listing 5.9   Terminating a single child process (thy_supervisor.ex)

```
defmodule ThySupervisor do
  use GenServer

  #######
  # API #
  #######

  def terminate_child(supervisor, pid) when is_pid(pid) do
    GenServer.call(supervisor, {:terminate_child, pid})
  end

  #####################
  # Callback Functions #
  #####################

  def handle_call({:terminate_child, pid}, _from, state) do
    case terminate_child(pid) do
      :ok ->
        new_state = state |> HashDict.delete(pid)
        {:reply, :ok, new_state}
      :error ->
        {:reply, {:error, "error terminating child"}, state}
    end
  end

  ####################
  # Private Functions #
  ####################

  defp terminate_child(pid) do
    Process.exit(pid, :kill)
    :ok
  end

end
```

You use `Process.exit(pid, :kill)` to terminate the child process. Remember how you set the supervisor to trap exits? When a child is forcibly killed using `Process.exit(pid, :kill)`, the supervisor receives a message in the form of `{:EXIT, pid, :killed}`. In order to handle this message, the `handle_info/3` callback is used in the following listing.

Listing 5.10   Handling `:EXIT` messages via `handle_info/3` (thy_supervisor.ex)

```
def handle_info({:EXIT, from, :killed}, state) do
  new_state = state |> HashDict.delete(from)
  {:noreply, new_state}
end
```

All you need to do is update the supervisor state by removing its entry in the `HashDict` and return the appropriate tuple in the callback.

RESTART_CHILD(PID, CHILD_SPEC)

Sometimes it's helpful to manually restart a child process. When you want to do so, you need to supply the process id and the child specification, as shown in listing 5.11. Why do you need the child specification passed in along with the process id? Because you may want to add more arguments, and they have to go in the child specification. The `restart_child/2` private function is a combination of `terminate_child/1` and `start_child/1`.

Listing 5.11   Restarting a child process (thy_supervisor.ex)

```
defmodule ThySupervisor do
  use GenServer

  #######
  # API #
  #######

  def restart_child(supervisor, pid, child_spec) when is_pid(pid) do
    GenServer.call(supervisor, {:restart_child, pid, child_spec})
  end

  ######################
  # Callback Functions #
  ######################

  def handle_call({:restart_child, old_pid}, _from, state) do
    case HashDict.fetch(state, old_pid) do
      {:ok, child_spec} ->
        case restart_child(old_pid, child_spec) do
          {:ok, {pid, child_spec}} ->
            new_state = state
                        |> HashDict.delete(old_pid)
                        |> HashDict.put(pid, child_spec)
            {:reply, {:ok, pid}, new_state}
          :error ->
            {:reply, {:error, "error restarting child"}, state}
        end
```

```
      _ ->
        {:reply, :ok, state}
    end
end

#####################
# Private Functions #
#####################

defp restart_child(pid, child_spec) when is_pid(pid) do
  case terminate_child(pid) do
    :ok ->
      case start_child(child_spec) do
        {:ok, new_pid} ->
          {:ok, {new_pid, child_spec}}
        :error ->
          :error
      end
    :error ->
      :error
  end
end

end
```

COUNT_CHILDREN(SUPERVISOR)

This function returns the number of children linked to the supervisor. The implementation is straightforward, as the next listing shows.

Listing 5.12   Counting the number of child processes (thy_supervisor.ex)

```
defmodule ThySupervisor do
  use GenServer

  #######
  # API #
  #######

  def count_children(supervisor) do
    GenServer.call(supervisor, :count_children)
  end

  #####################
  # Callback Functions #
  #####################

  def handle_call(:count_children, _from, state) do
    {:reply, HashDict.size(state), state}
  end

end
```

WHICH_CHILDREN(SUPERVISOR)

This is similar to count_children/1's implementation. Because the implementation is simple, it's fine to return the entire state. See the following listing.

Listing 5.13   Simple implementation of `which_children/1` (thy_supervisor.ex)

```
defmodule ThySupervisor do
  use GenServer

  #######
  # API #
  #######

  def which_children(supervisor) do
    GenServer.call(supervisor, :which_children)
  end

  #####################
  # Callback Functions #
  #####################

  def handle_call(:which_children, _from, state) do
    {:reply, state, state}
  end

end
```

TERMINATE(REASON, STATE)

This callback is called to shut down the supervisor process. Before you terminate the supervisor process, you need to terminate all the children it's linked to, which is handled by the `terminate_children/1` private function, shown in the next listing.

Listing 5.14   Terminating the supervisor (thy_supervisor.ex)

```
defmodule ThySupervisor do
  use GenServer

  #####################
  # Callback Functions #
  #####################

  def terminate(_reason, state) do
    terminate_children(state)
    :ok
  end

  #####################
  # Private Functions #
  #####################

  defp terminate_children([]) do
    :ok
  end

  defp terminate_children(child_specs) do
    child_specs |> Enum.each(fn {pid, _} -> terminate_child(pid) end)
  end

  defp terminate_child(pid) do
    Process.exit(pid, :kill)
    :ok
  end

end
```

5.3.4   *Handling crashes*

I've saved the best for last. What happens when one of the child processes crashes? If you were paying attention, the supervisor receives a message that looks like {:EXIT, pid, reason}. Once again, you use the handle_info/3 callback to handle the exit messages.

There are two cases to consider (other than :killed, which you handled in terminate_child/1). The first case is when the process exited normally. The supervisor doesn't have to do anything in this case except update its state, as the next listing shows.

> **Listing 5.15   Doing nothing when a child process exits normally (thy_supervisor.ex)**

```
def handle_info({:EXIT, from, :normal}, state) do
  new_state = state |> HashDict.delete(from)
  {:noreply, new_state}
end
```

The second case, shown in the following listing, is when the process has exited abnormally and hasn't been forcibly killed. In that case, the supervisor should automatically restart the failed process.

> **Listing 5.16   Restarting a child process that exits abnormally (thy_supervisor.ex)**

```
def handle_info({:EXIT, old_pid, _reason}, state) do
  case HashDict.fetch(state, old_pid) do
    {:ok, child_spec} ->
      case restart_child(old_pid, child_spec) do
        {:ok, {pid, child_spec}} ->
          new_state = state
                      |> HashDict.delete(old_pid)
                      |> HashDict.put(pid, child_spec)
          {:noreply, new_state}
        :error ->
          {:noreply, state}
      end
    _ ->
      {:noreply, state}
  end
end
```

This function is nothing new. It's almost the same implementation as restart_child/2, except that the child specification is reused.

5.3.5   *Full supervisor source*

The following listing shows the full source of your hand-rolled supervisor in all its glory.

Listing 5.17   Full implementation of thy_supervisor.ex

```elixir
defmodule ThySupervisor do
  use GenServer

  #######
  # API #
  #######

  def start_link(child_spec_list) do
    GenServer.start_link(__MODULE__, [child_spec_list])
  end

  def start_child(supervisor, child_spec) do
    GenServer.call(supervisor, {:start_child, child_spec})
  end

  def terminate_child(supervisor, pid) when is_pid(pid) do
    GenServer.call(supervisor, {:terminate_child, pid})
  end

  def restart_child(supervisor, pid, child_spec) when is_pid(pid) do
    GenServer.call(supervisor, {:restart_child, pid, child_spec})
  end

  def count_children(supervisor) do
    GenServer.call(supervisor, :count_children)
  end

  def which_children(supervisor) do
    GenServer.call(supervisor, :which_children)
  end

  ######################
  # Callback Functions #
  ######################

  def init([child_spec_list]) do
    Process.flag(:trap_exit, true)
    state = child_spec_list
            |> start_children
            |> Enum.into(HashDict.new)

    {:ok, state}
  end

  def handle_call({:start_child, child_spec}, _from, state) do
    case start_child(child_spec) do
      {:ok, pid} ->
        new_state = state |> HashDict.put(pid, child_spec)
        {:reply, {:ok, pid}, new_state}
      :error ->
        {:reply, {:error, "error starting child"}, state}
    end
  end

  def handle_call({:terminate_child, pid}, _from, state) do
    case terminate_child(pid) do
      :ok ->
        new_state = state |> HashDict.delete(pid)
```

```elixir
        {:reply, :ok, new_state}
      :error ->
        {:reply, {:error, "error terminating child"}, state}
  end
end

def handle_call({:restart_child, old_pid}, _from, state) do
  case HashDict.fetch(state, old_pid) do
    {:ok, child_spec} ->
      case restart_child(old_pid, child_spec) do
        {:ok, {pid, child_spec}} ->
          new_state = state
                      |> HashDict.delete(old_pid)
                      |> HashDict.put(pid, child_spec)
          {:reply, {:ok, pid}, new_state}
        :error ->
          {:reply, {:error, "error restarting child"}, state}
      end
    _ ->
      {:reply, :ok, state}
  end
end

def handle_call(:count_children, _from, state) do
  {:reply, HashDict.size(state), state}
end

def handle_call(:which_children, _from, state) do
  {:reply, state, state}
end

def handle_info({:EXIT, from, :normal}, state) do
  new_state = state |> HashDict.delete(from)
  {:noreply, new_state}
end

def handle_info({:EXIT, from, :killed}, state) do
  new_state = state |> HashDict.delete(from)
  {:noreply, new_state}
end

def handle_info({:EXIT, old_pid, _reason}, state) do
  case HashDict.fetch(state, old_pid) do
    {:ok, child_spec} ->
      case restart_child(old_pid, child_spec) do
        {:ok, {pid, child_spec}} ->
          new_state = state
                      |> HashDict.delete(old_pid)
                      |> HashDict.put(pid, child_spec)
          {:noreply, new_state}
        :error ->
          {:noreply, state}
      end
    _ ->
      {:noreply, state}
  end
end
```

```elixir
  def terminate(_reason, state) do
    terminate_children(state)
    :ok
  end

  #####################
  # Private Functions #
  #####################
  defp start_children([child_spec|rest]) do
    case start_child(child_spec) do
      {:ok, pid} ->
        [{pid, child_spec}|start_children(rest)]
      :error ->
        :error
    end
  end

  defp start_children([]), do: []

  defp start_child({mod, fun, args}) do
    case apply(mod, fun, args) do
      pid when is_pid(pid) ->
        Process.link(pid)
        {:ok, pid}
      _ ->
        :error
    end
  end

  defp terminate_children([]) do
    :ok
  end

  defp terminate_children(child_specs) do
    child_specs |> Enum.each(fn {pid, _} -> terminate_child(pid) end)
  end

  defp terminate_child(pid) do
    Process.exit(pid, :kill)
    :ok
  end

  defp restart_child(pid, child_spec) when is_pid(pid) do
    case terminate_child(pid) do
      :ok ->
        case start_child(child_spec) do
          {:ok, new_pid} ->
            {:ok, {new_pid, child_spec}}
          :error ->
            :error
        end
      :error ->
        :error
    end
  end
end
```

5.4   *A sample run (or, "Does it really work?")*

Before you put your supervisor through its paces, create a new file called lib/thy
_worker.ex, as shown in the next listing.

Listing 5.18   Example worker to be used with `ThySupervisor` (lib/thy_worker.ex)

```
defmodule ThyWorker do
  def start_link do
    spawn(fn -> loop end)
  end

  def loop do
    receive do
      :stop -> :ok

      msg ->
        IO.inspect msg
        loop
    end
  end
end
```

You begin by creating a supervisor:

```
iex> {:ok, sup_pid} = ThySupervisor.start_link([])
{:ok, #PID<0.86.0>}
```

Create a process and add it to the supervisor. You save the pid of the newly spawned
child process:

```
iex> {:ok, child_pid} = ThySupervisor.start_child(sup_pid, {ThyWorker,
➥ :start_link, []})
```

Let's see what links are present in the supervisor:

```
iex(3)> Process.info(sup_pid, :links)
{:links, [#PID<0.82.0>, #PID<0.86.0>]}
```

Interesting—two processes are linked to the supervisor process. The first is obviously
the child process you just spawned. What about the other one?

```
iex> self
#PID<0.82.0>
```

A little thought should reveal that because the supervisor process is spawned and
linked by the shell process, it has the shell's pid in its link set.

   Now, kill the child process:

```
iex> Process.exit(child_pid, :crash)
```

What happens when you inspect the link set of the supervisor again?

```
iex> Process.info(sup_pid, :links)
{:links, [#PID<0.82.0>, #PID<0.90.0>]}
```

Sweet! The supervisor automatically took care of spawning and linking the new child process. To convince yourself, you can peek at the supervisor's state:

```
iex> ThySupervisor.which_children(sup_pid)
#HashDict<[{#PID<0.90.0>, {ThyWorker, :start_link, []}}]>
```

5.5 Summary

In this chapter, you worked through several examples that highlighted the following:

- The "Let it crash" philosophy means delegating error detection and handling to another process and not coding too defensively.
- Links set up bidirectional relationships between processes that serve to propagate exit signals when a crash happens in one of the processes.
- Monitors set up a unidirectional relationship between processes so that the monitoring process is notified when a monitored process dies.
- Exit signals can be trapped by system processes that convert exit signals into normal messages.
- You implemented a simple supervisor process using processes and links.

Fault tolerance
with Supervisors

6

This chapter covers

- Using the OTP `Supervisor` behavior
- Working with Erlang Term Storage (ETS)
- Using `Supervisor`s with normal processes and other OTP behaviors
- Implementing a basic worker-pool application

In the previous chapter, you built a naïve `Supervisor` made from primitives provided by the Elixir language: monitors, links, and processes. You should now have a good understanding of how `Supervisor`s work under the hood.

After teasing you in the previous chapter, in this chapter I'll finally show you how to use the real thing: the OTP `Supervisor` behavior. The sole responsibility of a `Supervisor` is to observe an attached child process, check to see if it goes down, and take some action if that happens.

The OTP version offers a few more bells and whistles than your previous implementation of a `Supervisor`. Take *restart strategies*, for example, which dictate how a `Supervisor` should restart the children if something goes wrong. `Supervisor` also offers options for limiting the number of restarts within a specific timeframe; this is especially useful for preventing infinite restarts.

To really understand Supervisors, it's important to try them for yourself. Therefore, instead of boring you with every single Supervisor option, I'll walk you through building the worker-pool application shown in its full glory (courtesy of the Observer application) in figure 6.1.

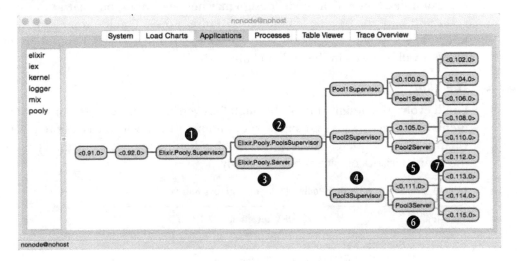

Figure 6.1   The completed worker-pool application

In the figure, **1** is the top-level Supervisor. It supervises **2** another Supervisor (PoolsSupervisor) and **3** a GenServer (Pooly.Server). PoolsSupervisor in turn supervises three other PoolSupervisors (one of them is marked **4**). These Supervisors have unique names. Each PoolSupervisor supervises a worker Supervisor **5** (represented by its process id) and a GenServer **6**. Finally, the workers **7** do the grunt work. If you're wondering what the GenServers are for, they're primarily needed to maintain state for the Supervisor at the same level. For example, the GenServer at **6** helps maintain the state for the Supervisor at **5**.

6.1   *Implementing Pooly: a worker-pool application*

You're going to build a worker pool over the course of two chapters. What is a worker pool? It's something that manages a pool (surprise!) of workers. You might use a worker pool to manage access to a scarce resource. It could be a pool of Redis connections, web-socket connections, or even GenServer workers.

For example, suppose you spawn 1 million processes, and each process needs a connection to the database. It's impractical to open 1 million database connections. To get around this, you can create a pool of database connections. Each time a process needs a database connection, it will issue a request to the pool. Once the process is done with the database connection, it's returned to the pool. In effect, resource allocation is delegated to the worker-pool application.

The worker-pool application you'll build is not trivial. If you're familiar with the Poolboy library, much of its design has been adapted for this example. (No worries if you haven't heard of or used Poolboy; it isn't a prerequisite.)

This will be a rewarding exercise because it will get you thinking about concepts and issues that wouldn't arise in simpler examples. You'll get hands-on with the `Supervisor` API, too. As such, this example is slightly more challenging than the previous examples. Some of the code/design may not be obvious, but that's mostly because you don't have the benefit of hindsight. But fret not—I'll guide you every step of the way. All I ask is that you work through the code by typing it on your computer; enlightenment will be yours by the end of chapter 7!

6.1.1   *The plan*

You'll evolve the design of Pooly through four versions. This chapter covers the fundamentals of `Supervisor` and starts you building a basic version (version 1) of Pooly. Chapter 7 is completely focused on building Pooly's various features. Table 6.1 lists the characteristics of each version of Pooly.

Table 6.1   The changes that Pooly will undergo across four versions

Version	Characteristics
1	Supports a *single* pool Supports a *fixed* number of workers No recovery when consumer and/or worker processes fail
2	Supports a *single* pool Supports a *fixed* number of workers Recovery when consumer and/or worker processes fail
3	Supports *multiple* pools Supports a *variable* number of workers
4	Supports *multiple* pools Supports a *variable* number of workers Variable-sized pool allows for worker overflow Queuing for consumer processes when all workers are busy

To give you an idea how the design will evolve, figure 6.2 illustrates versions 1 and 2, and figure 6.3 illustrates versions 3 and 4. Rectangles represent `Supervisors`, ovals represent `GenServers`, and circles represent the worker processes. From the figures, it should be obvious why it's called a supervision *tree*.

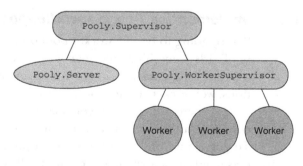

Figure 6.2   Versions 1 and 2 of Pooly

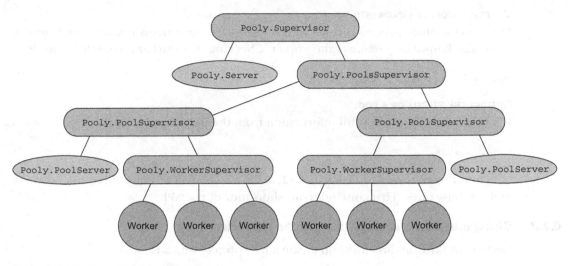

Figure 6.3   Versions 3 and 4 of Pooly

6.1.2   *A sample run of Pooly*

Before we get into the actual coding, it's instructive to see how to use Pooly. This section uses version 1.

STARTING A POOL

In order to start a pool, you must give it a *pool configuration* that provides the information needed for Pooly to initialize the pool:

```
pool_config = [
  mfa: {SampleWorker, :start_link, []},
  size: 5
]
```

This tells the pool to create five SampleWorkers. To start the pool, do this:

```
Pooly.start_pool(pool_config)
```

CHECKING OUT WORKERS

In Pooly lingo, *checking out* a worker means requesting and getting a worker from the pool. The return value is a pid of an available worker:

```
worker_pid = Pooly.checkout
```

Once a *consumer process* has a worker_pid, the process can do whatever it wants with it. What happens if no more workers are available? For now, :noproc is returned. You'll have more sophisticated ways of handling this in later versions.

CHECKING WORKERS BACK INTO THE POOL

Once a consumer process is done with the worker, the process must return it to the pool, also known as *checking in* the worker. Checking in a worker is straightforward:

```
Pooly.checkin(worker_pid)
```

GETTING THE STATUS OF A POOL

It's helpful to get some useful information from the pool:

```
Pooly.status
```

For now, this returns a tuple such as {3, 2}. This means there are three free workers and two busy ones. That concludes our short tour of the API.

6.1.3 Diving into Pooly, version 1: laying the groundwork

Go to your favorite directory and create a new project with mix:

```
% mix new pooly
```

> **NOTE**   The source code for the different versions of this project has been split into branches. For example, to check out version 3, cd into the project folder and do a git checkout version-3.

---

mix and the --sup option

You may be aware that mix includes an option called --sup. This option generates an OTP application skeleton including a supervision tree. If this option is left out, the application is generated without a Supervisor and application callback. For example, you may be tempted to create Pooly like so:

```
% mix new pooly --sup
```

But because you're just learning, you'll opt for the flagless version.

The first version of Pooly will support only a single pool of fixed workers. There will also be no recovery handling when either the consumer or the worker process fails. By the end of this version, Pooly will look like figure 6.4.

As you can see, the application consists of a top-level Supervisor (Pooly.Supervisor) that supervises two other processes: a GenServer

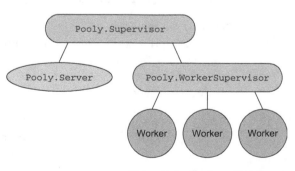

Figure 6.4   Pooly version 1

process (`Pooly.Server`) and a worker `Supervisor` (`Pooly.WorkerSupervisor`). Recall from chapter 5 that `Supervisors` can themselves be supervised because `Supervisors` are processes.

How do I begin?

Whenever I'm designing an Elixir program that may have many supervision hierarchies, I always make a sketch first. That's because (as you'll find out soon) there are quite a few things to keep straight. Probably more so than in other languages, you must have a rough design in mind, which forces you to think slightly ahead.

Figure 6.5 illustrates how Pooly version 1 works. When it starts, only `Pooly.Server` is attached to `Pooly.Supervisor` ❶. When the pool is started with a pool configuration, `Pooly.Server` first verifies that the pool configuration is valid.

After that, it sends a `:start_worker_supervisor` to `Pooly.Supervisor` ❷. This message instructs `Pooly.Supervisor` to start `Pooly.WorkerSupervisor`. Finally, `Pooly.WorkerSupervisor` is told to start a number of worker processes based on the size specified in the pool configuration ❸.

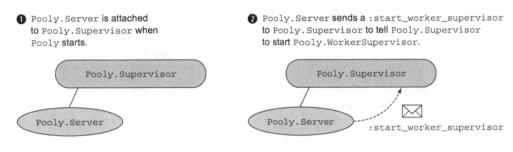

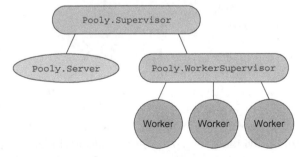

Figure 6.5 How Pooly's various components are initialized

6.2   *Implementing the worker Supervisor*

You'll first create a worker `Supervisor`. This `Supervisor` is in charge of monitoring all the spawned workers in the pool. Create worker_supervisor.ex in lib/pooly. Just like a `GenServer` behavior (or any other OTP behavior, for that matter), you use the `Supervisor` behavior like this:

```
defmodule Pooly.WorkerSupervisor do
  use Supervisor
end
```

Listing 6.1 defines the good old `start_link/1` function that serves as the main entry point when creating a `Supervisor` process. This `start_link/1` function is a wrapper function that calls `Supervisor.start_link/2`, passing in the module name and the arguments.

Like `GenServer`, when you define `Supervisor.start_link/2`, you should next implement the corresponding `init/1` callback function. The arguments passed to `Supervisor.start_link/2` are then passed to the `init/1` callback.

Listing 6.1   Validating and destructuring arguments (lib/pooly/worker_supervisor.ex)

```
defmodule Pooly.WorkerSupervisor do
  use Supervisor

  #######
  # API #
  #######

  def start_link({_,_,_} = mfa) do        ◄───┐   ❶ Pattern-matches the
    Supervisor.start_link(__MODULE__, mfa)          arguments to make sure
  end                                               they're a tuple containing
                                                    three elements
  #############
  # Callbacks #
  #############                      ❷ Pattern-matches the
                                      individual elements from
  def init({m,f,a}) do        ◄───┐   the three-element tuple
    # ...
  end
end
```

You first declare that `start_link` takes a three-element tuple ❶: the module, a function, and a list of arguments of the worker process. Notice the beauty of pattern matching at work here. Saying `{_,_,_}` = mfa essentially does two things. First, it asserts that the input argument must be a three-element tuple. Second, the input argument is referenced by `mfa`. You could have written it as `{m,f,a}`. But because you aren't using the individual elements, you pass along the entire tuple using `mfa`.

`mfa` is then passed along to the `init/1` callback. This time, you need to use the individual elements of the tuple, so you assert that the expected input argument is `{m,f,a}` ❷. The `init/1` callback is where the actual initialization occurs.

6.2.1 Initializing the Supervisor

Let's take a closer look at the `init/1` callback in the next listing, where most of the interesting bits happen in a `Supervisor`.

> **Listing 6.2 Initializing the `Supervisor` (lib/pooly/worker_supervisor.ex)**

```elixir
defmodule Pooly.WorkerSupervisor do

  #############
  # Callbacks #
  #############

  def init({m,f,a} = x) do
    worker_opts = [restart: :permanent,      ◁──   Specifies that the
                   function: f]                     worker is always to
                                                    be restarted
    children = [worker(m, a, worker_opts)]    ◁──   Specifies the function
                                                    to start the worker
    opts     = [strategy: :simple_one_for_one,
                max_restarts: 5,              ◁──   Creates a list
                max_seconds: 5]                     of the child
                                                    processes
    supervise(children, opts)   ◁──   Specifies the options
  end                                 for the supervisor
end                                   Helper function to
                                      create the child
                                      specification
```

Let's decipher the listing. In order for a `Supervisor` to initialize its children, you must give it a *child specification*. A child specification (covered briefly in chapter 5) is a recipe for the `Supervisor` to spawn its children.

The child specification is created with `Supervisor.Spec.worker/3`. The `Supervisor` `.Spec` module is imported by the `Supervisor` behavior by default, so there's no need to supply the fully qualified version.

The return value of the `init/1` callback must be a *supervisor specification*. In order to construct a supervisor specification, you use the `Supervisor.Spec.supervise/2` function.

`supervise/2` takes two arguments: a *list* of children and a *keyword list* of options. In listing 6.2, these are represented by `children` and `opts`, respectively. Before you get into defining children, let's discuss the second argument to `supervise/2`.

6.2.2 Supervision options

The example defines the following options to `supervise/2`:

```elixir
opts = [strategy: :simple_one_for_one,
        max_restarts: 5,
        max_seconds: 5]
```

You can set a few options here. The most important is the *restart strategy*, which we'll look at next.

6.2.3   *Restart strategies*

Restart strategies dictate how a `Supervisor` restarts a child/children when something goes wrong. In order to define a restart strategy, you include a `strategy` key. There are four kinds of restart strategies:

- `:one_for_one`
- `:one_for_all`
- `:rest_for_one`
- `:simple_one_for_one`

Let's take a quick look at each of them.

:ONE_FOR_ONE

If the process dies, only that process is restarted. None of the other processes are affected.

:ONE_FOR_ALL

Just like the Three Musketeers, if *any* process dies, all the processes in the supervision tree die along with it. After that, all of them are restarted. This strategy is useful if all the processes in the supervise tree depend on each other.

:REST_FOR_ONE

If one of the processes dies, the rest of the processes that were started *after* that process are terminated. After that, the process that died and the rest of the child processes are restarted. Think of it like dominoes arranged in a circular fashion.

:SIMPLE_ONE_FOR_ONE

The previous three strategies are used to build a static supervision tree. This means the workers are specified up front via the child specification.

In `:simple_one_for_one`, you specify only one entry in the child specification. Every child process that's spawned from this `Supervisor` is the same kind of process.

The best way to think about the `:simple_one_for_one` strategy is like a factory method (or a constructor in OOP languages), where the workers that are produced are alike. `:simple_one_for_one` is used when you want to dynamically create workers.

The `Supervisor` initially starts out with empty workers. Workers are then dynamically attached to the `Supervisor`. Next, let's look at the other options that allow you to fine-tune the behavior of `Supervisors`.

6.2.4   *max_restarts and max_seconds*

`max_restarts` and `max_seconds` translate to the maximum number of restarts the `Supervisor` can tolerate within a maximum number of seconds before it gives up and terminates. Why have these options? The main reason is that you don't want your `Supervisor` to infinitely restart its children when something is genuinely wrong (such as a programmer error). Therefore, you may want to specify a threshold at which the `Supervisor` should give up. Note that by default, `max_restarts` and `max_seconds` are set to 3 and 5 respectively. In listing 6.2, you specify that the Supervisor should give up if there are more than five restarts within five seconds.

6.2.5 *Defining children*

It's now time to learn how to define children. In the example code, the children are specified in a list:

```
children = [worker(m, a, worker_opts)]
```

What does this tell you? It says that this Supervisor has one child, or one kind of child in the case of a :simple_one_for_one restart strategy. (It doesn't make sense to define multiple workers when in general you don't know how many workers you want to spawn when using a :simple_one_for_one restart strategy.)

The worker/3 function creates a child specification for a worker, as opposed to its sibling supervisor/3. This means if the child isn't a Supervisor, you should use worker/3. If you're supervising a Supervisor, then use supervisor/3. You'll use both variants shortly.

Both variants take the module, arguments, and options. The first two are exactly what you'd expect. The third argument is more interesting.

CHILD SPECIFICATION DEFAULT OPTIONS

When you leave out the options

```
children = [worker(m, a)]
```

Elixir will supply the following options by default:

```
[id: module,
 function: :start_link,
 restart: :permanent,
 shutdown: :infinity,
 modules: [module]]
```

function should be obvious—It's the f of mfa. Sometimes a worker's main entry point is some function other than start_link. This is the place to specify the custom function to be called.

You'll use two restart values throughout the Pooly application:

- :permanent—The child process is always restarted.
- :temporary—The child process is never restarted.

In worker_opts, you specify :permanent. This means any crashed worker is always restarted.

CREATING A SAMPLE WORKER

To test this, you need a sample worker. Create sample_worker.ex in lib/pooly and fill it with the code in the following listing.

Listing 6.3   Worker used to test Pooly (lib/pooly/sample_worker.ex)

```elixir
defmodule SampleWorker do
  use GenServer

  def start_link(_) do
    GenServer.start_link(__MODULE__, :ok, [])
  end

  def stop(pid) do
    GenServer.call(pid, :stop)
  end

  def handle_call(:stop, _from, state) do
    {:stop, :normal, :ok, state}
  end
end
```

SampleWorker is a simple GenServer that does little except have functions that control its lifecycle:

```elixir
iex> {:ok, worker_sup} = Pooly.WorkerSupervisor.start_link({SampleWorker,
➥:start_link, []})
```

Now you can create a child:

```elixir
iex> Supervisor.start_child(worker_sup, [[]])
```

The return value is a two-element tuple that looks like {:ok, #PID<0.132.0>}.

Add a few more children to the Supervisor. Next, let's see all the children that the worker Supervisor is supervising, using Supervisor.which_children/1:

```elixir
iex> Supervisor.which_children(worker_sup)
```

The result is a list that looks like this:

```elixir
[{:undefined, #PID<0.98.0>, :worker, [SampleWorker]},
 {:undefined, #PID<0.101.0>, :worker, [SampleWorker]}]
```

You can also count the number of children:

```elixir
iex> Supervisor.count_children(worker_sup)
```

The return result should be self-explanatory:

```elixir
%{active: 2, specs: 1, supervisors: 0, workers: 2}
```

Now to see the Supervisor in action! Create another child, but this time, save a reference to it:

```elixir
iex> {:ok, worker_pid} = Supervisor.start_child(worker_sup, [[]])
```

Supervisor.which_children(worker_sup) should look like this:

```elixir
[{:undefined, #PID<0.98.0>, :worker, [SampleWorker]},
 {:undefined, #PID<0.101.0>, :worker, [SampleWorker]},
```

```
{:undefined, #PID<0.103.0>, :worker, [SampleWorker]}]
```

Stop the worker you just created:

```
iex> SampleWorker.stop(worker_pid)
```

Let's inspect the state of the worker `Supervisor`'s children:

```
iex(8)> Supervisor.which_children(worker_sup)
[{:undefined, #PID<0.98.0>, :worker, [SampleWorker]},
 {:undefined, #PID<0.101.0>, :worker, [SampleWorker]},
 {:undefined, #PID<0.107.0>, :worker, [SampleWorker]}]
```

Whoo-hoo! The `Supervisor` automatically restarted the stopped worker! I still get a warm, fuzzy feeling whenever a `Supervisor` restarts a failed child automatically. Getting something similar in other languages usually require a lot more work. Next, we'll look at implementing `Pooly.Server`.

6.3 *Implementing the server: the brains of the operation*

In this section, you'll work on the brains of the application. In general, you want to leave the `Supervisor` with as little logic as possible because less code means a smaller chance of things breaking.

Therefore, you'll introduce a `GenServer` process that will handle most of the interesting logic. The server process must communicate with both the top-level `Supervisor` and the worker `Supervisor`. One way is to use *named processes*, as shown in figure 6.6.

In this case, both processes can refer to each other by their respective names. But a more general solution is to have the server process contain a reference to the top-level `Supervisor` and the worker `Supervisor` as part of its state (see figure 6.7). Where will the server get references to both supervisors? When the top-level `Supervisor` starts the server, the `Supervisor` can pass its own pid to the server. This is exactly what you'll do when you get to the implementation of the top-level `Supervisor`.

Now, because the server has a reference to the top-level `Supervisor`, the server can tell it to start a child using the `Pooly.WorkerSupervisor` module. The server will pass in the relevant bits of the pool configuration and `Pooly.WorkerSupervisor` will handle the rest.

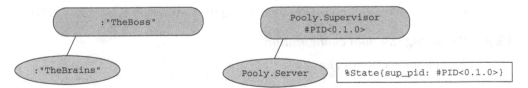

Figure 6.6   Named processes allow other processes to reference them by name.

Figure 6.7   A reference to the supervisor is stored in the state of the Pooly server.

The server process also maintains the state of the pool. You already know that the server has to store references to the top-level Supervisor and the worker Supervisor. What else should it store? For starters, it needs to store details about the pool, such as what kind of workers to create and how many of them. The pool configuration provides this information.

6.3.1 Pool configuration

The server accepts a pool configuration that comes in a keyword list. In this version, an example pool configuration looks like this:

```
[mfa: {SampleWorker, :start_link, []}, size: 5]
```

As I mentioned earlier, the key mfa stands for *m*odule, *f*unction, and list of *a*rguments of the pool of worker(s) to be created. size is the number of worker processes to create.

Enough jibber-jabber[1]— let's see some code! Create a file called server.ex, and place it in lib/pooly.

For now, you'll make Pooly.Server a *named process*, which means you can reference the server process using the module name (Pooly.Server.status instead of Pool.Server.status(pid)). The next listing shows how this is done.

> **Listing 6.4 Starting the server process with sup and pool_config (lib/pooly/servertex)**

```
defmodule Pooly.Server do
  use GenServer
  import Supervisor.Spec

  #######
  # API #
  #######

  def start_link(sup, pool_config) do
    GenServer.start_link(__MODULE__, [sup, pool_config], name: __MODULE__)
  end

end
```

The server process needs both the reference to the top-level Supervisor process and the pool configuration, which you pass in as [sup, pool_config]. Now you need to implement the init/1 callback. The init/1 callback has two responsibilities: validating the pool configuration and initializing the state, as all good init callbacks do.

6.3.2 Validating the pool configuration

A valid pool configuration looks like this:

```
[mfa: {SampleWorker, :start_link, []}, size: 5]
```

---

[1] This was written with the voice of Mr. T in mind.

This is a keyword list with two keys, mfa and size. Any other key will be ignored. As the function goes through the pool-configuration keyword list, the state is gradually built up, as shown in the next listing.

Listing 6.5 Setting up the server state (lib/pooly/server.ex)

```elixir
defmodule Pooly.Server do
  use GenServer                         ❶ Struct that maintains the
                                           state of the server
  defmodule State do
    defstruct sup: nil, size: nil, mfa: nil
  end

  #############
  # Callbacks #
  #############                          ❷ Callback invoked when
                                           GenServer.start_link/3
  def init([sup, pool_config]) when is_pid(sup) do    is called
    init(pool_config, %State{sup: sup})
  end                                   ❸ Pattern match for the
                                           mfa option; stores it in
  def init([{:mfa, mfa}|rest], state) do   the server's state
    init(rest,  %{state | mfa: mfa})
  end                                   ❹ Pattern match for the
                                           size option; stores it in
  def init([{:size, size}|rest], state) do  the server's state
    init(rest, %{state | size: size})
  end

  def init([_|rest], state) do          ❺ Ignores all other options
    init(rest, state)
  end                                   ❻ Base case when the
                                           options list is empty
  def init([], state) do
    send(self, :start_worker_supervisor)
    {:ok, state}                        ❼ Sends a message to start
  end                                      the worker supervisor
end
```

This listing sets up the state of the server. First you declare a struct that serves as a container for the server's state ❶. Next is the callback when GenServer.start _link/3 is invoked ❷.

The init/1 callback receives the pid of the top-level Supervisor along with the pool configuration. It then calls init/2, which is given the pool configuration along with a new state that contains the pid of the top-level Supervisor.

Each element in a keyword list is represented by a two-element tuple, where the first element is the key and the second element is the value. For now, you're interested in remembering the mfa and size values of the pool configuration (❸, ❹). If you want to add more fields to the state, you add more function clauses with the appropriate pattern. You ignore any options that you don't care about ❺.

Finally, once you've gone through the entire list ❻, you expect that the state has been initialized. Remember that one of the valid return values of init/1 is {:ok, state}. Because init/1 calls init/2, and the empty list case ❻ is the last function clause invoked, it should return {:ok, state}.

What is the curious-looking line at ❼? Once you reach ❻, you're confident that the state has been built. That's when you can start the worker Supervisor that you implemented previously. The server process is sending a message to itself. Because send/2 returns immediately, the init/1 callback isn't blocked. You don't want init/1 to time out, do you?

The number of init/1 functions can look overwhelming, but don't fret. Individually, each function is as small as it gets. Without pattern matching in the function arguments, you'd need to write a large conditional to capture all the possibilities.

6.3.3   *Starting the worker Supervisor*

When the server process sends a message to itself using send/2, the message is handled using handle_info/2, as shown in the next listing.

Listing 6.6   Callback handler to start the worker Supervisor (lib/pooly/server.ex)

```
defmodule Pooly.Server do

  sup: nil, worker_sup: nil, size: nil, workers: nil, mfa: nil

  #############
  # Callbacks #
  #############

  def handle_info(:start_worker_supervisor, state = %{sup: sup, mfa: mfa,
    size: size}) do
    {:ok, worker_sup} = Supervisor.start_child(sup,
  supervisor_spec(mfa))
    workers = prepopulate(size, worker_sup)
    {:noreply, %{state | worker_sup: worker_sup, workers: workers}}
  end

  ####################
  # Private Functions #
  ####################

  defp supervisor_spec(mfa) do
    opts = [restart: :temporary]
    supervisor(Pooly.WorkerSupervisor, [mfa], opts)
  end

end
```

Starts the worker Supervisor process via the top-level Supervisor ❶

Creates "size" number of workers that are supervised with the newly created Supervisor ❷

Updates the state with the worker Supervisor pid and its supervised workers ❸

Specifies that the process to be specified is a Supervisor, instead of a worker ❹

There's quite a bit going on in this listing. Because the state of the server process contains the top-level Supervisor pid (sup), you invoke Supervisor.start_child/2 with the Supervisor pid and a Supervisor specification ❶. After that, you pass the pid of the newly created worker Supervisor pid (worker_sup) and use it to start size number of workers ❷. Finally, you update the state with the worker Supervisor pid and newly created workers ❸.

You return a tuple with the worker `Supervisor` pid as the second element ❶. The `Supervisor` specification consists of a worker `Supervisor` as a child ❹. Notice that instead of

```
worker(Pooly.WorkerSupervisor, [mfa], opts)
```

you use the `Supervisor` variant:

```
supervisor(Pooly.WorkerSupervisor, [mfa], opts)
```

Here, you pass in `restart: :temporary` as the `Supervisor` specification. This means the top-level `Supervisor` won't automatically restart the worker `Supervisor`. This seems a bit odd. Why? The reason is that you want to do something more than have the `Supervisor` restart the child. Because you want some custom recovery rules, you turn off the `Supervisor`'s default behavior of automatically restarting downed workers with `restart: :temporary`.

Note that this version doesn't deal with worker recovery if crashes occur. The later versions will fix this. Let's deal with prepopulating workers next.

6.3.4 *Prepopulating the worker Supervisor with workers*

Given a `size` option in the pool configuration, the worker `Supervisor` can prepopulate itself with a pool of workers. The `prepopulate/2` function in the following listing takes a `size` and the worker `Supervisor` pid and builds a list of `size` number of workers.

> **Listing 6.7 Prepopulating the worker `Supervisor` (lib/pooly/server.ex)**

```
defmodule Pooly.Server do

  #####################
  # Private Functions #
  #####################

  defp prepopulate(size, sup) do
    prepopulate(size, sup, [])
  end

  defp prepopulate(size, _sup, workers) when size < 1 do
    workers
  end

  defp prepopulate(size, sup, workers) do
    prepopulate(size-1, sup, [new_worker(sup) | workers])    ⟵─┐ Creates a list of
  end                                                            workers attached
                                                                 to the worker
  defp new_worker(sup) do                                        Supervisor
    {:ok, worker} = Supervisor.start_child(sup, [[]])    ⟵──┐ Dynamically creates
    worker                                                     a worker process
  end                                                          and attaches it to
                                                               the Supervisor
end
```

6.3.5   *Creating a new worker process*

The new_worker/1 function in listing 6.7 is worth a look. Here, you use Supervisor .start_child/2 again to spawn the worker processes. Instead of passing in a child specification, you pass in a *list of arguments*.

The two flavors of Supervisor.start_child/2

There are two flavors of Supervisor.start_child/2. The first takes a child specification:

```
{:ok, sup} = Supervisor.start_child(sup, supervisor_spec(mfa))
```

The other flavor takes a list of arguments:

```
{:ok, worker} = Supervisor.start_child(sup, [[]])
```

Which flavor should you use? Pooly.WorkerSupervisor uses a :simple_one _for_one restart strategy. This means the child specification has already been pre-defined, which means the first flavor is out—the second one is what you want.

The second version lets you pass additional arguments to the worker. Under the hood, the arguments defined in the child specification when creating Pooly .WorkerSupervisor are concatenated on the list passed in to the Supervisor .start_child/2, and the result is then passed along to the worker process during initialization.

The return result of new_worker/2 is the pid of the newly created worker. You haven't yet implemented a way to get a worker out of a pool or put a worker back into the pool. These two actions are also known as *checking out* and *checking in* a worker, respectively. But before you do that, we need to take a brief detour and talk about ETS.

Just enough ETS

In this chapter and the next, you'll use Erlang Term Storage (ETS). This sidebar will give you just enough background to understand the ETS-related code in this chapter and the next.

ETS is in essence a very efficient in-memory database built specially to store Erlang/Elixir data. It can store large amounts of data without breaking a sweat. Data access is also done in constant time. It comes free with Erlang, which means you have to use :ets to access it from Elixir.

CREATING A NEW ETS TABLE

You create a table using :ets.new/2. Let's create a table to store my Mum's favorite artists, their date of birth, and the genre in which they perform:

```
iex> :ets.new(:mum_faves, [])
12308
```

The most basic form takes an atom representing the name of the table and an empty list of options. The return value of `:ets.new/2` is a table ID, which is akin to a pid. The process that created the ETS table is called the *owner process*. In this case, the `iex` process is the owner. The most common options are related to the ETS table's type, its access rights, and whether it's named.

ETS TABLE TYPES

ETS tables come in four flavors:

- `:set`—The default. Its characteristics are the set data structure you may have learned about in CS101 (unordered, with each unique key mapping to an element).
- `:ordered_set`—A sorted version of `:set`.
- `:bag`—Rows with the same keys are allowed, but the rows must be different.
- `:duplicate_bag`—Same as `:bag` but without the row-uniqueness restriction.

In this chapter and the next, you'll use `:set`, which essentially means you don't have to specify the table type in the list of options. If you wanted to be specific, you'd create the table like so:

```
iex> :ets.new(:mum_faves, [:set])
```

ACCESS RIGHTS

Access rights control which processes can read from and write to the ETS table. There are three options:

- `:protected`—The owner process has full read and write permissions. All other processes can only read from the table. This is the default.
- `:public`—There are no restrictions on reading and writing.
- `:private`—Only the owner process can read from and write to the table.

You'll use `:private` tables in this chapter because you'll be storing pool-related data that other pools have no business knowing about. Let's say my Mum is shy about her eclectic music tastes, and she wants to make the table private:

```
iex> :ets.new(:mum_faves, [:set, :private])
```

NAMED TABLES

When you created the ETS table, you supplied an atom. This is slightly misleading because you can't use `:mum_faves` to refer to the table without supplying the `:named_table` option. Therefore, to use `:mum_faves` instead of an unintelligible reference like `12308`, you can do this:

```
iex> :ets.new(:mum_faves, [:set, :private, :named_table])
     :mum_faves
```

Note that if you try to run this line again, you'll get

```
iex> :ets.new(:mum_faves, [:set, :private, :named_table])
  ** (ArgumentError) argument error
        (stdlib) :ets.new(:mum_faves, [:set, :private, :named_table])
```

That's because names should be a unique reference to an ETS table.

(continued)

INSERTING AND DELETING DATA

You insert data using the `:ets.insert/2` function. The first argument is the table identifier (the number or the name), and the second is the data. The data comes in the form of a tuple, where the first element is the key and the second can be any arbitrarily nested term. Here are a few of Mum's favorites:

```
iex> :ets.insert(:mum_faves, {"Michael Bolton", 1953, "Pop"})
true
iex> :ets.insert(:mum_faves, {"Engelbert Humperdinck", 1936, "Easy
       Listening"})
true
iex> :ets.insert(:mum_faves, {"Justin Beiber", 1994, "Teen"})
true
iex> :ets.insert(:mum_faves, {"Jim Reeves", 1923, "Country"})
true
iex> :ets.insert(:mum_faves, {"Cyndi Lauper", 1953, "Pop"})
true
```

You can look at what's in the table using `:ets.tab2list/1`:

```
iex> :ets.tab2list(:mum_faves)
[{"Michael Bolton", 1953, "Pop"},
 {"Cyndi Lauper", 1953, "Pop"},
 {"Justin Beiber", 1994, "Teen"},
 {"Engelbert Humperdinck", 1936, "Easy Listening"},
 {"Jim Reeves", 1923, "Country"}]
```

Note that the return result is a list, and the elements in the list are unordered. All right, I lied. My Mum isn't really a Justin Beiber fan.[a] Let's rectify this:

```
iex> :ets.delete(:mum_faves, "Justin Beiber")
true
```

LOOKING UP DATA

A table is of no use if you can't retrieve data. The simplest way to do that is to use the key. What's Michael Bolton's birth year? Let's find out:

```
iex> :ets.lookup(:mum_faves, "Michael Bolton")
[{"Michael Bolton", 1953, "Pop"}]
```

Why is the result a list? Recall that ETS supports other types, such as :duplicate_bag, which allows for duplicated rows. Therefore, the most general data structure to represent this is the humble list.

What if you want to search by the year instead? You can use `:ets.match/2`:

```
iex> :ets.match(:mum_faves, {:"$1", 1953, :"$2"})
[["Michael Bolton", "Pop"], ["Cyndi Lauper", "Pop"]]
```

---

a. She isn't a Cyndi Lauper fan, either, but I was listening to "Girls Just Want to Have Fun" while writing this.

You pass in a pattern, which looks slightly strange at first. Because you're only querying using the year, you use `:"$N"` as a placeholder, where N is an integer. This corresponds to the order in which the elements in each matching result are presented. Let's swap the placeholders:

```
iex> :ets.match(:mum_faves, {:"$2", 1953, :"$1"})
[["Pop", "Michael Bolton"], ["Pop", "Cyndi Lauper"]]
```

You can clearly see that the genre comes before the artist name. What if you only cared about returning the artist? You can use an underscore to omit the genre:

```
iex> :ets.match(:mum_faves, {:"$1", 1953, :"_"})
[["Michael Bolton"], ["Cyndi Lauper"]]
```

There's much more to learn about ETS, but this is all the information you need to understand the ETS bits of the code in this book.

6.3.6 *Checking out a worker*

When a consumer process checks out a worker from the pool, you need to handle a few key logistical issues:

- What is the pid of the consumer process?
- Which worker pid is the consumer process using?

The consumer process needs to be monitored by the server because if it dies, the server process must know about it and take recovery action. Once again, you aren't implementing the recovery code yet, but laying the groundwork.

You also need to know which worker is assigned to which consumer process so that you can pinpoint which consumer process used which worker pid. Th next listing shows the implementation of checking out workers.

Listing 6.8 Checking out a worker (lib/pooly/server.ex)

```
defmodule Pooly.Server do

  #######
  # API #
  #######

  def checkout do
    GenServer.call(__MODULE__, :checkout)
  end

  ##############
  # Callbacks #
  ##############

  def handle_call(:checkout, {from_pid, _ref}, %{workers: workers, monitors:
      monitors} = state) do
    case workers do
```

1 Pattern-matches the pid of the client, workers, and monitors

2 Handles the case when there are workers left to check out

```
              [worker|rest] ->
                ref = Process.monitor(from_pid)
                true = :ets.insert(monitors, {worker, ref})
                {:reply, worker, %{state | workers: rest}}

              [] ->
                {:reply, :noproc, state}
            end
          end

      end
```

Updates the monitors in the ETS table ❹

Gets the server process to monitor ❸ the client process

You use an ETS table to store the monitors. The implementation of the callback function is interesting. There are two cases to handle: either you have workers left that can be checked out ❷, or you don't. In the latter case, you return {:reply, :noproc, state}, signifying that no processes are available. In most examples about GenServers, you see that the from parameter is ignored:

```
def handle_call(:checkout, _from, state) do
  # ...
end
```

In this instance, from is very useful. Note that from is a two-element tuple consisting of the client pid and a tag (a reference). At ❶, you care only about the pid of the client. You use the pid of the client (from_pid) and get the server process to monitor it ❸. Then you use the resulting reference and add it to the ETS table ❹. Finally, the state is updated with one less worker.

You now need to update the init/1 callback, as shown in the next listing, because you've introduced a new monitors field to store the ETS table.

Listing 6.9   Storing a reference to the ETS table (lib/pooly/server.ex)

```
defmodule Pooly.Server do

  #############
  # Callbacks #
  #############

  def init([sup, pool_config]) when is_pid(sup) do
    monitors = :ets.new(:monitors, [:private])
    init(pool_config, %State{sup: sup, monitors: monitors})
  end
end
```

Updates the state to store the monitors table

6.3.7   Checking in a worker

The reverse of checking out a worker is (wait for it) checking in a worker. The implementation shown in the next listing is the reverse of listing 6.8.

Listing 6.10   Checking in a worker (lib/pooly/server.ex)

```
defmodule Pooly.Server do

  #######
  # API #
  #######

  def checkin(worker_pid) do
    GenServer.cast(__MODULE__, {:checkin, worker_pid})
  end

  #############
  # Callbacks #
  #############

  def handle_cast({:checkin, worker}, %{workers: workers, monitors:
  ↪monitors} = state) do
    case :ets.lookup(monitors, worker) do
      [{pid, ref}] ->
        true = Process.demonitor(ref)
        true = :ets.delete(monitors, pid)
        {:noreply, %{state | workers: [pid|workers]}}
      [] ->
        {:noreply, state}
    end
  end

end
```

Given a worker pid (`worker`), the entry is searched for in the `monitors` ETS table. If an entry isn't found, nothing is done. If an entry is found, then the consumer process is de-monitored, the entry is removed from the ETS table, and the `workers` field of the server state is updated with the addition of the worker's pid.

6.3.8   *Getting the pool's status*

You want to have some insight into your pool. That's simple enough to implement, as the following listing shows.

Listing 6.11   Getting the status of the pool (lib/pooly/server.ex)

```
defmodule Pooly.Server do

  #######
  # API #
  #######

  def status do
    GenServer.call(__MODULE__, :status)
  end

  #############
  # Callbacks #
  #############
```

```
    def handle_call(:status, _from, %{workers: workers, monitors: monitors} =
➥state) do
      {:reply, {length(workers), :ets.info(monitors, :size)}, state}
    end

end
```

This gives you some information about the number of workers available and the number of checked out (busy) workers.

6.4 *Implementing the top-level Supervisor*

There's one last piece to write before you can claim that version 1 is feature complete.[2] Create supervisor.ex in lib/pooly; this is the top-level Supervisor. The full implementation is shown in the next listing.

Listing 6.12   Top-level Supervisor (lib/pooly/supervisor.ex)

```
defmodule Pooly.Supervisor do
  use Supervisor

  def start_link(pool_config) do
    Supervisor.start_link(__MODULE__, pool_config)
  end

  def init(pool_config) do
    children = [
      worker(Pooly.Server, [self, pool_config])
    ]

    opts = [strategy: :one_for_all]

    supervise(children, opts)
  end

end
```

As you can see, the structure of Pooly.Supervisor is similar to Pooly.WorkerSupervisor. The start_link/1 function takes pool_config. The init/1 callback receives the pool configuration.

The children list consists of Pooly.Server. Recall that Pooly.Server.start _link/2 takes two arguments: the pid of the top-level Supervisor process (the one you're working on now) and the pool configuration.

What about the worker Supervisor? Why aren't you supervising it? It should be clear that because the server starts the worker Supervisor, it isn't included here at first.

The restart strategy you use here is :one_for_all. Why not, say, :one_for_one? Think about it for a moment. What happens when the server crashes? It loses all of its state. When the server process restarts, the state is essentially a blank slate. Therefore, the state of the server is inconsistent with the actual pool state.

---

[2] A rare occurrence in the software industry.

What happens if the worker Supervisor crashes? The pid of the worker Supervisor will be different, along with the worker processes. Once again, the state of the server is inconsistent with the actual pool state.

There's a dependency between the server process and the worker Supervisor. If either goes down, it should take the other down with it—hence the :one_for_all restart strategy.

6.5 *Making Pooly an OTP application*

Create a file called pooly.ex in lib. You'll be creating an OTP application, which serves as an entry point to Pooly. It will also contain convenience functions such as start_pool/1 so that clients can say Pooly.start_pool/2 instead of Pooly.Server.start_pool/2. First, add the code in the following listing to pooly.ex.

Listing 6.13   Pooly application (lib/pooly.ex)

```
defmodule Pooly do
  use Application

  def start(_type, _args) do
    pool_config = [mfa: {SampleWorker, :start_link, []}, size: 5]
    start_pool(pool_config)
  end

  def start_pool(pool_config) do
    Pooly.Supervisor.start_link(pool_config)
  end

  def checkout do
    Pooly.Server.checkout
  end

  def checkin(worker_pid) do
    Pooly.Server.checkin(worker_pid)
  end

  def status do
    Pooly.Server.status
  end

end
```

Pooly uses an OTP Application behavior. What you've done here is specify start/2, which is called first when Pooly is initialized. You predefine a pool configuration and a call to start_pool/1 out of convenience.

6.6 *Taking Pooly for a spin*

First, open mix.exs, and modify application/0:

```
defmodule Pooly.Mixfile do
  use Mix.Project

  def project do
    [app: :pooly,
```

```
      version: "0.0.1",
      elixir: "~> 1.0",
      build_embedded: Mix.env == :prod,
      start_permanent: Mix.env == :prod,
      deps: deps]
  end

  def application do
    [applications: [:logger],
            mod: {Pooly, []}]            ⟵——— Starts the Pooly application
  end

  defp deps do
    []
  end
end
```

Next, head to the project directory and launch `iex`:

```
% iex -S mix
```

Fire up Observer:

```
iex> :observer.start
```

Select the Applications tab and you'll see something similar to figure 6.8.

Let's start by killing a worker. (I hope you aren't reading this book aloud!) You can do this by right-clicking a worker process and selecting Kill Process, as shown in figure 6.9.

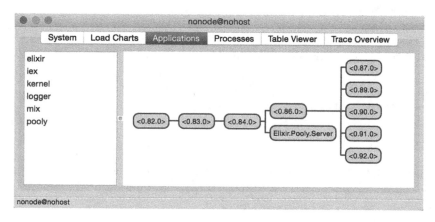

Figure 6.8   Version 1 of Pooly as seen in Observer

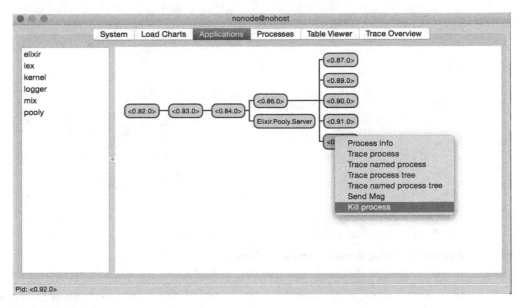

Figure 6.9   Killing a worker in Observer

The Supervisor spawns a new worker in the killed process's place (see figure 6.10). More important, the crash/exit of a single worker doesn't affect the rest of the supervision tree. In other words, the crash of that single worker is isolated to that worker and doesn't affect anything else.

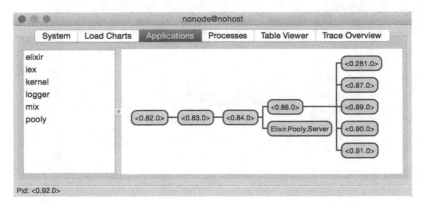

Figure 6.10   The Supervisor replaced a killed worker with a newly spawned worker.

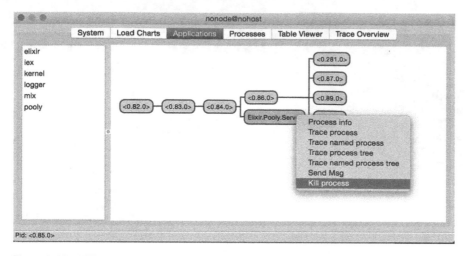

Figure 6.11   Killing the server process in Observer

Now, what happens if you kill `Pooly.Server`? Once again, right-click `Pooly.Server` and select Kill Process, as shown in figure 6.11.

This time, all the processes are killed and the top-level `Supervisor` restarts all of its child processes (see figure 6.12). Why does killing `Pooly.Server` cause everything under the top-level `Supervisor` to die? The mere description of the effect should yield an important clue. What's the restart strategy of the top-level `Supervisor`?

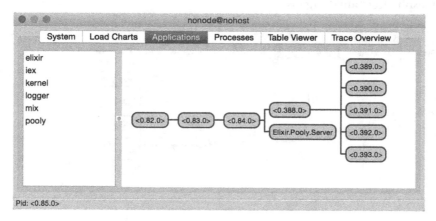

Figure 6.12   Killing the server restarted all the processes under the top-level `Supervisor`.

Let's jolt your memory a little:

```
defmodule Pooly.Supervisor do

  def init(pool_config) do
    # ...
    opts = [strategy: :one_for_all]
```

```
        supervise(children, opts)
    end

end
```

The :one_for_all restart strategy explains why killing Pooly.Server brings down (and restarts) the rest of the children.

6.7 *Exercises*

Take the following exercises for a spin:

1 What happens when you kill the WorkerSupervisor process in Observer? Can you explain why that happens?

2 Shut down and restart some values. Play around with the various shutdown and restart values. For example, in Pooly.WorkerSupervisor, try changing opts from

```
opts = [strategy: :simple_one_for_one,
        max_restarts: 5,
        max_seconds: 5]
```

to something like this:

```
opts = [strategy: :simple_one_for_one,
        max_restarts: 0,
        max_seconds: 5]
```

Next, try changing worker_opts from

```
worker_opts = [restart:  :permanent, function: f]
```

to

```
worker_opts = [restart:  :temporary, function: f]
```

Remember to set opts back to the original value.

6.8 *Summary*

In this chapter, you learned about the following:

- OTP Supervisor behavior
- Supervisor restart strategies
- Using ETS to store state
- How to construct Supervisor hierarchies, both static and dynamic
- The various Supervisor and child specification options
- Implementing a basic worker-pool application

You've seen how, by using different restart strategies, the Supervisor can dictate how its children restart. More important, depending again on the restart strategy, the Supervisor can isolate crashes to only the process affected.

Even though the first version of Pooly is simple, it allowed you to experiment with constructing both static and dynamic supervision hierarchies. In the former case, you declared in the supervision specification of `Pooly.Supervisor` that `Pooly.Server` is to be supervised. In the latter case, `Pooly.WorkerSupervisor` is only added to the supervision tree when `Pooly.Server` is initialized.

In the following chapter, you'll continue to evolve the design of Pooly while adding more features. At the same time, you'll explore more advanced uses of `Supervisor`.

Completing the
worker-pool application

7

This chapter covers

- Implementing the entire worker pool application
- Building multiple supervision hierarchies
- Dynamically creating Supervisors and workers

In this chapter, you'll continue to evolve the design of the Pooly application, which you started in chapter 6. By the end of this chapter, you'll have a full, working worker-pool application. You'll get to explore the Supervisor API more thoroughly and also explore more advanced (read: fun!) Supervisor topics.

In chapter 6, you were left with a rudimentary worker-pool application, if we can even call it that. In the following sections, you'll add some smarts to Pooly. For example, there's currently no way to handle crashes and restarts gracefully. The current version of Pooly can only handle a single pool with a fixed number of workers. Version 3 of Pooly will implement support for multiple pools and a variable number of worker processes.

Sometimes the pool must deal with an unexpected load. What happens when there are too many requests? What happens when all the workers are busy? In version

4, you'll make pools that are variable in size and allow for the *overflowing* of workers. You'll also implement queuing for consumer processes when all workers are busy.

7.1 Version 3: error handling, multiple pools, and multiple workers

How can you tell if a process crashes? You can either monitor it or link to it. This leads to the next question: which should you choose? To answer that question, let's think about what should happen when processes crash. There are two cases to consider:

- Crashes between a server process and a consumer process
- Crashes between a server process and a worker process

7.1.1 Case 1: crashes between the server and consumer process

A crash of the server process shouldn't affect a consumer process—and the reverse is also true! When a consumer process crashes, it shouldn't crash the server process. Therefore, monitors are the way to go.

You're already monitoring the consumer process each time a worker is checked out. What's left is to handle the :DOWN message of a consumer process, as the next listing shows.

> **Listing 7.1   Handling the consumer :DOWN message (lib/pooly/server.ex)**

```
defmodule Pooly.Server do

  #############
  # Callbacks #
  #############

  def handle_info({:DOWN, ref, _, _, _}, state = %{monitors: monitors,
  ➥workers: workers}) do
    case :ets.match(monitors, {:"$1", ref}) do
      [[pid]] ->
        true = :ets.delete(monitors, pid)
        new_state = %{state | workers: [pid|workers]}      ◁─┐ Returns the
        {:noreply, new_state}                                │ worker to the pool

      [[]] ->
        {:noreply, state}
    end
  end

end
```

When a consumer process goes down, you match the reference in the `monitors` ETS table, delete the monitor, and add the worker back into the state.

7.1.2 Case 2: crashes between the server and worker

If the server crashes, should it bring down the worker process? It should, because otherwise, the state of the server will be inconsistent with the pool's actual state. On the other hand, when a worker process crashes, should it bring down the server process? Of course not! What does this mean for you? Well, because of the bidirectional dependency, you should use *links*. But because the server should *not* crash when a worker process crashes, the server process should trap exits, as shown in the following listing.

Listing 7.2 Making the server process trap exits (lib/pooly/server.ex)

```
defmodule Pooly.Server do

  #############
  # Callbacks #
  #############
  def init([sup, pool_config]) when is_pid(sup) do        Sets the server
    Process.flag(:trap_exit, true)                        process to trap exits
    monitors = :ets.new(:monitors, [:private])
    init(pool_config, %State{sup: sup, monitors: monitors})
  end

end
```

With the server process trapping exits, you now handle `:EXIT` messages coming from workers, as shown in the next listing.

Listing 7.3 Handling worker `:EXIT` messages (lib/pooly/server.ex)

```
defmodule Pooly.Server do

  #############
  # Callbacks #
  #############

  def handle_info({:EXIT, pid, _reason}, state = %{monitors: monitors,
➥workers: workers, worker_sup: worker_sup}) do
    case :ets.lookup(monitors, pid) do
      [{pid, ref}] ->
        true = Process.demonitor(ref)
        true = :ets.delete(monitors, pid)
        new_state = %{state | workers: [new_worker(worker_sup)|workers]}
        {:noreply, new_state}

      [[]] ->
        {:noreply, state}
    end
  end

end
```

When a worker process exits unexpectedly, its entry is looked up in the `monitors` ETS table. If an entry doesn't exist, nothing needs to be done. Otherwise, the consumer process is no longer monitored, and its entry is removed from the `monitors` table. Finally, a new worker is created and added back into the workers field of the server state.

7.1.3   *Handling multiple pools*

After version 2, you have a basic worker pool in place. But any self-respecting worker-pool application should be able to handle multiple pools. Let's go through a few possible designs before you start coding. The most straightforward way would be to design the supervision tree as shown in figure 7.1.

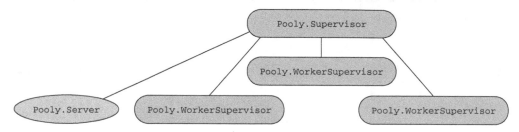

Figure 7.1   A possible design to handle multiple pools

Do you see a problem with this? You're essentially sticking more WorkerSupervisors into Pooly.Supervisor. This is a bad design. The issue is the *error kernel*, or the lack thereof.

Allow me to elaborate. Issues with any of the WorkerSupervisors shouldn't affect the Pooly.Server. It pays to think about what happens when a process crashes and what's affected. A potential fix could be to add another Supervisor to handle all of the WorkerSupervisors—say, a Pooly.WorkersSupervisor (just another level of indirection!). Figure 7.2 shows how it could look.

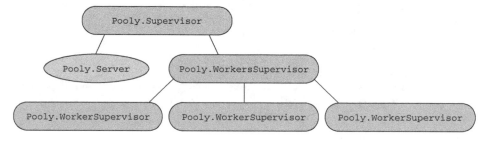

Figure 7.2   Another possible design. Can you identify the bottleneck?

Do you notice another problem? The poor Pooly.Server process has to handle every request meant for any pool. This means the server process may pose a bottleneck if messages to it come fast and furious, and they can potentially flood its mailbox. Pooly.Server also presents a single point of failure, because it contains the state of every pool. The death of the server process would mean all the worker Supervisors would have to be brought down. Consider the design in figure 7.3.

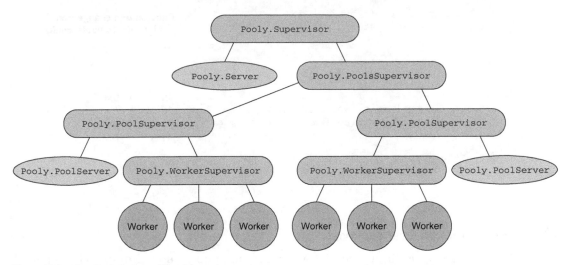

Figure 7.3   The final design of Pooly

The top-level `Supervisor` `Pooly.Supervisor` supervises a `Pooly.Server` and a `PoolsSupervisor`. The `PoolsSupervisor` in turn supervises many `PoolSupervisors`. Each `PoolSupervisor` supervises its own `PoolServer` and `WorkerSupervisor`.

As you've probably guessed, Pooly is going to undergo a design overhaul. To make things easier to follow, you'll implement the changes from top down.

7.1.4   Adding the application behavior to Pooly

The first file to change is lib/pooly.ex, the main entry point into Pooly, shown in the next listing. Because you're now supporting multiple pools, you want to refer to each pool by name. This means the various functions will also accept `pool_name` as a parameter.

Listing 7.4   Adding support for multiple pools (lib/pooly.ex)

```
defmodule Pooly do
  use Application

  def start(_type, _args) do
    pools_config =                              ◁──  Pluralization change from
      [                                              pool_config to pools_config
        [name: "Pool1",
          mfa: {SampleWorker, :start_link, []}, size: 2],
        [name: "Pool2",                              Pool configuration
          mfa: {SampleWorker, :start_link, []}, size: 3],    now takes the
        [name: "Pool3",                              configuration of
          mfa: {SampleWorker, :start_link, []}, size: 4],    multiple pools.
      ]                                              Pools also have
                                                     names.
    start_pools(pools_config)          ◁──  Pluralization change from
  end                                        pool_config to pools_config
```

```
def start_pools(pools_config) do
  Pooly.Supervisor.start_link(pools_config)
end

def checkout(pool_name) do
  Pooly.Server.checkout(pool_name)
end

def checkin(pool_name, worker_pid) do
  Pooly.Server.checkin(pool_name, worker_pid)
end

def status(pool_name) do
  Pooly.Server.status(pool_name)
end

end
```

Pluralization change from pool_config to pools_config

The rest of the APIs take pool_name as a parameter.

7.1.5   Adding the top-level Supervisor

Your next stop is the top-level Supervisor, lib/pooly/supervisor.ex. The top-level Supervisor is in charge of kick-starting Pooly.Server and Pooly.PoolsSupervisor. When Pooly.PoolsSupervisor starts, it starts up individual Pooly.PoolSupervisors that in turn start their own Pooly.Server and Pooly.WorkerSupervisor (see figure 7.4).

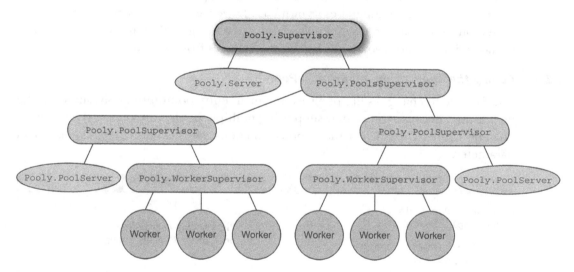

Figure 7.4   Starting from the top-level Supervisor

Pooly.Supervisor supervises two processes: Pooly.PoolsSupervisor (as yet unimplemented) and Pooly.Server. You therefore need to add these two processes to the Pooly.Supervisor's children list, as shown in the next listing.

Listing 7.5   Top-level Supervisor (lib/pooly/supervisor.ex)

```
defmodule Pooly.Supervisor do
  use Supervisor

  def start_link(pools_config) do
    Supervisor.start_link(__MODULE__, pools_config,
                            name: __MODULE__)
  end

  def init(pools_config) do
    children = [
      supervisor(Pooly.PoolsSupervisor, []),
      worker(Pooly.Server, [pools_config])
    ]

    opts = [strategy: :one_for_all]

    supervise(children, opts)
  end

end
```

Pooly.Supervisor is now a named process.

❶ Pluralization change from pool_config to pools_config

Pooly.Supervisor now supervises two children. Note that Pooly.Server no longer takes the pid Pooly.Supervisor because you can refer to it by name.

The major changes to Pooly.Supervisor are mainly adding Pooly.PoolsSupervisor as a child and giving Pooly.Supervisor a name. Recall that you're setting the name of Pooly.Supervisor to __MODULE__ ❶, which means you can refer to the process as Pooly.Supervisor instead of pid. Therefore, you don't need to pass in self (see version 2 of Pooly.Supervisor) into Pooly.Server.

7.1.6   *Adding the pools Supervisor*

Create pools_supervisor.ex in lib/pooly. The next listing shows the implementation.

Listing 7.6   Pools Supervisor (lib/pooly/pools_supervisor.ex)

```
defmodule Pooly.PoolsSupervisor do
  use Supervisor

  def start_link do
    Supervisor.start_link(__MODULE__, [], name: __MODULE__)
  end

  def init(_) do
    opts = [
      strategy: :one_for_one
    ]

    supervise([], opts)
  end

end
```

❶ Starts the Supervisor and gives it the same name as the module

❷ Specifies the :one_for_one restart strategy option to pass in to supervise/2

Just like Pooly.Supervisor, you're giving Pooly.PoolsSupervisor a name ❶. Notice that this Supervisor has no child specifications. In fact, when it starts up, there are no pools attached to it. The reason is that just as in version 2, you want to validate the pool configuration before creating any pools. Therefore, the only information you supply is the restart strategy ❷. Why :one_for_one? Because a crash in any of the pools shouldn't affect every other pool.

7.1.7   *Making Pooly.Server dumber*

In versions 1 and 2, Pooly.Server was the brains of the entire operation. This is no longer the case. Some of Pooly.Server's job will be taken over by the dedicated Pooly.PoolServer (see figure 7.5).

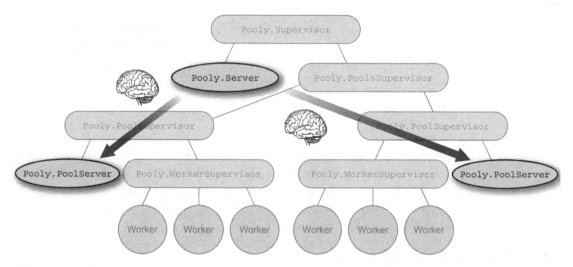

Figure 7.5   Logic from the top-level pool server from the previous version will be moved into individual pool servers.

Most of the APIs are the same from previous versions, with the addition of pool_name. Open lib/pooly/server.ex, and replace the previous implementation with the code in the following listing.

Listing 7.7   Top-level pool server (lib/pooly/server.ex)

```elixir
defmodule Pooly.Server do
  use GenServer
  import Supervisor.Spec

  #######
  # API #
  #######

  def start_link(pools_config) do
    GenServer.start_link(__MODULE__, pools_config, name: __MODULE__)
  end

  def checkout(pool_name) do
    GenServer.call(:"#{pool_name}Server", :checkout)      # ❶  Uses a dynamically
  end                                                     #      constructed atom to
                                                          #      refer to the respective
  def checkin(pool_name, worker_pid) do                   #      pool server
```

```
    GenServer.cast(:"#{pool_name}Server", {:checkin, worker_pid})
  end

  def status(pool_name) do
    GenServer.call(:"#{pool_name}Server", :status)
  end
```

Uses a dynamically
constructed atom to refer to
the respective pool server ❶

```
  #############
  # Callbacks #
  #############

  def init(pools_config) do
    pools_config |> Enum.each(fn(pool_config) ->
      send(self, {:start_pool, pool_config})
    end)
```

Iterates through the
configuration and
❷ sends the :start_pool
message to itself

```
    {:ok, pools_config}
  end

  def handle_info({:start_pool, pool_config}, state) do
    {:ok, _pool_sup} = Supervisor.start_child(Pooly.PoolsSupervisor,
➥supervisor_spec(pool_config))
    {:noreply, state}
  end
```

On receiving the message,
passes pool_config to
PoolsSupervisor ❸

```
  #####################
  # Private Functions #
  #####################

  defp supervisor_spec(pool_config) do
    opts = [id: :"#{pool_config[:name]}Supervisor"]
    supervisor(Pooly.PoolSupervisor, [pool_config], opts)
  end

end
```

❹ Helper function to
generate a unique
Supervisor spec (due
to the "id" option)

In this version, `Pooly.Server`'s job is to delegate all the requests to the respective pools and to start the pools and attach the pools to `Pooly.PoolsSupervisor`. You assume that each individual pool server is named `:"#{pool_name}Server"` ❶. Notice that the name is an *atom*! Sadly, I've lost hours (and hair) to this because I failed to read the documentation properly.

The `pools_config` is iterated ❷, and the `{:start_pool, pool_config}` message is sent. The message is handled ❸, and `Pooly.PoolsSupervisor` is told to start a child based on the given `pool_config`.

There is one tiny caveat to look out for. Notice that you make sure each `Pooly.PoolSupervisor` is started with a unique `Supervisor` specification ID ❹. If you forget to do this, you'll get a cryptic error message such as the following:

```
12:08:16.336 [error] GenServer Pooly.Server terminating
Last message: {:start_pool, [name: "Pool2", mfa: {SampleWorker,
➥:start_link, []}, size: 2]}
State: [[name: "Pool1", mfa: {SampleWorker, :start_link, []}, size: 2],
➥[name: "Pool2", mfa: {SampleWorker, :start_link, []}, size: 2]]
```

```
** (exit) an exception was raised:
    ** (MatchError) no match of right hand side value: {:error,
➥{:already_started, #PID<0.142.0>}}
        (pooly) lib/pooly/server.ex:38: Pooly.Server.handle_info/2
        (stdlib) gen_server.erl:593: :gen_server.try_dispatch/4
        (stdlib) gen_server.erl:659: :gen_server.handle_msg/5
        (stdlib) proc_lib.erl:237: :proc_lib.init_p_do_apply/3
```

The clue here is `{:error, {:already_started, #PID<0.142.0>}}`. I spent a couple of hours trying to figure this out before stumbling onto this solution. But what happens when a `Pooly.PoolSupervisor` starts with a given `pool_config`?

7.1.8 *Adding the pool Supervisor*

`Pooly.PoolSupervisor` takes the place of `Pooly.Supervisor` from previous versions (see figure 7.6). As such, you only need to make a few minor changes. First, you'll initialize each `Pooly.PoolSupervisor` with a name. Second, you need to tell `Pooly.PoolSupervisor` to use `Pooly.PoolServer` instead. See the following listing.

Listing 7.8   Individual pool `Supervisor` (lib/pooly/pool_supervisor.ex)

```
defmodule Pooly.PoolSupervisor do
  use Supervisor

  def start_link(pool_config) do
    Supervisor.start_link(__MODULE__, pool_config,
➥name: :"#{pool_config[:name]}Supervisor")        ❶ Starts the Supervisor
  end                                                  with a unique name

  def init(pool_config) do
    opts = [
      strategy: :one_for_all
    ]                                               ❷ The module name
                                                       passed to the child
    children = [                                       specification has
      worker(Pooly.PoolServer, [self, pool_config])    changed to PoolServer.
    ]

    supervise(children, opts)
  end

end
```

You give individual pool `Supervisor`s a name ❶, although this isn't strictly necessary. It helps you easily pinpoint the pool `Supervisor`s when viewing them in Observer.

The child specification is changed from `Pooly.Server` to `Pooly.PoolServer` ❷. You're passing the same parameters. Even though you're naming `Pooly.PoolSupervisor`, you will not use the name in `Pooly.PoolServer` so that you can reuse much of the implementation of `Pooly.Server` from version 2.

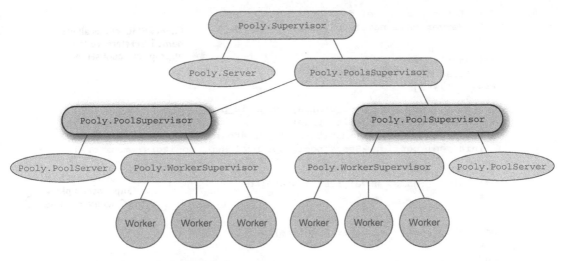

Figure 7.6 Implementing the individual pool Supervisors

7.1.9 *Adding the brains for the pool*

As noted in the previous section, much of the logic remains unchanged, except in places to support multiple pools. In the interest of saving trees and screen real estate, functions that are exactly the same as Pooly.Server version 2 have their implementation stubbed out with # .... In other words, if you're following along, you can copy and paste the implementation of Pooly.Server version 2 to Pooly.PoolServer.

The next listing shows the implementation of Pooly.PoolServer.

Listing 7.9 Individual pool server (lib/pooly/pool_server.ex)

```
defmodule Pooly.PoolServer do
  use GenServer
  import Supervisor.Spec

  defmodule State do
    defstruct pool_sup: nil, worker_sup: nil, monitors: nil, size: nil,
  ➥workers: nil, name: nil, mfa: nil
  end

  def start_link(pool_sup, pool_config) do
    GenServer.start_link(__MODULE__, [pool_sup, pool_config], name:
  ➥name(pool_config[:name]))
  end

  def checkout(pool_name) do
    GenServer.call(name(pool_name), :checkout)
  end

  def checkin(pool_name, worker_pid) do
    GenServer.cast(name(pool_name), {:checkin, worker_pid})
  end
```

❶ GenServer.start_link/3 now takes the pool Supervisor's pid.

❷ Client API functions all use name/1 to reference the appropriate pool server.

```
def status(pool_name) do
  GenServer.call(name(pool_name), :status)
end
```

⎤   **Client API functions all use**
    name/l to reference the
❷   **appropriate pool server.**

```
#############
# Callbacks #
###########j

def init([pool_sup, pool_config]) when is_pid(pool_sup) do
  Process.flag(:trap_exit, true)
  monitors = :ets.new(:monitors, [:private])
  init(pool_config, %State{pool_sup: pool_sup, monitors: monitors})    ◁
end
```

Stores the pool
Supervisor's pid in
the GenServer's state ❸

```
def init([{:name, name}|rest], state) do
  # ...
end

def init([{:mfa, mfa}|rest], state) do
  # ...
end

def init([{:size, size}|rest], state) do
  # ...
end

def init([], state) do
  send(self, :start_worker_supervisor)
  {:ok, state}
end
```

◁   **Sends a message to self**
    to kick-start the worker
❹   **Supervisor process**

```
def init([_|rest], state) do
  # ...
end

def handle_call(:checkout, {from_pid, _ref}, %{workers: workers,
⟼monitors: monitors} = state) do
  # ...
end

def handle_call(:status, _from, %{workers: workers, monitors: monitors} =
⟼state) do
  # ...
end

def handle_cast({:checkin, worker}, %{workers: workers, monitors:
⟼monitors} = state) do
  # ...
end

def handle_info(:start_worker_supervisor, state = %{pool_sup: pool_sup,
⟼name: name, mfa: mfa, size: size}) do
  {:ok, worker_sup} = Supervisor.start_child(pool_sup,
    supervisor_spec(name, mfa))
  workers = prepopulate(size, worker_sup)
  {:noreply, %{state | worker_sup: worker_sup, workers: workers}}
end
```

Tells the pool Supervisor to start a   **Prepopulates the worker Supervisor**
❺ **worker supervisor as a child process**   **with worker processes** ❻

```elixir
def handle_info({:DOWN, ref, _, _, _}, state = %{monitors: monitors,
  workers: workers}) do
  # ...
end

def handle_info({:EXIT, pid, _reason}, state = %{monitors: monitors,
  workers: workers, pool_sup: pool_sup}) do
  case :ets.lookup(monitors, pid) do
    [{pid, ref}] ->
      true = Process.demonitor(ref)
      true = :ets.delete(monitors, pid)
      new_state = %{state | workers: [new_worker(pool_sup)|workers]}
      {:noreply, new_state}

    _ ->
      {:noreply, state}
  end
end

def terminate(_reason, _state) do
  :ok
end

#####################
# Private Functions #
#####################

defp name(pool_name) do
  :"#{pool_name}Server"
end

defp prepopulate(size, sup) do
  # ...
end

defp prepopulate(size, _sup, workers) when size < 1 do
  # ...
end

defp prepopulate(size, sup, workers) do
  # ...
end

defp new_worker(sup) do
  # ...
end

defp supervisor_spec(name, mfa) do
  opts = [id: name <> "WorkerSupervisor", restart: :temporary]
  supervisor(Pooly.WorkerSupervisor, [self, mfa], opts)
end

end
```

Returns the name of the pool server ❼ **as an atom**

Returns a child specification for the ❽ **worker Supervisor**

There are a few notable changes. The server's start_link/2 function takes the pool Supervisor as the first argument ❶. The pid of the pool Supervisor is saved in the state of the server process ❸. Also, note that the state of the server has been extended to store the pid of the pool Supervisor and worker Supervisor:

```
defmodule State do
  defstruct pool_sup: nil, worker_sup: nil, monitors: nil, size: nil,
            workers: nil, name: nil, mfa: nil
end
```

Once the server is done processing the pool configuration, it will eventually send the
:start_worker_supervisor message to itself ❹. This message is handled by the
handle_info/2 callback. The pool Supervisor is told to start a worker Supervisor as
a child ❺, using the child specification defined at ❽. In addition to mfa, you also pass
in the pid of the server process. Once the pid of the worker Supervisor is returned,
it's used to pre-populate itself with workers ❻. You use name/1 ❼ to reference the
appropriate pool server to call the appropriate functions ❷.

7.1.10 *Adding the worker supervisor for the pool*

The last piece is the worker Supervisor, which is tasked with managing the individual
workers (see figure 7.7). It manages any crashing workers. There's a subtle detail: during initialization, the worker Supervisor creates a link to its corresponding pool
server. Why bother? If either the pool server or worker Supervisor goes down, there's
no point in either continuing to exist. Let's look at the full implementation in listing
7.10 for details.

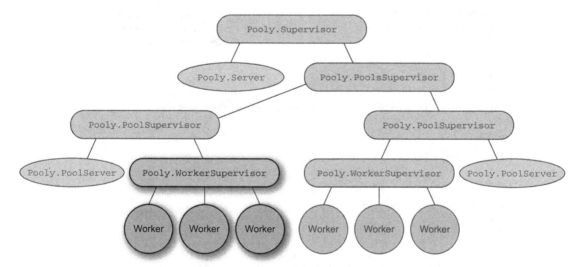

Figure 7.7   Implementing the individual pool's worker Supervisor

Listing 7.10   Pool's worker Supervisor (lib/pooly/worker_supervisor.ex)

```
defmodule Pooly.WorkerSupervisor do
  use Supervisor

  def start_link(pool_server, {_,_,_} = mfa) do
    Supervisor.start_link(__MODULE__, [pool_server, mfa])
  end
```

**Starts the
Supervisor with
the pid of the
pool server and a
module, function,
arguments tuple**

```
def init([pool_server, {m,f,a}]) do
  Process.link(pool_server)
  worker_opts = [restart:  :temporary,
                 shutdown: 5000,
                 function: f]

  children = [worker(m, a, worker_opts)]
  opts     = [strategy:     :simple_one_for_one,
              max_restarts: 5,
              max_seconds:  5]

  supervise(children, opts)
end
```
end

The only changes are the additional `pool_server` argument and the linking of `pool_server` to the worker `Supervisor` process. Why? As previously mentioned, there's a dependency between the processes, and the pool server needs to be notified when the worker `Supervisor` goes down. Similarly, if the worker `Supervisor` crashes, it should also take down the pool server.

In order for the pool server to handle the message, you need to add another `handle_info/2` callback in lib/pooly/pool_server.ex, as the following listing shows.

> **Listing 7.11   Detecting if the worker `Supervisor` goes down (lib/pooly/pool_server.ex)**

```
defmodule Pooly.PoolServer do

  #############
  # Callbacks #
  #############
  def handle_info({:EXIT, worker_sup, reason}, state = %{worker_sup:
➥worker_sup}) do
    {:stop, reason, state}
  end

end
```

Whenever the worker `Supervisor` exits, it will also terminate the pool server for the same reason that it terminated the worker `Supervisor`.

7.1.11 *Taking it for a spin*

Let's make sure you wired everything up correctly. First, open lib/pooly.ex to configure the pool. Make sure the `start/2` function looks like the following listing.

> **Listing 7.12   Configuring Pooly to start three pools of various sizes (lib/pooly.ex)**

```
defmodule Pooly do
  use Application

  def start(_type, _args) do
    pools_config =
```

```
    [
      [name: "Pool1", mfa: {SampleWorker, :start_link, []}, size: 2],
      [name: "Pool2", mfa: {SampleWorker, :start_link, []}, size: 3],
      [name: "Pool3", mfa: {SampleWorker, :start_link, []}, size: 4]
    ]

    start_pools(pools_config)
  end

  # ...
end
```

You tell Pooly to create three pools, each with a given size and type of worker. For simplicity (laziness, really), you're using `SampleWorker` in all three pools. In a fresh terminal session, launch `iex` and start Observer:

```
% iex -S mix
iex> :observer.start
```

Bear witness to the glorious supervision tree you have created, shown in figure 7.8.

Now, starting from the leaves (lowest/rightmost) of the supervision tree, try right-clicking the process and killing it. You'll again notice that a new process takes over.

Work your way higher. What happens when, say, `Pool3Server` is killed? You'll notice that the corresponding `WorkerSupervisor` and the workers under it are all killed and then respawned. It's important to note that `Pool3Server` is a brand-new process.

Go even higher. What happens when you kill a `PoolSupervisor`? As expected, everything under it is killed, another `PoolSupervisor` is respawned, and everything under it respawns, too. Notice what doesn't happen: the rest of the application

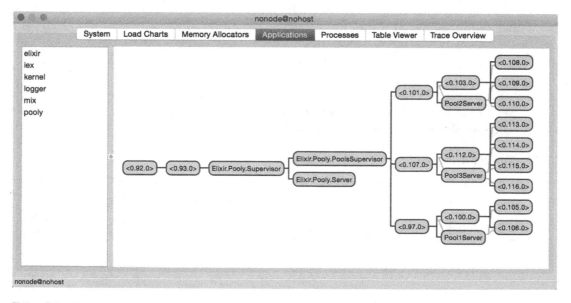

Figure 7.8   The Pooly supervision tree as seen in Observer

remains unaffected. Isn't that wonderful? When crashes happen, as they inevitably will, having a nicely layered supervision hierarchy allows the error to be handled in an isolated way so it doesn't affect the rest of the application.

7.2 Version 4: implementing overflowing and queuing

In the final version of Pooly, you're going to extend it a little to support a variable number of workers by specifying a *maximum overflow*. I also want to introduce the notion of *queuing up* workers. That is, when the maximum overflow limit has been reached, Pooly can queue up workers for consumers that are willing to *block and wait* for a next available worker.

7.2.1 Implementing maximum overflow

As usual, in order to specify the maximum overflow, you add a new field to the pool configuration. In lib/pooly.ex, modify pools_config in start/2 to look as shown in the next listing.

Listing 7.13   Implementing maximum overflow (lib/pooly.ex)

```
defmodule Pooly do

  def start(_type, _args) do
    pools_config =
      [
        [name: "Pool1",
         mfa: {SampleWorker, :start_link, []},
         size: 2,
         max_overflow: 3
        ],
        [name: "Pool2",
         mfa: {SampleWorker, :start_link, []},
         size: 3,
         max_overflow: 0
        ],
        [name: "Pool3",
         mfa: {SampleWorker, :start_link, []},
         size: 4,
         max_overflow: 0
        ]

      ]

    start_pools(pools_config)
  end

end
```

Specifies the maximum overflow in the pool configuration

Now that you have a new option for the pool configuration, you must head over to lib/pooly/pool_server.ex to add support for max_overflow. This includes the following:

- Adding an entry called max_overflow in State

- Adding an entry called `overflow` in `State` to keep track of the current overflow count
- Adding a function clause in `init/2` to handle `max_overflow`

The next listing shows the additions.

Listing 7.14   Adding a maximum overflow option (lib/pooly/pool_server.ex)

```elixir
defmodule Pooly.PoolServer do

  defmodule State do
    defstruct pool_sup: nil, worker_sup: nil, monitors: nil, size: nil,
    ➥workers: nil, name: nil, mfa: nil, overflow: nil, max_overflow: nil
  end

  #############
  # Callbacks #
  #############

  def init([{:name, name}|rest], state) do
    # ...
  end

  # ... more init/1 definitions
  def init([{:max_overflow, max_overflow}|rest], state) do
    init(rest, %{state | max_overflow: max_overflow})
  end

  def init([], state) do
    #...
  end

  def init([_|rest], state) do
    # ...
  end

end
```

Next, let's consider the case of an actual overflow. An overflow is said to happen if the total number of busy workers exceeds `size` *and* is within the limits of `max_overflow`. When can overflows happen? When a worker is checked out. Therefore, the only place to look is `handle_call({:checkout, block}, from, state)`, as shown in the next listing.

Listing 7.15   Handling overflows during checking out (lib/pooly/pool_server.ex)

```elixir
defmodule Pooly.PoolServer do

  #############
  # Callbacks #
  #############

  def handle_call({:checkout, block}, {from_pid, _ref} = from, state) do
    %{worker_sup:   worker_sup,
      workers:      workers,
```

```
         monitors:      monitors,
         overflow:      overflow,
         max_overflow: max_overflow} = state

    case workers do
      [worker|rest] ->
        # ...
        {:reply, worker, %{state | workers: rest}}

      [] when max_overflow > 0 and overflow < max_overflow ->
        {worker, ref} = new_worker(worker_sup, from_pid)
        true = :ets.insert(monitors, {worker, ref})
        {:reply, worker, %{state | overflow: overflow+1}}

      [] ->
        {:reply, :full, state};
    end
  end

end
```

❶ Checks whether within overflow limits

Handling this case is simple. You check whether you're within the limits of overflowing ❶. If so, a new worker is created and the necessary bookkeeping information is added to the monitors ETS table. A reply containing the worker pid is given to the consumer process, along with an increment of the overflow count.

7.2.2 *Handling worker check-ins*

Now that you can handle overflow, how do you handle worker check-ins? In version 2, all you did was add the worker pid back into the workers field of the PoolServer state:

```
{:noreply, %{state | workers: [pid|workers]}}
```

But when handling a check-in of an overflowed worker, you don't want to add it back into the workers field. It's sufficient to dismiss the worker. You'll implement a helper function to handle check-ins, as shown in the following listing.

Listing 7.16 Handling worker overflows (lib/pooly/pool_server.ex)

```
defmodule Pooly.PoolServer do

  ######################
  # Private Functions #
  ######################

  def handle_checkin(pid, state) do
    %{worker_sup:    worker_sup,
      workers:       workers,
      monitors:      monitors,
      overflow:      overflow} = state

    if overflow > 0 do
      :ok = dismiss_worker(worker_sup, pid)
      %{state | waiting: empty, overflow: overflow-1}
    else
```

```
        %{state | waiting: empty, workers: [pid|workers], overflow: 0}
    end
  end

  defp dismiss_worker(sup, pid) do
    true = Process.unlink(pid)
    Supervisor.terminate_child(sup, pid)
  end

end
```

handle_checkin/2 checks that the pool is indeed overflowed when a worker is being checked back in. If so, it delegates to dismiss_worker/2 to terminate the worker and decrement overflow. Otherwise, the worker is added back into workers as before.

The function for dismissing workers isn't difficult to understand. All you need to do is unlink the worker from the pool server and tell the worker Supervisor to terminate the child. Now you can update handle_cast({:checkin, worker}, state), as shown in the next listing.

Listing 7.17   Updating the check-in callback (lib/pooly/pool_server.ex)

```
defmodule Pooly.PoolServer do

  #############
  # Callbacks #
  #############

  def handle_cast({:checkin, worker}, %{monitors: monitors} = state) do
    case :ets.lookup(monitors, worker) do
      [{pid, ref}] ->
        # ...
        new_state = handle_checkin(pid, state)    ◁─┐ Update this line to use
        {:noreply, new_state}                        │ handle_checkin/2.

      [] ->
        {:noreply, state}
    end
  end
end
```

7.2.3   *Handling worker exits*

What happens when an overflowed worker exits? Let's turn to the callback function handle_info({:EXIT, pid, _reason}, state). Similar to the case when handling worker check-ins, you delegate the task of handling worker exits to a helper function in the next listing.

Listing 7.18   Computing the state for worker exits (lib/pooly/pool_server.ex)

```
defmodule Pooly.PoolServer do

  #####################
  # Private Functions #
  #####################
```

```
defp handle_worker_exit(pid, state) do
  %{worker_sup:    worker_sup,
    workers:       workers,
    monitors:      monitors,
    overflow:      overflow} = state

  if overflow > 0 do
    %{state | overflow: overflow-1}
  else
    %{state | workers: [new_worker(worker_sup)|workers]}
  end
end
end
```

The logic is the reverse of `handle_checkin/2`, as shown in listing 7.19. You check whether the pool is overflowed, and if so, you decrement the counter. Because the pool is overflowed, you don't bother to add the worker back into the pool. On the other hand, if the pool isn't overflowed, you need to add a worker back into the worker list.

Listing 7.19   Handling worker exits (lib/pooly/pool_server.ex)

```
defmodule Pooly.PoolServer do

  ############
  # Callbacks #
  ############

  def handle_info({:EXIT, pid, _reason}, state = %{monitors: monitors,
  ➥workers: workers, worker_sup: worker_sup}) do
    case :ets.lookup(monitors, pid) do
      [{pid, ref}] ->
        # ...
        new_state = handle_worker_exit(pid, state)      ◁─┐ Update this line to use
        {:noreply, new_state}                              │ handle_worker_exit/2.

      _ ->
        {:noreply, state}
    end
  end

end
```

7.2.4   *Updating status with overflow information*

Let's give `Pooly` the ability to report whether it's overflowed. The pool will have three states: `:overflow`, `:full`, and `:ready`. The following listing shows the updated implementation of `handle_call(:status, from, state)`.

Listing 7.20   Adding overflow information to the status (lib/pooly/pool_server.ex)

```
defmodule Pooly.PoolServer do

  ############
  # Callbacks #
  ############
```

```
  def handle_call(:status, _from, %{workers: workers, monitors: monitors} =
➥state) do
    {:reply, {state_name(state), length(workers), :ets.info(monitors,
➥:size)}, state}
  end

  #####################
  # Private Functions #
  #####################

  defp state_name(%State{overflow: overflow, max_overflow: max_overflow,
➥workers: workers}) when overflow < 1 do
    case length(workers) == 0 do
      true ->
        if max_overflow < 1 do
          :full
        else
          :overflow
        end
      false ->
        :ready
    end
  end

  defp state_name(%State{overflow: max_overflow, max_overflow:
➥max_overflow}) do
    :full
  end

  defp state_name(_state) do
    :overflow
  end

end
```

7.2.5   *Queuing worker processes*

For the last bit of Pooly, you're going to handle the case where consumers are willing to wait for a worker to be available. In other words, the consumer process is willing to block until the worker pool frees up a worker. For this to work, you need to queue up worker processes and match a newly freed worker process with a waiting consumer process.

A BLOCKING CONSUMER

A consumer must tell Pooly if it's willing to block. You can do this by extending the API for checkout in lib/pooly.ex:

```
defmodule Pooly do
  @timeout 5000

  #######
  # API #
  #######

  def checkout(pool_name, block \\ true, timeout \\ @timeout) do
    Pooly.Server.checkout(pool_name, block, timeout)
  end

end
```

In this new version of checkout, you add two extra parameters: block and timeout. Head over to lib/pooly/server.ex, and update the checkout function accordingly:

```
defmodule Pooly.Server do

  #######
  # API #
  #######

  def checkout(pool_name, block, timeout) do
    Pooly.PoolServer.checkout(pool_name, block, timeout)
  end

end
```

Now to the real meat of the implementation, lib/pooly/pooly_server.ex, shown in the following listing.

Listing 7.21 Using a queue for waiting consumers (lib/pooly/pool_server.ex)

```
defmodule Pooly.PoolServer do

  defmodule State do
    defstruct pool_sup: nil, ..., waiting: nil, ..., max_overflow: nil   #A
  end

  #############
  # Callbacks #
  #############

  def init([pool_sup, pool_config]) when is_pid(pool_sup) do
    Process.flag(:trap_exit, true)
    monitors = :ets.new(:monitors, [:private])
    waiting  = :queue.new
    state    = %State{pool_sup: pool_sup, monitors: monitors,
                      waiting: waiting, overflow: 0}

    init(pool_config, state)
  end

  #######
  # API #
  #######

  def checkout(pool_name, block, timeout) do
    GenServer.call(name(pool_name), {:checkout, block}, timeout)
  end

end
```

> Updates the state to store the queue of waiting consumers

> Adds block and timeout callbacks for checkout

First, you update the state with a waiting field. That will store the queue of consumers. Although Elixir doesn't come with a queue data structure, it doesn't need to. Erlang comes with a queue implementation. There's a bigger lesson in this: whenever something is missing from Elixir, instead of reaching for a third-party library,[1] find out whether Erlang has the functionality you need. This highlights the wonderful interoperability between Erlang and Elixir.

---

[1] Or even worse, building one yourself (unless it's for educational purposes)!

Queues in Erlang

The queue implementation that Erlang provides is interesting. I'll let the examples do the talking. Let's look at the basics of using a queue: creating a queue, adding items to a queue, and removing items from a queue. In a fresh `iex` session, create a queue:

```
iex(1)> q = :queue.new
{[], []}
```

Notice that the return value is a tuple of two elements—lists, to be more precise. Why two? To answer that question, add a couple of items to the queue:

```
iex(2)> q = :queue.in("uno", q)
{["uno"], []}

iex(3)> q = :queue.in("dos", q)
{["dos"], ["uno"]}

iex(4)> q = :queue.in("tres", q)
{["tres", "dos"], ["uno"]}
```

The first element (the head of the queue) is the *second* element of the tuple, and the remainder of the queue is represented by the *first* element. Now, try removing an element from the queue:

```
iex(5)> :queue.out(q)
{{:value, "uno"}, {["tres"], ["dos"]}}
```

This is an interesting-looking tuple. Let's break it down a little:

```
{{:value, "uno"}, ...}
```

This tagged tuple (with `:value`) contains the value of the first element of the queue. Now for the other part:

```
{..., {["tres"], ["dos"]}}
```

This tuple is the new queue, after the first element has been removed. The representation of the new queue is the same as the one you saw earlier, with the first element being the second element of the tuple and the remaining part of the queue in the first element.

Yes, I know it's slightly confusing, but hang in there. Arranging the result this way makes sense because, remember, data structures are immutable in Elixir/Erlang land. Also, this is a perfect case for pattern matching:

```
iex(6)> {{:value, head}, q} = :queue.out(q)
{{:value, "uno"}, {["tres"], ["dos"]}}

iex(7)> {{:value, head}, q} = :queue.out(q)
{{:value, "dos"}, {[], ["tres"]}}

iex(8)> {{:value, head}, q} = :queue.out(q)
{{:value, "tres"}, {[], []}}
```

> What happens when you try to get something out of an empty queue?
>
> ```
> iex(9)> {{:value, head}, q} = :queue.out(q)
> ** (MatchError) no match of right hand side value: {:empty, {[], []}}
> ```
>
> Whoops! For an empty queue, the return value is a tuple that contains :empty as the first element. This concludes our brief detour of using the queue; this is all you need to understand the examples that follow.

Next, you'll add block and timeout to the invocation of the callback function in the following listing.

Listing 7.22 Handling waiting consumers (lib/pooly/pool_server.ex)

```
defmodule Pooly.PoolServer do

  ##############
  # Callbacks #
  ##############

  def handle_call({:checkout, block}, {from_pid, _ref} = from, state) do
    %{worker_sup:   worker_sup,
      workers:      workers,
      monitors:     monitors,
      waiting:      waiting,                              ❶ Updates state
      overflow:     overflow,                                with waiting
      max_overflow: max_overflow} = state

    case workers do
      [worker|rest] ->
        # ...

      [] when max_overflow > 0 and overflow < max_overflow ->
        # ...

      [] when block == true ->                            ❷ Adds a waiting
        ref = Process.monitor(from_pid)                     consumer to
        waiting = :queue.in({from, ref}, waiting)           the queue
        {:noreply, %{state | waiting: waiting}, :infinity}

      [] ->
        {:reply, :full, state};
    end
  end

end
```

You add two things:

- waiting to the state ❶
- Handling the case when a consumer is willing to block ❷

Let's deal with the case when you're overflowed and there's a request for a worker where the consumer is willing to wait. This case is covered next.

HANDLING A CONSUMER THAT'S WILLING TO BLOCK

When a consumer is willing to block, you'll first monitor it. That's because if it crashes for some reason, you must know about it and remove it from the queue.

Next, you add to the `waiting` queue a tuple of the form `{from, ref}`. `from` is the same `from` of the callback. Note that `from` is a *tuple*, containing a tuple of the consumer pid and a tag, itself a reference.

Finally, note that the reply is a `:noreply`, with `:infinity` as the timeout. Returning `:noreply` means `GenServer.reply(from_pid, message)` must be called from somewhere else. Because you don't know how long you must wait, you pass in `:infinity`.

Where do you need to call `GenServer.reply/2`? In other words, when do you need to reply to the consumer process? During a check-in of a worker! Time to update `handle_checkin/2`. This time, you'll use the `waiting` queue and pattern matching, as shown in the following listing.

Listing 7.23   Handling a check-in that's willing to block (lib/pooly/pool_server.ex)

```elixir
defmodule Pooly.PoolServer do

  #####################
  # Private Functions #
  #####################

  def handle_checkin(pid, state) do
    %{worker_sup:    worker_sup,
      workers:       workers,
      monitors:      monitors,
      waiting:       waiting,
      overflow:      overflow} = state

    case :queue.out(waiting) do
      {{:value, {from, ref}}, left} ->
        true = :ets.insert(monitors, {pid, ref})
        GenServer.reply(from, pid)
        %{state | waiting: left}

      {:empty, empty} when overflow > 0 ->
        :ok = dismiss_worker(worker_sup, pid)
        %{state | waiting: empty, overflow: overflow-1}

      {:empty, empty} ->
        %{state | waiting: empty, workers: [pid|workers], overflow: 0}
    end
  end
end
```

> Replies to the consumer process when a worker is available

Depending on the output of the queue, you have to handle three cases. The first case is when the queue isn't empty. This means you have at least one consumer process waiting for a worker. You insert a three-element tuple into the `monitors` ETS table. Now you can finally tell the consumer process that you have an available worker using `GenServer.reply/2`.

The second case is when there are no consumers currently waiting, but you're in an overflow state. This means you have to decrement the `overflow` count by 1.

The last case to handle is when there are no consumers currently waiting and you're not in an overflow state. For this, you can add the worker back into the workers field.

GETTING A WORKER FROM WORKER EXITS

There's another way a waiting consumer can get a worker: if some other worker process exits. The modification is simple. Head to handle_worker_exit/2, as shown in the next listing.

> **Listing 7.24 Handling worker exits (lib/pooly/pool_server.ex)**

```
defmodule Pooly.PoolServer do

  #####################
  # Private Functions #
  #####################

  defp handle_worker_exit(pid, state) do
    %{worker_sup:   worker_sup,
      workers:      workers,
      monitors:     monitors,
      waiting:      waiting,
      overflow:     overflow} = state

    case :queue.out(waiting) do
      {{:value, {from, ref}}, left} ->
        new_worker = new_worker(worker_sup)
        true = :ets.insert(monitors, {new_worker, ref})
        GenServer.reply(from, new_worker)
        %{state | waiting: left}

      {:empty, empty} when overflow > 0 ->
        %{state | overflow: overflow-1, waiting: empty}

      {:empty, empty} ->
        workers = [new_worker(worker_sup) | workers]
        %{state | workers: workers, waiting: empty}
    end
  end
end
```

Similar to handle_checkin/2, you use pattern matching from the result of :queue.out/1. The first case is when you have a waiting consumer process. Because a worker has crashed or exited, you create a new one and hand it to the consumer process. The rest of the cases are self-explanatory.

7.2.6 *Taking it for a spin*

Now to reap the fruits of your labor. Configure the pool as follows:

```
defmodule Pooly do

  def start(_type, _args) do
    pools_config =
      [
        [name: "Pool1",
         mfa: {SampleWorker, :start_link, []},
```

```
       size: 2,
       max_overflow: 1
       ],
       [name: "Pool2",
       mfa: {SampleWorker, :start_link, []},
       size: 3,
       max_overflow: 0
       ],
       [name: "Pool3",
       mfa: {SampleWorker, :start_link, []},
       size: 4,
       max_overflow: 0
       ]
     ]

    start_pools(pools_config)
  end
end
```

Here, only `Pool1` has overflow configured. Open a new `iex` session:

```
% iex -S mix
iex(1)> w1 = Pooly.checkout("Pool1")
#PID<0.97.0>

iex(2)> w2 = Pooly.checkout("Pool1")
#PID<0.96.0>

iex(3)> w3 = Pooly.checkout("Pool1")
#PID<0.111.0>
```

With max overflow set to 1, the pool can handle one extra worker. What happens when you try to check out another worker? The client will be blocked indefinitely or time-out, depending on how you try to check out the worker. For example, doing this will block indefinitely:

```
iex(4)> Pooly.checkout("Pool1", true, :infinity)
```

On the other hand, doing this will time out after five seconds:

```
iex(5)> Pooly.checkout("Pool1", true, 5000)
```

If you're following along, you'll realize that the session is blocked. Before you continue, open lib/pooly/sample_worker.ex, and add the `work_for/2` function and its corresponding callback, as the following listing shows.

Listing 7.25 Simulating processing (lib/pooly/sample_worker.ex)

```
defmodule SampleWorker do
  use GenServer

    # ...

  def work_for(pid, duration) do
```

```
      GenServer.cast(pid, {:work_for, duration})
    end

    def handle_cast({:work_for, duration}, state) do
      :timer.sleep(duration)
      {:stop, :normal, state}
    end

end
```

This function simulates a short-lived worker by telling the worker to sleep for some time and then exiting normally. Restart the session as you did earlier. Check out three workers:

```
iex(1)> w1 = Pooly.checkout("Pool1")
#PID<0.97.0>

iex(2)> w2 = Pooly.checkout("Pool1")
#PID<0.96.0>

iex(3)> w3 = Pooly.checkout("Pool1")
#PID<0.111.0>
```

This time, tell the first worker to work for 10 seconds:

```
iex(4)> SampleWorker.work_for(w1, 10_000)
:ok
```

Now, try to check out a worker. Because you've exceeded the maximum overflow, the pool will cause the client to block:

```
iex(5)> Pooly.checkout("Pool1", true, :infinity)
```

Ten seconds later, the console prints out a pid:

```
#PID<0.114.0>
```

Success! Even though you were in an overflowed state, once the first worker has completed its job, another slot became available and was handled by the waiting client.

7.3   *Exercises*

1 *Restart strategies*—Play around with the different restart strategies. For example, pick one Supervisor and change its restart strategy to something different. Launch :observer.start, and see what happens. Did the Supervisor restart the child/children processes as you expected?

2 *Transactions*—There's a limitation with this implementation. It's assumed that all consumers behave like good citizens of the pool and check workers back in when they're finished with them. In general, the pool shouldn't make assumptions like this, because it's easy to cause a shortage of workers. To get around this, Poolboy has *transactions*. Here's the skeleton for you to complete:

```
defmodule Pooly.Server do

  def transaction(pool_name, fun, timeout) do
    worker = <FILL ME IN>
    try do
      <FILL ME IN>
    after
      <FILL ME IN>
    end
  end

end
```

3 Currently, it's possible to check in the same worker multiple times. Fix this!

7.4   Summary

Believe it or not, you're finished with `Pooly`! If you've made it this far, you deserve a break. Not only that, you've re-implemented 96.777% of Poolboy, but in Elixir. This is probably the most complicated example in this book. But I'm pretty sure that after working through it, you've gained a deeper appreciation of `Supervisors` and how they interact with other processes, as well as how `Supervisors` can be structured in a layered way to provide fault tolerance.

If you struggled with chapters 6 and 7, don't worry;[2] there's nothing wrong with you. I struggled with grasping these concepts, too. Pooly has a lot of moving parts. But if you step back and look at the code again, it's amazing how everything fits together. In this chapter, you learned about the following:

- Using the OTP `Supervisor` behavior
- Building multiple supervision hierarchies
- Dynamically creating `Supervisors` and workers using the OTP `Supervisor` API
- A grand tour of building a non-trivial application using a mixture of `Supervisors` and `GenServers`

In the next chapter, you look at an equally exciting topic: distribution.

---

[2]   If you didn't, I don't want to hear about it.

Distribution
and load balancing

8

This chapter and the next will be the most fun chapters (I say that about every chapter). In this chapter, we'll explore the distribution capabilities of the Erlang VM. You'll learn about the distribution primitives that let you create a cluster of nodes and spawn processes remotely. The next chapter will explore failover and takeover in a distributed system.

In order to demonstrate all these concepts, you'll build two applications. The first is a command-line tool to perform load testing on websites. Yes, this could very well be used for evil purposes, but I'll leave you to your own exploits.

The other is an application that will demonstrate how a cluster handles failures by having another node automatically step up to take the place of a downed node. To take things further, it will also demonstrate how a node yields control when a previously downed node of higher priority rejoins the cluster.

8.1   Why distributed?

There are at least two good reasons to create a distributed system. When the application you're building has exceeded the physical capabilities of a single machine, you have a choice between either upgrading that single machine or adding another machine. There are limits to how much you can upgrade a single machine. There are also physical limits to how much a single machine can handle. Examples include the number of opened file handles and network connections. Sometimes a machine has to be brought down for scheduled maintenance or upgrades. With a distributed system, you can design the load to be spread across multiple machines. In other words, you're achieving load balancing.

Fault tolerance is the other reason to consider building a distributed system. This is the case when one or more nodes are monitoring the node that's running the application. If that node goes down, the next node in line will automatically take over that node. Having such a setup means you eliminate a single point of failure (unless all your nodes are hosted on a single machine!).

Make no mistake—distributed systems are still difficult, given the nature of the problem. It's up to you to contend with the tradeoffs and issues that come up with distributed systems, such as net splits. But Elixir and the Erlang VM offer tools you can wield to make it much easier to build distributed systems.

8.2   Distribution for load balancing

In this section, you'll learn how to build a distributed load tester. The load tester you're building basically creates a barrage of GET requests to an end point and measures the response time. Because there's a limit to the number of open network connections a single physical machine can make, this is a perfect use case for a distributed system. In this case, the number of web requests needed is spread evenly across each node in the cluster.

8.2.1   An overview of Blitzy, the load tester

Before you begin learning about distribution and implementing Blitzy, let's briefly see what it can do. Blitzy is a command-line program. Here's an example of unleashing Blitzy on an unsuspecting victim:

```
% ./blitzy -n 100 http://www.bieberfever.com
[info]  Pummeling http://www.bieberfever.com with 100 requests
```

This example creates 100 workers, each of which makes an HTTP GET request to www.bieberfever.com; you then measure the response time and count the number of successful requests. Behind the scenes, Blitzy creates a cluster and splits the workers across the nodes in the cluster. In this case, 100 workers are split across 4 nodes. Therefore, 25 workers are running on each node (see figure 8.1).

1. Start 100 workers.

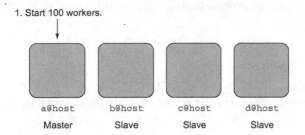

2. Start 25 workers.

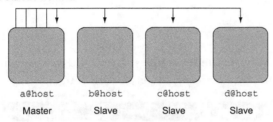

3. Each node reports the result back to the master node

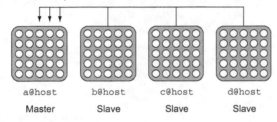

Figure 8.1 The number of requests is split across the available nodes in the cluster. Once a node has received results from all of its workers, the respective node reports back to the worker.

Once all the workers from each individual node have finished, the result is sent over the master node (see figure 8.1). The master node then aggregates and reports the results:

```
Total workers    : 1000
Successful reqs  : 1000
Failed res       : 0
Average (msecs)  : 3103.478963
Longest (msecs)  : 5883.235
Shortest (msecs) : 25.061
```

When I'm planning to write a distributed application, I always begin with the non-distributed version first to keep things slightly simpler. Once you have the non-distributed bits working, you can then move on to the distribution layer. Jumping straight into building an application with distribution in mind for a first iteration usually turns out badly.

That's the approach you'll take when developing Blitzy in this chapter. You'll begin with baby steps:

1   Build the non-concurrent version.
2   Build the concurrent version.
3   Build a distributed version that can run on two virtual machine instances.
4   Build a distributed version that can run on two separate machines connected to a network.

8.2.2   *Let the mayhem begin!*

Give the project a good name:

```
% mix new blitzy
```

In the next listing, let's pull in some dependencies that you'd know to include in mix.exs if you had a crystal ball. (Fortunately, I'm here to tell you!)

Listing 8.1   Setting up the dependencies for Blitzy (mix.exs)

```
defmodule Blitzy.Mixfile do
  use Mix.Project

  def project do
    [app: :blitzy,
     version: "0.0.1",
     elixir: "~> 1.1-rc1",
     deps: deps]
  end

  def application do
    [mod: {Blitzy, []},
     applications: [:logger, :httpoison, :timex]]      Adds the prerequisite
  end                                                   applications.

  defp deps do
    [
      {:httpoison, "~> 0.9.0"},           HTTPoison is an
      {:timex,     "~> 3.0"},             HTTP client.
      {:tzdata, "~> 0.1.8", override: true}         Timex is a
    ]                                                date/time library.
  end
end
```

If you're wondering about tzdata and the override: true:, you need this because newer versions of tzdata don't play nicely with escripts. (Escripts will be explained later in the chapter.) Don't forget to add the correct entries in application/0.

Always read the README!

I wouldn't know to include the correct entries in application/0 if I hadn't read the installation instructions given in the respective READMEs of the libraries. Failure to do so will often lead to confusing errors.

8.2.3 *Implementing the worker process*

Begin with the worker process. The worker fetches the web page and computes how long the request takes. Create lib/blitzy/worker.ex as shown in the following listing.

> **Listing 8.2   Implementing the worker (lib/blitzy/worker.ex)**

```
defmodule Blitzy.Worker do
  use Timex
  require Logger

  def start(url) do
    {timestamp, response} = Duration.measure(fn -> HTTPoison.get(url) end)
    handle_response({Duration.to_milliseconds(timestamp), response})
  end

  defp handle_response({msecs, {:ok, %HTTPoison.Response{status_code:
  ➥code}}})
  when code >= 200 and code <= 304 do
    Logger.info "worker [#{node}-#{inspect self}] completed in #{msecs}
  ➥msecs"
    {:ok, msecs}
  end

  defp handle_response({_msecs, {:error, reason}}) do
    Logger.info "worker [#{node}-#{inspect self}] error due to #{inspect
  ➥reason}"
    {:error, reason}
  end

  defp handle_response({_msecs, _}) do
    Logger.info "worker [#{node}-#{inspect self}] errored out"
    {:error, :unknown}
  end

end
```

For example, you could instead have used HTTPotion's `HTTPotion.get/1`:

```
Blitzy.Worker.start("http://www.bieberfever.com", &HTTPotion.get/1)
```

The HTTP request function is then invoked in the body of `Time.measure/1`. Notice the slightly different syntax: `func.(url)` instead of `func(url)`. The dot is important because you need to tell Elixir that `func` is pointing to another function and not to that function itself.

`Time.measure/1` is a handy function from Timex that measures the time taken for a function to complete. Once that function completes, `Time.measure/1` returns a tuple containing the time taken and the return value of that function. Note that all measurements are in milliseconds.

The tuple returned from `Time.measure/1` is then passed to `handle_response/1`. Here, you're expecting that whatever function you pass into `start/2` will give you a return result containing a tuple in either of the following formats:

- `{:ok, %{status_code: code}`
- `{:error, reason}`

In addition to getting a successful response, you also check that the status code falls between 200 and 304. If you get an error response, you return a tuple tagged with :error along with the reason for the error. Finally, you handle all other cases.

8.2.4   *Running the worker*

Let's try running the worker:

```
iex(1)> Blitzy.Worker.start("http://www.bieberfever.com")
{:ok, 2458.665}
```

Awesome! Hitting Justin Bieber's fan site takes around 2.4 seconds. Notice that this was the amount of time you had to wait to get the result back, too. How then can you execute, say, 1,000 concurrent requests? Use spawn/spawn_link!

Although that can work, you also need a way to aggregate the return results of the worker to calculate the average time taken for all successful requests made by the workers, for example. Well, you could pass the caller process into the argument of the Blitzy.Worker.start function and send a message to the caller process once the result is available. In turn, the caller process must wait for incoming messages from 1,000 workers.

Here's a quick sketch of how to accomplish this. It introduces a Blitzy.Caller module:

```
defmodule Blitzy.Caller do
  def start(n_workers, url) do
    me = self

    1..n_workers
    |> Enum.map(fn _ -> spawn(fn -> Blitzy.Worker.start(url, me) end) end)
    |> Enum.map(fn _ ->
      receive do
        x -> x
      end
    end)
  end
end
```

The caller module takes two arguments: the number of workers to create and the URL to load-test against. This code may not be intuitive, so let's go through it bit by bit.

You first save a reference to the calling process in me. Why? Because if you use self instead of me in spawn, then self refers to the newly spawned process and not the calling process. To convince yourself, try this:

```
iex(1)> self
#PID<0.159.0>

iex(2)> spawn(fn -> IO.inspect self end)
#PID<0.162.0>
```

Next, you spawn n_workers number of workers. The result of

```
1..n_workers
|> Enum.map(fn _ -> spawn(fn -> Blitzy.Worker.start(url, me) end) end)
```

is a list of worker pids. You expect the pids to send the caller process the results (more on that in the next section), so you wait for an equal number of messages:

```
worker_pids
|> Enum.map(fn _ ->
    receive do
    x -> x
    end
end)
```

You only need to make a slight modification to `Blitzy.Worker.start/1`, as shown in the following listing.

Listing 8.3 Sending worker process results to the caller process (lib/worker.ex)

```
defmodule Blitzy.Worker do
    use Timex
    require Logger                        Adds a caller
    def start(url) do            <──┘     argument
        {timestamp, response} = Duration.measure(fn -> HTTPoison.get(url) end)
        handle_response({Duration.to_milliseconds(timestamp), response})
    end

    defp handle_response({msecs, {:ok, %HTTPoison.Response{status_code: code}}})
    when code >= 200 and code <= 304 do
        Logger.info "worker [#{node}-#{inspect self}] completed in #{msecs} msecs"
        {:ok, msecs}
    end

    defp handle_response({_msecs, {:error, reason}}) do
        Logger.info "worker [#{node}-#{inspect self}] error due to #{inspect reason}"
        {:error, reason}
    end

    defp handle_response({_msecs, _}) do         <───────────────┐
        Logger.info "worker [#{node}-#{inspect self}] errored out"
        {:error, :unknown}              When the result is
    end                              computed, sends the result
end                                        to the caller process
```

These modifications allow the `Blitzy.Worker` process to send its results to the caller process.

If it sounds messy and is beginning to make your head hurt a little, then you're in good company. Although honestly it isn't that difficult; spawning a bunch of tasks concurrently and waiting for the result from each of the spawned workers shouldn't be that hard, especially because this is a common use case. Fortunately, this is where `Tasks` come in.

8.3   *Introducing Tasks*

A `Task` is an abstraction in Elixir to execute one particular computation. This computation is usually simple and self-contained and requires no communication/coordination with other processes. To appreciate how `Tasks` can make the previous scenario easier, let's look at an example.

You can create an asynchronous `Task` by invoking `Task.async/1`:

```
iex> task = Task.async(fn ->
➥Blitzy.Worker.start("http://www.bieberfever.com") end)
```

You get back a `Task` struct:

```
%Task{pid: #PID<0.154.0>, ref: #Reference<0.0.3.67>}
```

At this point, the `Task` is asynchronously executing in the background. To get the value from the `Task`, you need to invoke `Task.await/1`, as the next listing shows.

Listing 8.4   Creating 10 `Tasks`, each running a Blitzy worker process

```
iex> Task.await(task)
{:ok, 3362.655}
```

What happens if the `Task` is still computing? The caller process is blocked until the `Task` finishes. Let's try it:

```
iex> worker_fun = fn -> Blitzy.Worker.start("http://www.bieberfever.com") end
#Function<20.54118792/0 in :erl_eval.expr/5>

iex> tasks = 1..10 |> Enum.map(fn _ -> Task.async(worker_fun) end)
```

The return result is a list of 10 `Task` structs:

```
[%Task{pid: #PID<0.184.0>, ref: #Reference<0.0.3.1071>},
 %Task{pid: #PID<0.185.0>, ref: #Reference<0.0.3.1072>},
 %Task{pid: #PID<0.186.0>, ref: #Reference<0.0.3.1073>},
 %Task{pid: #PID<0.187.0>, ref: #Reference<0.0.3.1074>},
 %Task{pid: #PID<0.188.0>, ref: #Reference<0.0.3.1075>},
 %Task{pid: #PID<0.189.0>, ref: #Reference<0.0.3.1076>},
 %Task{pid: #PID<0.190.0>, ref: #Reference<0.0.3.1077>},
 %Task{pid: #PID<0.191.0>, ref: #Reference<0.0.3.1078>},
 %Task{pid: #PID<0.192.0>, ref: #Reference<0.0.3.1079>},
 %Task{pid: #PID<0.193.0>, ref: #Reference<0.0.3.1080>}]
```

There are now 10 asynchronous workers hitting the site. Grab the results:

```
iex> result = tasks |> Enum.map(&Task.await(&1))
```

Depending on your network connection, the shell process may be blocked for a while before you get something like this:

```
[ok: 95.023, ok: 159.591, ok: 190.345, ok: 126.191, ok: 125.554, ok:
109.059, ok: 139.883, ok: 125.009, ok: 101.94, ok: 124.955]
```

Isn't this awesome? Not only can you create asynchronous processes to create your workers, but you also have an easy way to collect results from them.

Hang on to your seats, because this is only going to get better! There's no need to go through the hassle of passing in the caller's pid and setting up receive blocks. With `Tasks`, this is all handled for you.

In lib/blitzy.ex, create a `run/2` function that creates and waits for the worker `Tasks`, as shown in the following listing.

Listing 8.5 Convenience function to run Blitzy workers in `Tasks` (lib/blitzy.ex)

```
defmodule Blitzy do

  def run(n_workers, url) when n_workers > 0 do
    worker_fun = fn -> Blitzy.Worker.start(url) end

    1..n_workers
      |> Enum.map(fn _ -> Task.async(worker_fun) end)
      |> Enum.map(&Task.await(&1))
  end

end
```

You can now invoke `Blitzy.run/2` and get the results in a list:

```
iex> Blitzy.run(10, "http://www.bieberfever.com")
```

```
[ok: 71.408, ok: 69.315, ok: 72.661, ok: 67.062, ok: 74.63, ok: 65.557,
 ok: 201.591, ok: 78.879, ok: 115.75, ok: 66.681]
```

There's a tiny issue, though. Observe what happens when you bump up the number of workers to 1,000:

```
iex> Blitzy.run(1000, "http://www.bieberfever.com")
```

This results in the following:

```
(exit) exited in: Task.await(%Task{pid: #PID<0.231.0>, ref:
  #Reference<0.0.3.1201>}, 5000)
    ** (EXIT) time out
    (elixir) lib/task.ex:274: Task.await/2
    (elixir) lib/enum.ex:1043: anonymous fn/3 in Enum.map/2
    (elixir) lib/enum.ex:1385: Enum."-reduce/3-lists^foldl/2-0-"/3
    (elixir) lib/enum.ex:1043: Enum.map/2
```

The problem is that `Task.await/2` times out after five seconds (the default). You can easily fix this by giving `:infinity` to `Task.await/2` as the timeout value, as shown in the next listing.

Listing 8.6 Making a `Task` wait forever (lib/blitzy.ex)

```
defmodule Blitzy do

  def run(n_workers, url) when n_workers > 0 do
    worker_fun = fn -> Blitzy.Worker.start(url) end

    1..n_workers
      |> Enum.map(fn _ -> Task.async(worker_fun) end)
      |> Enum.map(&Task.await(&1, :infinity))       ◁── Lets Task.await/2
  end                                                    wait forever

end
```

Specifying infinity isn't a problem in this case because the HTTP client will time out if the server takes too long. You can delegate this decision to the HTTP client and not the Task.

Finally, you need to compute the average time taken. In lib/blitzy.ex, shown in the next listing, `parse_results/1` handles computing some simple statistics and formatting the results into a human-friendly format.

Listing 8.7   Computing simple statistics from the workers (lib/blitzy.ex)

```elixir
defmodule Blitzy do

  # ...

  defp parse_results(results) do
    {successes, _failures} =
      results
        |> Enum.partition(fn x ->          ⟵——— Enum.partition/2
            case x do
              {:ok, _} -> true
              _        -> false
            end
          end)

    total_workers = Enum.count(results)
    total_success = Enum.count(successes)
    total_failure = total_workers - total_success

    data = successes |> Enum.map(fn {:ok, time} -> time end)
    average_time  = average(data)
    longest_time  = Enum.max(data)
    shortest_time = Enum.min(data)

    IO.puts """
    Total workers   : #{total_workers}
    Successful reqs : #{total_success}
    Failed res      : #{total_failure}
    Average (msecs) : #{average_time}
    Longest (msecs) : #{longest_time}
    Shortest (msecs) : #{shortest_time}
    """
  end

  defp average(list) do
    sum = Enum.sum(list)
    if sum > 0 do
      sum / Enum.count(list)
    else
      0
    end
  end

end
```

The most interesting part is the use of `Enum.partition/2`. This function takes a collection and a predicate function, and it results in two collections. The first collection contains all the elements where the predicate function returned a truthy value when applied. The second collection contains the rejects. In this case, because a successful request looks like {:ok, _} and an unsuccessful request looks like {:error, _}, you can pattern-match on {:ok, _}.

8.4 Onward to distribution!

We'll revisit Blitzy in a bit. Let's learn how to build a cluster in Elixir! One of the killer features of the Erlang VM is distribution—that is, the ability to have multiple Erlang runtimes talking to each other. Sure, you can probably do it in other languages and platforms, but most will cause you to lose faith in computers and humanity in general, just because they weren't built with distribution in mind.

8.4.1 Location transparency

Processes in an Elixir/Erlang cluster are *location transparent* (see figure 8.2) This means it's just as easy to send a message between processes on a single node as it is to do so on a different node, as long as you know the process id of the recipient process. This makes it incredibly easy to have processes communicate across nodes because there's fundamentally no difference, at least from the developer's point of view.

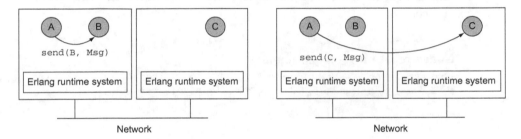

Figure 8.2 Location transparency means essentially no difference between sending a message to a process on the same node and to a process on a remote server.

8.4.2 An Elixir node

A *node* is a system running the Erlang VM with a given name. A name is represented as an atom such as :justin@bieber.com, much like an email address. Names come in two flavors: *short* and *long*. Using short names assumes that all the nodes will be located within the same IP domain. In general, this is easier to set up and is what you'll stick with in this chapter.

8.4.3 Creating a cluster

The first step in creating a cluster is to start an Erlang system in distributed mode, and to do that, you must give it a name. In a fresh terminal, fire up iex—but this time, give it a short name (--sname NAME):

```
$ iex --sname barry
iex(barry@imac)>
```

Notice that the `iex` prompt now has the short name and the hostname of the local machine. To get the node name of the local machine, a call to `Kernel.node/0` will do the trick:

```
iex(barry@imac)> node
:barry@imac
```

Alternatively, `Node.self/0` gives you the same result, but I prefer `node` because it's much shorter.

Now, in two other separate terminal windows, repeat the process but give each of them different names. Start the second node:

```
$ iex --sname robin
iex(robin@imac)>
```

And now the third one:

```
$ iex --sname maurice
iex(maurice@imac)>
```

At this point, the nodes are still in isolation—they don't know about each other's existence.

> ### Nodes must have unique names!
> If you start a node with a name that has already been registered, the VM will throw a fit. A corollary to this is that you can't mix long and short names.

8.4.4 Connecting nodes

Go to the `barry` node, and connect to `robin` using `Node.connect/1`:

```
iex(barry@imac)> Node.connect(:robin@imac)
true
```

`Node.connect/1` returns `true` if the connection is successful. To list all the nodes `barry` is connected to, use `Node.list/0`:

```
iex(barry@imac)> Node.list
[:robin@imac]
```

Note that `Node.list/1` doesn't list the current node, only nodes it's connected to. Now, go to the `robin` node, and run `Node.list/0` again:

```
iex(robin@imac)> Node.list
[:barry@imac]
```

No surprises here. Connecting `barry` to `robin` means a bidirectional connection is set up. Next, from `robin`, let's connect to `maurice`:

```
iex(robin@imac)> Node.connect(:maurice@imac)
true
```

Check the nodes that `robin` is connected to:

```
iex(robin@imac)> Node.list
[:barry@imac, :maurice@imac]
```

Let's check back to `barry`. You didn't explicitly run `Node.connect(:maurice@imac)` on `barry`. What should you see?

```
iex(barry@imac)> Node.list
[:robin@imac, :maurice@imac]
```

8.4.5 *Node connections are transitive*

Sweet! Node connections are *transitive.* This means that even though you didn't connect `barry` to `maurice` explicitly, this was done because `barry` is connected to `robin` and `robin` is connected to `maurice`, so `barry` is connected to `maurice` (see figure 8.3).

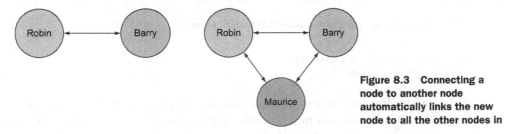

Figure 8.3 Connecting a node to another node automatically links the new node to all the other nodes in

Disconnecting a node disconnects it from all the members of the cluster. A node may disconnect, for example, if `Node.disconnect/1` is called or if the node dies due to a network disruption.

8.5 *Remotely executing functions*

Now that you know how to connect nodes to a cluster, let's do something useful. First close all previously opened `iex` sessions because you're going to create your cluster again from scratch. Before that, though, head to lib/worker.ex and make a one-line addition to the `start/3` function, as shown in the following listing.

> **Listing 8.8 Adding a line to print the current node (lib/worker.ex)**

```
defmodule Blitzy.Worker do

  def start(url, func \\ &HTTPoison.get/1) do          Prints the current node
    IO.puts "Running on #node-#{node}"              ◁──
    {timestamp, response} = Duration.measure(fn -> func.(url) end)
```

```
        handle_response({Duration. Duration.to_milliseconds (timestamp),
          response})
      end
      # ... same as before
    end
```

This time, go to `blitzy`'s directory in three different terminals. Do this in the first terminal

```
% iex --sname barry -S mix
```

and this in the second terminal

```
% iex --sname robin -S mix
```

and this in the third:

```
% iex --sname maurice -S mix
```

Next, you connect all the nodes together. For example, do this from the `maurice` node:

```
iex(maurice@imac)> Node.connect(:barry@imac)
true
```

```
iex(maurice@imac)> Node.connect(:robin@imac)
true
```

```
iex(maurice@imac)> Node.list
[:barry@imac, :robin@imac]
```

Now for the fun bit—you're going to run `Blitzy.Worker.start` on all three nodes. Let that sink it for a moment because it's *super* awesome. Note that the rest of the commands will be performed on the `maurice` node. Although you're free to perform them on any node, some of the output will be different.

First you store all the references of every member of the cluster (including the current node) into `cluster`:

```
iex(maurice@imac)> cluster = [node | Node.list]
[:maurice@imac, :barry@imac, :robin@imac]
```

Then you can use the `:rpc.multicall` function to run `Blitzy.Worker.start/1` on all three nodes:

```
iex(maurice@imac)> :rpc.multicall(cluster, Blitzy.Worker, :start,
  ➥["http://www.bieberfever.com"])
"Running on #node-maurice@imac"
"Running on #node-robin@imac"
"Running on #node-barry@imac"
```

The return result looks like this:

```
{[ok: 2166.561, ok: 3175.567, ok: 2959.726], []}
```

In fact, you don't even need to specify the cluster:

```
iex(maurice@imac)> :rpc.multicall(Blitzy.Worker, :start,
➥["http://www.bieberfever.com"])
"Running on #node-maurice@imac"
"Running on #node-barry@imac"
"Running on #node-robin@imac"
{[ok: 1858.212, ok: 737.108, ok: 1038.707], []}
```

Notice that the return value is a tuple of two elements. All successful calls are captured in the first element, and a list of bad (unreachable) nodes is given in the second argument.

How do you execute multiple workers in multiple nodes, while being able to aggregate the results and present them afterward? You solved that when you implemented `Blitzy.run/2` using `Task.async/1` and `Task.await/2`:

```
iex(maurice@imac)> :rpc.multicall(Blitzy, :run, [5,
➥"http://www.bieberfever.com"], :infinity)
```

The return result is three lists, each with five elements:

```
{[[ok: 92.76, ok: 71.179, ok: 138.284, ok: 78.159, ok: 139.742],
  [ok: 120.909, ok: 75.775, ok: 146.515, ok: 86.986, ok: 129.492],
  [ok: 147.873, ok: 171.228, ok: 114.596, ok: 120.745, ok: 130.114]],
 []}
```

There are many interesting functions in the Erlang documentation for the RPC module, such as `:rpc.pmap/3` and `parallel_eval/1`. I encourage you to experiment with them later. For now, let's turn our attention back to Blitzy.

8.6   *Making Blitzy distributed*

You'll create a simple configuration file that the master node will use to connect to the cluster's nodes. Open config/config.exs, and add the code in the following listing.

> **Listing 8.9   Configuration file for the entire cluster (config/config.exs)**

```
use Mix.Config

config :blitzy, master_node: :"a@127.0.0.1"

config :blitzy, slave_nodes: [:"b@127.0.0.1",
                              :"c@127.0.0.1",
                              :"d@127.0.0.1"]
```

8.6.1   *Creating a command-line interface*

Blitzy is a command-line program, so let's build a command-line interface for it. Create a new file called cli.ex, and place it in lib. This is how you want to invoke Blitzy:

```
./blitzy -n [requests] [url]
```

[requests] is an integer that specifies the number of workers to create, and [url] is a string that specifies the endpoint. Also, a help message should be presented if the user fails to supply the correct format. In Elixir, it's easy to wire this up.

Head over to mix.exs, and modify project/0. Create an entry called escript, and add the code from the following listing.

Listing 8.10 Adding escript to the project function (mix.exs)

```
defmodule Blitzy.Mixfile do

  def project do
    [app: :blitzy,
     version: "0.0.1",
     elixir: "~> 1.1",
     escript: [main_module: Blitzy.CLI], #1
     deps: deps]
  end

end
```

This points mix to the right module when you call mix escript.build to generate the Blitzy command-line program. The module pointed to by main_module is expected to have a main/1 function. Let's provide that and a few other functions in the next listing.

Listing 8.11 Handling input arguments using OptionParser (lib/cli.ex)

```
use Mix.Config
defmodule Blitzy.CLI do
  require Logger

  def main(args) do
    args
      |> parse_args
      |> process_options
  end

  defp parse_args(args) do
    OptionParser.parse(args, aliases: [n: :requests],
                             strict: [requests: :integer])
  end

  defp process_options(options, nodes) do
    case options do
      {[requests: n], [url], []} ->
        # perform action

      _ ->
        do_help

    end
  end

end
```

Most command-line programs in Elixir have the same general structure: taking in arguments, parsing them, and processing them. Thanks to the pipeline operator, you can express this as follows:

```
args
    |> parse_args
    |> process_options
```

args is a tokenized list of arguments. For example, given this

```
% ./blitzy -n 100 http://www.bieberfever.com
```

then args is

```
["-n", "100", "http://www.bieberfever.com"]
```

This list is then passed to parse_args/1, which is a thin wrapper for Option-Parser.parse/2. OptionParser.parse/2 does most of the heavy lifting. It accepts a list of arguments and returns the parsed values, the remaining arguments, and the invalid options. Let's see how to decipher this:

```
OptionParser.parse(args, aliases: [n: :requests],
                         strict: [requests: :integer])
```

First you alias --requests to n. This is a way to specify shorthand for switches. Option-Parser expects all switches to start with --<switch>, and single-character switches -<switch> should be appropriated aliased. For example, OptionParser treats this as invalid:

```
iex> OptionParser.parse(["-n", "100"])
{[], [], [{"-n", "100"}]}
```

You can tell it's invalid because it's the third list that's populated. On the other hand, if you added double dashes to the switch (the longhand version), then OptionParser happily accepts it:

```
iex(d@127.0.0.1)12> OptionParser.parse(["--n", "100"])
{[n: "100"], [], []}
```

You can also assert constraints on the types of the value of the switch. The value of -n must be an integer. Hence, you specify this in the strict option as in listing 8.11. Note once again that you're using the longhand name of the switch.

Once you're finished parsing the arguments, you can hand the results to process_options/1. In this function, you take advantage of the fact that Option-Parser.parse/2 returns a tuple with three elements, each of which is a list. See the following listing.

Listing 8.12   Declaring the format of the arguments the program expects (lib/cli.ex)

```elixir
defp process_options(options) do
  case options do
    {[requests: n], [url], []} ->      ◁─┐  Pattern-matching the
      # To be implemented later.         │  exact format you expect
    _ ->
      do_help

  end
end
```

You also pattern-match the exact format the program expects. Examine the pattern a little more closely:

```elixir
{[requests: n], [url], []}
```

Can you point out a few properties you're asserting on the arguments?

- `--requests` or `-n` contains a single value that's also an integer.
- There's also a URL.
- There are no invalid arguments. This is specified by the empty list in the third element.

If for any reason the arguments are invalid, you'll invoke the `do_help` function to present a friendly message, as shown in the following listing.

Listing 8.13   Help function for when the user gets the arguments wrong (lib/cli.ex)

```elixir
defp do_help do
  IO.puts """
  Usage:
  blitzy -n [requests] [url]

  Options:
  -n, [--requests]       # Number of requests

  Example:
  ./blitzy -n 100 http://www.bieberfever.com
  """
  System.halt(0)
end
```

For now, nothing happens when the arguments are valid. Let's fill in the missing pieces.

8.6.2 Connecting to the nodes

You created a configuration in config/config.exs previously, specifying the master and slave nodes. How do you access the configuration from your application? It's pretty simple:

```elixir
iex(1)> Application.get_env(:blitzy, :master_node)
:"a@127.0.0.1"
```

```
iex(2)> Application.get_env(:blitzy, :slave_nodes)
[:"b@127.0.0.1", :"c@127.0.0.1", :"d@127.0.0.1"]
```

Note that nodes b, c, and d need to be started in distributed mode with the matching names before the command (./blitzy -n 100 http://www.bieberfever.com) is executed. You need to modify the main/1 function in lib/cli.ex, as shown in the following listing.

Listing 8.14   Modifying `main` to read from the configuration file (lib/cli.ex)

```
defmodule Blitzy.CLI do

  def main(args) do
    Application.get_env(:blitzy, :master_node)      Starts the master node
      |> Node.start                                 in distributed mode

    Application.get_env(:blitzy, :slave_nodes)      Connects to the slave nodes
      |> Enum.each(&Node.connect(&1))

    args
      |> parse_args                                 Passes a list of all the nodes in the
      |> process_options([node|Node.list])   ◁─┘   cluster into process_options/2
  end

end
```

You read the configuration from config/config.exs. First you start the master node in distributed mode and assign it the name a@127.0.0.1. Next, you connect to the slave nodes. Then you pass the list of all the nodes in the cluster in to process_options/2, which now takes two arguments (previously it took only one). Let's modify that in the next listing.

Listing 8.15   Now takes the list of nodes in the cluster and hands it to `do_requests`

```
defmodule Blitzy.CLI do
  # ...

  defp process_options(options, nodes) do
    case options do
      {[requests: n], [url], []} ->              The list of nodes is passed
        do_requests(n, url, nodes)         ◁─┘  into do_requests/3.

      _ ->
        do_help

    end
  end

end
```

The list of nodes is passed into the do_requests/3 function, which is the main workhorse:

```
defmodule Blitzy.CLI do
  # ...
```

```
defp do_requests(n_requests, url, nodes) do
  Logger.info "Pummeling #{url} with #{n_requests} requests"

  total_nodes  = Enum.count(nodes)
  req_per_node = div(n_requests, total_nodes)

  nodes
  |> Enum.flat_map(fn node ->
       1..req_per_node |> Enum.map(fn _ ->
         Task.Supervisor.async({Blitzy.TasksSupervisor, node},
  Blitzy.Worker, :start, [url])
       end)
     end)
  |> Enum.map(&Task.await(&1, :infinity))
  |> parse_results
end

end
```

> Computes the number of workers to spawn per node

This code is relatively terse, but fear not! You'll return to it shortly. For now, let's take a short detour and look at `Task Supervisors`.

8.6.3 *Supervising Tasks with Tasks.Supervisor*

You don't want a crashing `Task` to bring down the entire application. This is especially the case when you're spawning thousands of `Tasks` (or more!). By now, you should know that the answer is to place the `Tasks` under supervision (see figure 8.4).

Happily, Elixir comes equipped with a `Task`-specific `Supervisor`, aptly called `Task.Supervisor`. This `Supervisor` is a `:simple_one_for_one` where all supervised `Tasks` are temporary (they aren't restarted when crashed). To use `Task.Supervisor`, you need to create lib/supervisor.ex, as the following listing shows.

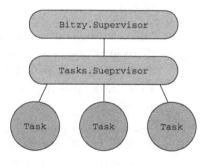

Figure 8.4   The Blitzy supervision tree

Listing 8.16   Setting up the top-level supervision tree (lib/supervisor.ex)

```
defmodule Blitzy.Supervisor do
  use Supervisor

  def start_link(:ok) do
    Supervisor.start_link(__MODULE__, :ok)
  end

  def init(:ok) do
    children = [
      supervisor(Task.Supervisor, [[name: Blitzy.TasksSupervisor]])
    ]

    supervise(children, [strategy: :one_for_one])
  end

end
```

You create a top-level supervisor (`Blitzy.Supervisor`) that supervises a `Task.Supervisor`, which you name `Blitzy.TasksSupervisor`. Now you need to start `Blitzy.Supervisor` when the application starts. Here's lib/blitzy.ex:

```
defmodule Blitzy do
  use Application

  def start(_type, _args) do
    Blitzy.Supervisor.start_link(:ok)
  end

end
```

The `start/2` function starts the top-level supervisor, which will then start the rest of the supervision tree.

8.6.4 *Using a Task Supervisor*

Let's take a closer look at this piece of code because it illustrates how you use `Task.Supervisor` to spread the workload across all the nodes and how to use `Task.await/2` to retrieve the results:

```
nodes
|> Enum.flat_map(fn node ->
    1..req_per_node |> Enum.map(fn _ ->
      Task.Supervisor.async({Blitzy.TasksSupervisor, node}, Blitzy.Worker,
  ➥:start, [url])
    end)
  end)
|> Enum.map(&Task.await(&1, :infinity))
|> parse_results
```

This is probably the most complicated line:

```
Task.Supervisor.async({Blitzy.TasksSupervisor, node}, Blitzy.Worker,
  ➥:start, [url])
```

This is similar to starting a `Task`:

```
Task.async(Blitzy.Worker, :start, ["http://www.bieberfever.com"])
```

But there are a few key differences. First, starting the `Task` from `Task.Supervisor` makes it, well, supervised! Second, take a closer look at the first argument. You're passing in a tuple containing the module name and the node. In order words, you're remotely telling each node's `Blitzy.TasksSupervisor` to spawn workers. That's amazing! `Task.Supervisor.async/3` returns the same thing as `Task.async/3`, a `Task` struct:

```
%Task{pid: #PID<0.154.0>, ref: #Reference<0.0.3.67>}
```

Therefore, you can call `Task.await/2` to wait for the results to be returned from each worker. Now that the hard bits are out of the way, you can better understand what this code is trying to do. Given a node, you spawn `req_per_node` number of workers:

```
1..req_per_node |> Enum.map(fn _ ->
   Task.Supervisor.async({Blitzy.TasksSupervisor, node}, Blitzy.Worker,
 ➥:start, [url])
end)
```

To do this on all the nodes, you have to somehow map the nodes. You could use
Enum.map/2:

```
nodes
|> Enum.map(fn node ->
     1..req_per_node |> Enum.map(fn _ ->
       Task.Supervisor.async({Blitzy.TasksSupervisor, node}, Blitzy.Worker,
 ➥:start, [url])
     end)
   end)
```

But this result would be a nested list of `Task` structs because the result of the inner
`Enum.map/2` is a list of `Task` structs. Instead, you want `Enum.flat_map/2` (see figure
8.5). It takes an arbitrarily nested list, flattens the list, and then applies a function to
each element of the flattened list.

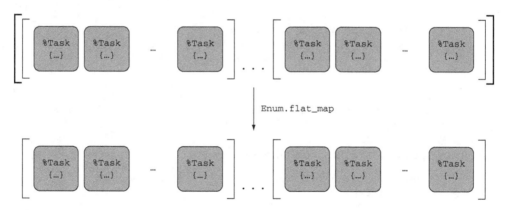

**Figure 8.5   Using `flat_map` to flatten the list of `Task` structs, and then mapping each `Task`
struct to the Blitzy task `Supervisor`**

Here's the code:

```
nodes
|> Enum.flat_map(fn node ->
     1..req_per_node |> Enum.map(fn _ ->
       Task.Supervisor.async({Blitzy.TasksSupervisor, node}, Blitzy.Worker,
 ➥:start, [url])
     end)
   end)
```

Because you have a flattened list of `Task.Structs`, you can hand it to `Task.await/2`:

```
nodes
|> Enum.flat_map(fn node ->
```

```
      # A list of Task structs
  end) # A list of Task structs (due to flat map)
|> Enum.map(&Task.await(&1, :infinity))
|> parse_results
```

`Task.await/2` essentially collects the results from all the nodes from the master node. When this is finished, you hand the list to `parse_results/1` as before.

8.6.5 *Creating the binary with mix escript.build*

Almost there! The last step is to generate the binary. In the project directory, run the following `mix` command:

```
% mix escript.build
Compiled lib/supervisor.ex
Compiled lib/cli.ex
Generated blitzy app
Generated escript blitzy with MIX_ENV=dev
```

The last line tells you that the `blitzy` binary has been created. If you list all the files in your directory, you'll find `blitzy`:

```
% ls
README.md     blitzy      deps            lib         mix.lock    test
_build        config      erl_crash.dump mix.exs      priv
```

8.6.6 *Running Blitzy!*

Finally! Before you start the binary, you have to start three other nodes. Recall that these are the slave nodes. In three separate terminals, start the slave nodes:

```
% iex --name b@127.0.0.1 -S mix

% iex --name c@127.0.0.1 -S mix

% iex --name d@127.0.0.1 -S mix
```

Now you can run `blitzy`. In another terminal, run the `blitzy` command:

```
% ./blitzy -n 10000 http://www.bieberfever.com
```

You'll see all four terminals populated with messages like this:

```
10:34:17.702 [info]  worker [b@127.0.0.1-#PID<0.2584.0>] completed in
58585.746 msecs
```

Figure 8.6 shows an example on my machine.

Finally, when everything is finished, the result is reported on the terminal where you launched the `./blitzy` command:

```
Total workers    : 10000
Successful reqs  : 9795
Failed res       : 205
Average (msecs)  : 31670.991222460456
Longest (msecs)  : 58585.746
Shortest (msecs) : 3141.722
```

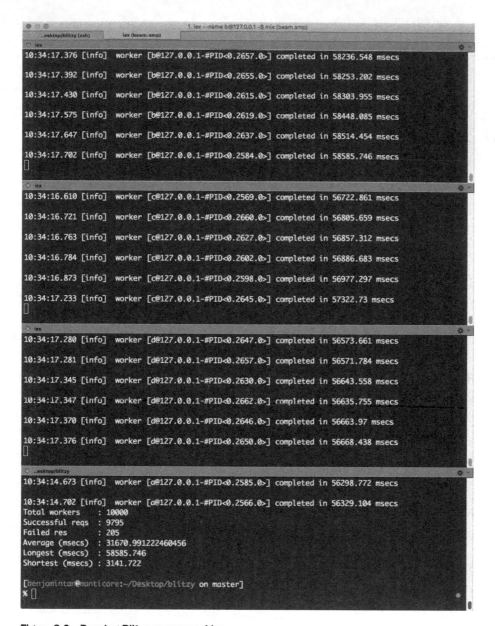

Figure 8.6   Running Blitzy on my machine

8.7 Summary

In this chapter, you got a broad overview of what distributed Elixir can offer. Here's the quick rundown:

- The built-in functions Elixir and the Erlang VM provide for building distributed systems
- Implementing a distributed application that demonstrates load-balancing
- How to use Tasks for short-lived computations
- Implementing a command-line application

In the next chapter, you continue with your adventures in distribution. You'll explore how distribution and fault tolerance go hand in hand.

Distribution and fault tolerance

In the previous chapter, we looked at the basics of distribution in Elixir. In particular, you now know how to set up a cluster. We also looked at Tasks, which are an abstraction over GenServers that makes it easy to write short-lived computations.

The next concept we'll explore is fault tolerance with respect to distribution. For this, you'll build an application that will demonstrate how a cluster handles failures by having another node automatically stepping up to take the place of a downed node. To take things further, it will also demonstrate how a node yields control when a previously downed node of higher priority rejoins the cluster. In other words, you'll build an application that demonstrates the *failover* and *takeover* capabilities of distributed Elixir.

9.1 Distribution for fault tolerance

Failover happens when a node running an application goes down, and that application is restarted on another node automatically, given some timeout period. *Takeover* happens when a node has a higher priority (defined in a list) than the currently running node, causing the lower-priority node to stop and the application to be restarted on the higher-priority node. Failovers and takeovers are cool (in programming, at least) because it seems like black magic when you see them in action. Once you know the mechanics, they will seem pretty straightforward, but no less cool.

9.1.1 An overview of the Chucky application

The application you're going to build is deliberately simple because the main objective is to learn how to wire up an OTP application to be fault-tolerant using failovers and takeovers. You'll build *Chucky*, a distributed and fault-tolerant application that provides fun "facts" about martial artist and actor Chuck Norris. This is an example run of Chucky:

```
iex(1)> Chucky.fact
"Chuck Norris's keyboard doesn't have a Ctrl key because nothing controls
Chuck Norris."

iex(2)> Chucky.fact
"All arrays Chuck Norris declares are of infinite size, because Chuck
Norris knows no bounds."
```

9.2 Building Chucky

Chucky is a simple OTP application. The meat of the application lies in a GenServer. You'll first build that, followed by implementing the Application behavior. Finally, you'll see how to hook everything up to use failover and takeover.

9.2.1 Implementing the server

You know the drill:

```
% mix new chucky
```

Next, create lib/server.ex, as shown in the next listing.

> **Listing 9.1   Implementing the main Chucky server (lib/server.ex)**

```
defmodule Chucky.Server do
  use GenServer

  #######
  # API #                                             Globally registers the
  #######                                             GenServer in the cluster

  def start_link do
    GenServer.start_link(__MODULE__, [], [name: {:global, __MODULE__}])  ⟵
  end
```

```
  def fact do
    GenServer.call({:global, __MODULE__}, :fact)
  end

  #############
  # Callbacks #
  #############

  def init([]) do
    :random.seed(:os.timestamp)
    facts = "facts.txt"
              |> File.read!
              |> String.split("\n")

    {:ok, facts}
  end

  def handle_call(:fact, _from, facts) do
    random_fact = facts
                    |> Enum.shuffle
                    |> List.first

    {:reply, random_fact, facts}
  end

end
```

Calls (and casts) to a globally registered GenServer have an extra :global.

Most of this code shouldn't be hard to understand, although the usage of :global in Chucky.Server.start_link/0 and Chucky.Server.fact/1 is new. In Chucky.Server .start_link/0, you register the name of the module using {:global, __MODULE__}. This has the effect of registering Chucky.Server onto the global_name_server process. This process is started each time a node starts. This means there isn't a single "special" node that keeps track of the name tables. Instead, each node will have a replica of the name tables.

Because you've globally registered this module, calls (and casts) also have to be prefixed with :global. Therefore, instead of writing

```
def fact do
  GenServer.call(__MODULE__, :fact)
end
```

you do this:

```
def fact do
  GenServer.call({:global, __MODULE__}, :fact)
end
```

The init/1 callback reads a file called facts.txt, splits it up based on newlines, and initializes the state of Chucky.Server to be the list of facts. Store facts.txt in the project root directory; you can grab a copy of the file from the project's GitHub repository. The handle_call/3 callback picks a random entry from its state (the list of facts) and returns it.

9.2.2 Implementing the Application behavior

Next, you'll implement the Application behavior that will serve as the entry point to the application. In addition, instead of creating an explicit Supervisor, you can create one from within Chucky.start/2. You do so by importing Supervisor.Spec, which exposes the worker/2 function (that creates the child specification) you can pass into the Supervisor.start_link function at the end of start/2. Create lib/chucky.ex as shown in the next listing.

Listing 9.2 Implementing the Application behavior (lib/chucky.ex)

```
defmodule Chucky do
  use Application
  require Logger

  def start(type, _args) do
    import Supervisor.Spec
    children = [
      worker(Chucky.Server, [])
    ]

    case type do
      :normal ->
        Logger.info("Application is started on #{node}")

      {:takeover, old_node} ->
        Logger.info("#{node} is taking over #{old_node}")

      {:failover, old_node} ->
        Logger.info("#{old_node} is failing over to #{node}")
    end

    opts = [strategy: :one_for_one, name: {:global, Chucky.Supervisor}]
    Supervisor.start_link(children, opts)
  end

  def fact do
    Chucky.Server.fact
  end
end
```

This is a simple Supervisor that supervises Chucky.Server. Like Chucky.Server, Chucky.Supervisor is globally registered and therefore is registered with :global.

9.2.3 Application type arguments

Notice that you're using the type argument start/2, which you usually ignore. For non-distributed applications, the value of type is usually :normal. It's when you start playing with takeover and failover that things start to get interesting.

If you look up the Erlang documentation for the data types type expects, you'll see the result shown in figure 9.1.

DATA TYPES

```
start_type() = normal
             | {takeover, Node :: node()}
             | {failover, Node :: node()}
```

Figure 9.1 **The different options** `type` **can take. Note the** `takeover` **and** `failover` **options.**

These are the three cases for which you pattern-match in listing 9.2. The pattern match succeeds for {:takeover, node} and {:failover, node} if the application is started in distribution mode.

Without going into too much detail (that happens in the next section), when a node is started because it's taking over another node (because it has higher priority), the node in {:takeover, node} is the node being taken over. In a similar vein, when a node is started because another node dies, node {:failover, node} is the node that died.

Until now, you haven't written any failover- or takeover-specific code yet. You'll tackle that next.

9.3   *An overview of failover and takeover in Chucky*

Before we go into specifics, let's talk about the behavior of the cluster. In this example, you'll configure a cluster of three nodes. For ease of reference, and due to a lack of imagination on my part, you'll name the nodes a@<host>, b@<host>, and c@< host>, where <host> is the hostname. I'll refer to the nodes as a, b, and c for the remainder of this section.

Node a is the master node, and b and c are the slave nodes. In the figures that follow, the node with the thicker ring is the master node. The others are the slave nodes.

The *order* in which the nodes are started matters. In this case, a starts first, followed by b and c. The cluster is fully initialized when all the nodes have started. In other words, only after a, b, and c are initialized is the cluster usable.

All three nodes have Chucky *compiled* (this is an important detail). But when the cluster starts, only one application is started, and it's started on the master node (surprise!). This means that although requests can be made from any node in the cluster, only the master node serves back that request (see figure 9.2).

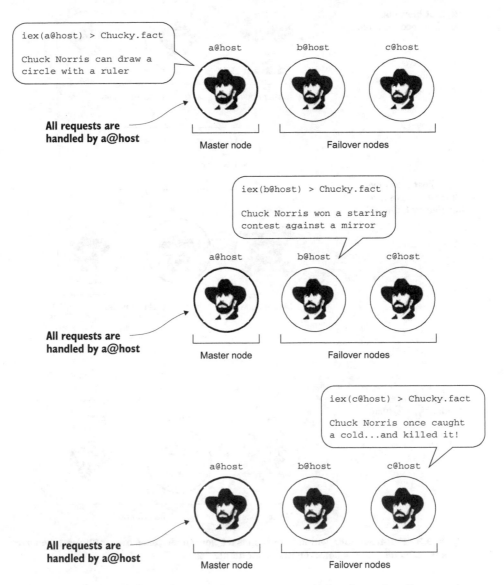

Figure 9.2   All requests are handled by `a@host`, no matter which node receives the request.

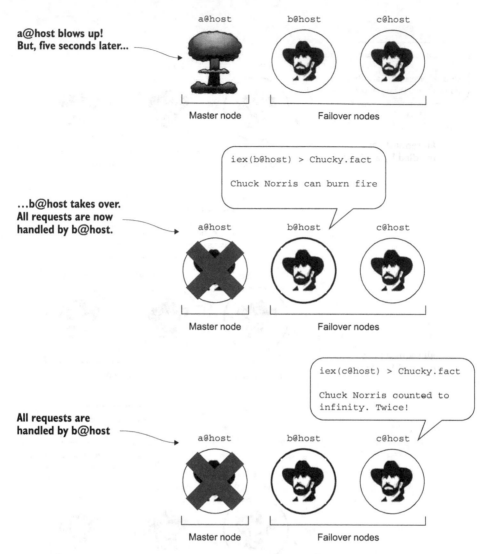

Figure 9.3 **If a@host fails, within five seconds a failover node takes over. b@host takes over automatically once it has detected that a@host has failed**

Now let's make things interesting. When a fails, the remaining nodes will, after a time-out period, detect the failure. Node b will then spin up the application (see figure 9.3).

What if b fails? Then c is next in line to spin up the application.

So far, these have been failover situations. Now, let's consider what happens when a restarts. Because a is the master node, it has the highest priority among all the nodes. Therefore, it initiates a takeover (see figure 9.4).

Whichever slave node is running, the application exits and yields control to the master node. How awesome is that? Next, let's walk through the steps to configure your distributed application for failover and takeover.

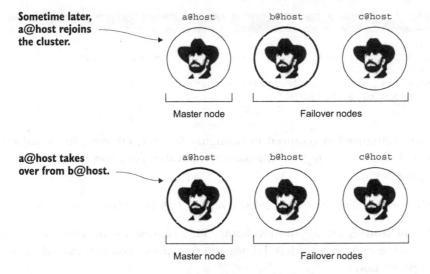

Figure 9.4   Once a@host is back, it initiates a takeover.

9.3.1   Step 1: determine the hostname(s) of the machine(s)

The first step is to find out the hostname of the machine(s) you'll be on. For example, here's how I did this on my Mac with OS X:

```
% hostname -s
manticore
```

9.3.2   Step 2: create configuration files for each of the nodes

Create configuration files for each of your nodes. To keep it simple, create these three files in the config directory:

- a.config
- b.config
- c.config

Notice that they're named *<name-of-node>*.config. You're free to give them any file-name you like, but I suggest sticking to this convention because each file will contain node-specific configuration details.

9.3.3   Step 3: fill the configuration files for each of the nodes

The configuration file for each node has a slightly complicated structure, but we'll examine it more closely in a moment. For now, enter the code in the following listing in config/a.config.

Listing 9.3   Configuration for a@host (config/a.config)

```
[{kernel,
  [{distributed, [{chucky, 5000, [a@manticore, {b@manticore,
     c@manticore}]}]},
   {sync_nodes_mandatory, [b@manticore, c@manticore]},
   {sync_nodes_timeout, 30000}
  ]}].
```

This is the configuration required to configure failover/takeover for a single node. Let's break it down, starting with the most complicated part, the distributed configuration parameter:

```
[{distributed, [{chucky, 5000, [a@manticore, {b@manticore, c@manticore}]}]}]
```

chucky is, of course, the application name. 5000 represents the timeout in milliseconds before the node is considered down and the application is restarted in the next-highest-priority node.

[a@manticore, {b@manticore, c@manticore}] lists the nodes in priority. In this case, a is first in line, followed by either b or c. Nodes defined in a tuple don't have a priority among themselves. For example, consider the following entry:

```
[a@manticore, {b@manticore, c@manticore}, d@manticore]
```

In this case, the highest priority is a, then b/c, followed by d.

Next are these configuration options:

- sync_nodes_mandatory—List of nodes that must be started within the time specified by sync_nodes_timeout.
- sync_nodes_optional—List of nodes that can be started within the time specified by sync_nodes_timeout. (Note that you don't use this option for this application.)
- sync_nodes_timeout—How long to wait for the other nodes to start (in milliseconds).

What's the difference between sync_nodes_mandatory and sync_nodes_optional? As its name suggests, the node being started will wait for all the nodes in sync_nodes_mandatory to start up, within the timeout limit set by sync_nodes_timeout. If even one fails to start, the node will terminate itself. The situation isn't as strict for sync_nodes_optional—the node will wait until the timeout elapses and will not terminate itself if any nodes aren't up.

For the remaining nodes, the configuration is almost the same, except for the sync_nodes_mandatory entry. It's very important that the rest of the configuration is unchanged. For example, having an inconsistent sync_nodes_timeout value would lead to undetermined cluster behavior.

The next listing shows the configuration for b.

Listing 9.4 Configuration for b@host (config/b.config)

```
[{kernel,
  [{distributed,
    [{chucky,
      5000,
      [a@manticore, {b@manticore, c@manticore}]}]},
   {sync_nodes_mandatory, [a@manticore, c@manticore]},
   {sync_nodes_timeout, 30000}
  ]}].
```

The configuration for c is shown in the following listing.

Listing 9.5 Configuration for c@host (config/c.config)

```
[{kernel,
  [{distributed,
    [{chucky,
      5000,
      [a@manticore, {b@manticore, c@manticore}]}]},
   {sync_nodes_mandatory, [a@manticore, b@manticore]},
   {sync_nodes_timeout, 30000}
  ]}].
```

9.3.4 Step 4: compile Chucky on all the nodes

The application should be compiled on the machine it's on. Compiling Chucky is easy enough:

```
% mix compile
```

Once again, remember to do this on every machine in the cluster.

9.3.5 Step 5: start the distributed application

Open three different terminals. On each of them, run the following commands:

- For a:

  ```
  % iex --sname a -pa _build/dev/lib/chucky/ebin --app chucky --erl
  ➥"-config config/a.config"
  ```

- For b:

  ```
  % iex --sname b -pa _build/dev/lib/chucky/ebin --app chucky --erl
  ➥"-config config/b.config"
  ```

- For c:

  ```
  % iex --sname c -pa _build/dev/lib/chucky/ebin --app chucky --erl
  ➥"-config config/c.config"
  ```

These commands are slightly cryptic but still decipherable:

- --sname <name> starts a distributed node and assigns a short name to it.

- -pa <path> prepends the given path to the Erlang code path. This path points to the BEAM files generated from Chucky after running mix compile. (The appends version is -pz.)
- --app <application> starts the application along with its dependencies.
- --erl <switches> contains switches passed to Erlang. In this example, -config config/c.config is used to configure OTP applications.

9.4   *Failover and takeover in action*

After all that hard work, let's see some action! You'll notice that when you start a (and even b), nothing happens until c is started. In each terminal, run Chucky.fact:

```
23:10:54.465 [info]  Application is started on a@manticore
iex(a@manticore)1> Chucky.fact
"Chuck Norris doesn't read, he just stares the book down untill it tells
him what he wants."

iex(b@manticore)1> Chucky.fact
"Chuck Norris can use his fist as his SSH key. His foot is his GPG key."

iex(c@manticore)1> Chucky.fact
"Chuck Norris never wet his bed as a child. The bed wet itself out of
fear."
```

Although it seems as though the application is running on each individual node, you can easily convince yourself that this isn't the case. Notice that in the first terminal, the message "Application is started on a@manticore" is printed out on a but not on the others.

There's another way to tell what applications are running on the current node. With Application.started_applications/1, you can clearly see that Chucky is running on a:

```
iex(a@manticore)1> Application.started_applications
[{:chucky, 'chucky', '0.0.1'}, {:logger, 'logger', '1.1.1'},
 {:iex, 'iex', '1.1.1'}, {:elixir, 'elixir', '1.1.1'},
 {:compiler, 'ERTS  CXC 138 10', '6.0.1'}, {:stdlib, 'ERTS  CXC 138 10',
     ➥'2.6'},
 {:kernel, 'ERTS  CXC 138 10', '4.1'}]
```

But Chucky is not running on b and c. Only the output of b is shown here because the output on both nodes is identical:

```
iex(b@manticore)1> Application.started_applications
[{:logger, 'logger', '1.1.1'}, {:iex, 'iex', '1.1.1'},
 {:elixir, 'elixir', '1.1.1'}, {:compiler, 'ERTS  CXC 138 10', '6.0.1'},
 {:stdlib, 'ERTS  CXC 138 10', '2.6'}, {:kernel, 'ERTS  CXC 138 10',
     ➥'4.1'}]
```

Now, terminate a by exiting iex (press Ctrl-C twice). In about five seconds, you'll notice that Chucky has automatically started in b:

```
iex(b@manticore)1>
23:16:42.161 [info]  Application is started on b@manticore
```

How awesome is that? The remaining nodes in the cluster determined that a was unreachable and presumed dead. Therefore, b assumed the responsibility of running Chucky. If you now run Application.started_applications/1 on b, you'll see something like this:

```
iex(b@manticore)2> Application.started_applications
[{:chucky, 'chucky', '0.0.1'}, {:logger, 'logger', '1.1.1'},
 {:iex, 'iex', '1.1.1'}, {:elixir, 'elixir', '1.1.1'},
 {:compiler, 'ERTS  CXC 138 10', '6.0.1'}, {:stdlib, 'ERTS  CXC 138 10',
     '2.6'},
 {:kernel, 'ERTS  CXC 138 10', '4.1'}]
```

On c, you can convince yourself that Chucky is still running:

```
iex(c@manticore)1> Chucky.fact
"The Bermuda Triangle used to be the Bermuda Square, until Chuck Norris
Roundhouse kicked one of the corners off."
```

Now, let's see some takeover action. What happens when a rejoins the cluster? Because a is the highest-priority node in the cluster, b will yield control to a. In other words, a will take over b. Start a again:

```
% iex --sname a -pa _build/dev/lib/chucky/ebin --app chucky --erl
  ➡"-config config/a.config"
```

In a, you'll see something like this:

```
23:23:36.695 [info]  a@manticore is taking over b@manticore
iex(a@manticore)1>
```

In b, you'll notice that the application has stopped:

```
iex(b@manticore)3>
23:23:36.707 [info]  Application chucky exited: :stopped
```

Of course, b can still dish out some Chuck Norris facts:

```
iex(b@manticore)4> Chucky.fact
"It takes Chuck Norris 20 minutes to watch 60 Minutes."
```

There you have it! You've seen one complete cycle of failover and takeover. In the next section, we'll look at connecting nodes that are in the same local area network.

9.5 *Connecting nodes in a LAN, cookies, and security*

Security wasn't a huge issue on the minds of Erlang designers when they were thinking about distribution. The reason was that nodes were used in their own internal/trusted networks. As such, things were kept simple.

In order for two nodes to communicate, all they need to do is share a *cookie*. This cookie is a plain text file usually stored in your home directory:

```
% cat ~/.erlang.cookie
XLVCOLWHHRIXHRRJXVCN
```

When you start nodes on the same machine, you don't have to worry about cookies because all the nodes share the same cookie in your home directory. But once you start connecting to other machines, you have to ensure that the cookies are all the same. There's an alternative, though: you can also explicitly call Node.set_cookie/2. In this section, you'll see how to connect to nodes that aren't on the same machine, but are on the same local network.

9.5.1 *Determining the IP addresses of both machines*

First, you need to find out the IP addresses of both machines. On Linux/Unix systems, you usually use ifconfig to do this. Also make sure they're both connected to the same LAN. This may mean plugging the machines into the same router/switch or having them connected to the same wireless endpoint. Here's some sample ifconfig output on one of my machines:

```
% ifconfig
lo0: flags=8049<UP,LOOPBACK,RUNNING,MULTICAST> mtu 16384
  options=3<RXCSUM,TXCSUM>
  inet6 ::1 prefixlen 128
  inet 127.0.0.1 netmask 0xff000000
  inet6 fe80::1%lo0 prefixlen 64 scopeid 0x1
  nd6 options=1<PERFORMNUD>
gif0: flags=8010<POINTOPOINT,MULTICAST> mtu 1280
stf0: flags=0<> mtu 1280
en0: flags=8863<UP,BROADCAST,SMART,RUNNING,SIMPLEX,MULTICAST> mtu 1500
  ether 10:93:e9:05:19:da
  inet6 fe80::1293:e9ff:fe05:19da%en0 prefixlen 64 scopeid 0x4
  inet 192.168.0.100 netmask 0xffffff00 broadcast 192.168.0.255
  nd6 options=1<PERFORMNUD>
  media: autoselect
  status: active
```

The numbers to look for are 192.168.0.100. When I performed the same steps on the other machine, the IP address was 192.168.0.103. Note that we're using IPv4 addresses here. If you were using IPv6 addresses, you'd have to use the IPv6 addresses for the following examples.

9.5.2 *Connecting the nodes*

Let's give this a go. On the first machine, start iex, but this time with the long name (--name) flag. Also, append @<ip-address> after the name:

```
% iex --name one@192.168.0.100
Erlang/OTP 18 [erts-7.1] [source] [64-bit] [smp:4:4] [async-threads:10]
[hipe] [kernel-poll:false] [dtrace]
```

```
Interactive Elixir (0.13.1-dev) - press Ctrl+C to exit (type h()
ENTER for help)
iex(one@192.168.0.100)1>
```

Perform the same steps on the second node:

```
% iex --name two@192.168.0.103
Erlang/OTP 18 [erts-7.1] [source] [64-bit] [smp:4:4] [async-threads:10]
[hipe] [kernel-poll:false] [dtrace]

Interactive Elixir (1.1.1) - press Ctrl+C to exit (type h() ENTER for help)

iex(two@192.168.0.103)1>
```

Now, try to connect one@192.168.0.100 and two@192.168.0.103:

```
iex(one@192.168.0.100)1> Node.connect :'two@192.168.0.103'
false
```

Wait, what? On two@192.168.0.103, you'll see a similar error report:

```
=ERROR REPORT==== 25-May-2014::22:32:25 ===
** Connection attempt from disallowed node 'one@192.168.0.100' **
```

What happened? Turns out, you're missing a key ingredient: the *cookie*.

9.5.3   *Remember the cookie!*

When you connect nodes on the same machine and you don't set any cookie with the
--cookie flag, the Erlang VM uses the generated one that sits in your home directory:

```
% cat ~/.erlang.cookie
XBYWEVWSNBAROAXWPTZX%
```

This means if you connect nodes without the cookie flag on the same local machine,
you usually won't run into problems.

On different machines, though, this is a problem. That's because the cookies are
probably different across the various machines. With this in mind, let's restart the
entire process. This time, though, you'll supply the same cookie value for every node.
Alternatively, you can copy the same .~/.erlang-cookie across all the nodes. Here,
you use the former technique. Do this on the first machine:

```
% iex --name one@192.168.0.100 --cookie monster
Erlang/OTP 18 [erts-7.1] [source] [64-bit] [smp:4:4] [async-threads:10]
[hipe] [kernel-poll:false] [dtrace]

Interactive Elixir (1.1.1) - press Ctrl+C to exit (type h() ENTER for help)
iex(one@192.168.0.100)1>
```

On the second machine, make sure you use the same cookie value:

```
% iex --name two@192.168.0.103 --cookie monster
Erlang/OTP 18 [erts-7.1] [source] [64-bit] [smp:4:4] [async-threads:10]
```

```
[hipe] [kernel-poll:false] [dtrace]

Interactive Elixir (1.1.1) - press Ctrl+C to exit (type h() ENTER for help)
iex(two@192.168.0.103)1>
```

Let's connect one@192.168.0.100 to two@192.168.0.103 again:

```
iex(one@192.168.0.100)1> Node.connect :'two@192.168.0.103'
true
```

Success! You've successfully set up an Elixir cluster over a LAN. As a sanity check, you can also do a Node.list/0. Recall that this function only lists its neighbors and therefore doesn't include the current node:

```
iex(one@192.168.0.100)2> Node.list
[:"two@192.168.0.103"]
```

9.6 *Summary*

It's essential to have proper failover and takeover implemented in an application that's expected to survive crashes. Unlike many languages and platforms, failover and takeover are baked into OTP. In this chapter, we continued our explorations of distribution. In particular, you learned about the following:

- Implementing a distributed application that demonstrates failover and takeover
- Configuring for failover and takeover
- Connecting nodes to a LAN
- Using cookies
- A few Chuck Norris jokes

In chapters 10 and 11, we'll look at testing in Elixir. Instead of covering unit testing, we'll explore property-based testing and how to test concurrent programs.

10

Dialyzer and
type specifications

This chapter covers

- What Dialyzer is and how it works
- Finding discrepancies in your code with Dialyzer
- Writing type specifications and defining your own types

Depending on your inclination, the mere mention of types may make you either shriek with joy or recoil in terror. Being a dynamically typed language, Elixir spares you from having to pepper your code base with types à la Haskell. Some may argue that this leads to a quicker development cycle. But Elixir programmers shouldn't be too smug. Statically typed languages can catch an entire class of errors at compile time that a dynamic language can only catch at runtime.

Fortunately, the fault-tolerance features baked into the language try to save us from ourselves. Languages without these features (Ruby, I'm looking at you) will crash. But it's your responsibility to make your software as reliable as possible. In this chapter, you'll learn how to exploit types to do that.

You'll be introduced to Dialyzer, a tool that comes bundled with the Erlang distribution. This power tool is used to weed out certain classes of software bugs. The best part? You don't have to do anything special to your code.

You'll learn some of the interesting theory behind how Dialyzer works, which will help you decipher its (sometimes cryptic) error messages. I'll also explain why Dialyzer isn't a silver bullet to solve all of your typing woes.

In the last part of this chapter, you'll learn how to make Dialyzer do a better job of hunting for bugs by sprinkling your code with types. By the time you're finished, you'll know how to integrate Dialyzer as part of your development workflow.

10.1   Introducing Dialyzer

Dialyzer stands for *DIscrepancy Analyze for ERlang* (whoever came up with the name deserves a raise for the awesome telecom-related acronym). Dialyzer is a tool that helps you find discrepancies in your code. What kind of discrepancies? Here's a list:

- Type errors
- Code that raises exceptions
- Unsatisfiable conditions
- Redundant code
- Race conditions

You'll see shortly how Dialyzer picks up these discrepancies. But first, it's helpful to understand how it works under the hood.

As I mentioned earlier, static languages can catch potential errors at compile time. Dynamic languages, by their very nature, can only detect these errors at runtime. Dialyzer attempts to bring some of the benefits of static type-checkers to a dynamic language like Elixir/Erlang.

One of the main objectives of Dialyzer is to not get in the way of existing programs. This means no Erlang (and Elixir) programmer should be expected to rewrite code just to accommodate Dialyzer. The result is a nice outcome: you don't need to give Dialyzer any additional information for it to do its work. That isn't to say you can't; as you'll see later, you can provide additional type information that helps Dialyzer do a better job of hunting down discrepancies.

10.2   Success typings

Dialyzer uses the notion of *success typings* to gather and infer type information. To understand what success typings are, you need to know a little about the Elixir type system.

A dynamic language such as Elixir requires a type system that's more relaxed than a static type system because functions can potentially take multiple types of arguments. Let's look at the Boolean and function, for example. In a static language such as Haskell, the and function is implemented like so:

```
and :: Bool -> Bool -> Bool                    ⟵—— Function type signature
and x y | x == True && y == True = True
        | otherwise = False
```

The type signature says that and is a function that accepts two Booleans as arguments and returns a Boolean. If the type checker sees anything other than Booleans as inputs to and, your program won't make it past compilation. Now, here's the Elixir version:

```elixir
defmodule MyBoolean do

  def and(true, true) do
    true
  end

  def and(false, _) do
    false
  end

  def and(_, false) do
    false
  end

end
```

Thanks to pattern matching, you can express and/2 as three function clauses. What are valid arguments to and/2? Both the first and second arguments accept true and false, and the return values are all Booleans.

The underscore (_), as you already know, means "anything under the Sun." Therefore, these are perfectly fine invocations of and/2:

```elixir
MyBoolean.and(false, "great success!")
MyBoolean.and([1, 2, 3], false)
```

A Haskell type checker won't allow a program like the Elixir version, because it doesn't allow "anything under the Sun" as a type. It can't handle the uncertainty.

Dialyzer, on the other hand, uses a different typing-inference algorithm called *success typings*. Success typings are optimistic. They always assume that all your functions are used correctly. In other words, your code is innocent until proven guilty.

Success typing starts by *over-approximating* the valid inputs to and outputs from your functions. At first it assumes that your function can take anything and return anything. But as the algorithm develops a better understanding of your code, it generates constraints. These constraints, in turn, restrict the input values and, as a consequence, the output. For example, if the algorithm sees x + y, then x and y must be numbers. Guards such as is_atom(z) provide additional constraints.

Once the constraints are generated, it's time to solve them, just like a puzzle. The solution to the puzzle is the success typing of the function. Conversely, if no solution is found, the constraints are *unsatisfiable*, and you have a type violation on your hands.

It's important to realize that because Dialyzer starts by always assuming that your code is correct, it doesn't guarantee that your code is type-safe. Now, before you get up and leave the room, a nice property arises from this: if Dialyzer finds something wrong, Dialyzer is guaranteed to be correct. So the first lesson of Dialyzer is as follows:

Dialyzer is always right if it says your code is wrong.

This is why when Dialyzer says that your code is messed up, it's 100% correct. Stricter type-checkers begin by assuming that your code is wrong and must type-check successfully before it's allowed to compile. This also means your code is guaranteed (more or less) to be type-safe.

To reiterate, Dialyzer won't discover all type violations. But if it finds a problem, then your code is guaranteed to be problematic. Now that you have some background on how success typings work, let's turn our attention to learning about types in Elixir.

Revealing types in Elixir

So far, we've discussed Elixir without much emphasis on exact types. This chapter pays more attention to types. If you're getting type errors and are confused, you can reach for two helpers: `i/1` and `t/1`.

USING I/1

From Elixir 1.2 onward, a handy helper in `iex` called `i/1` prints information about the given data type. For example, what's the difference between `"ohai"` and `'ohai'` (note the use of double and single quotes, respectively)? Let's find out:

```
iex> i("ohai")
Term
  "ohai"
Data type
  BitString
Byte size
  4
Description
  This is a string: a UTF-8 encoded binary. It's printed surrounded by
  "double quotes" because all UTF-8 codepoints in it are printable.
Raw representation
  <<111, 104, 97, 105>>
Reference modules
  String, :binary
```

And let's contrast this with `'ohai'`:

```
iex> i('ohai')
Term
  'ohai'
Data type
  List
Description
  This is a list of integers that is printed as a sequence of codepoints
  delimited by single quotes because all the integers in it represent
              valid
  ascii characters. Conventionally, such lists of integers are referred
              to as
  "char lists".
Raw representation
  [111, 104, 97, 105]
Reference modules
  List
```

In addition to `i/1`, there's another handy `iex` helper: `t/1`. `t/1` prints the types for the given module or for the given function/arity pair. This is handy if you want to know more about the types (possibly custom) used in a module. For example, let's investigate the types found in `Enum`:

```
iex> t Enum
@type t() :: Enumerable.t()
@type element() :: any()
@type index() :: non_neg_integer()
@type default() :: any()
```

Here, you can see that `Enum` has four defined types. `Enumerable.t` looks interesting. The `Enumerable` module also has a bunch of defined types:

```
iex> t Enumerable
@type acc() :: {:cont, term()} | {:halt, term()} | {:suspend, term()}
@type reducer() :: (term(), term() -> acc())
@type result() :: {:done, term()} | {:halted, term()} | {:suspended,
term(), continuation()}
@type continuation() :: (acc() -> result())
@type t() :: term()
```

10.3   *Getting started with Dialyzer*

Dialyzer can use either Erlang source code or debug-compiled BEAM bytecode. Obviously, this leaves you with the latter option. This means before you run Dialyzer, you must remember to do a `mix compile`.

Remember to compile first!

Since starting to use Dialyzer, I've lost count of the number of times I've forgotten this step. Fortunately, now that I've discovered Dialyxir (discussed shortly), I no longer have to manually compile my code.

Dialyzer comes installed with the Erlang distribution and exists as a command-line program:

```
% dialyzer
  Checking whether the PLT /Users/benjamintan/.dialyzer_plt is up-to-date...
dialyzer: Could not find the PLT: /Users/benjamintan/.dialyzer_plt
Use the options:
   --build_plt   to build a new PLT; or
   --add_to_plt  to add to an existing PLT

For example, use a command like the following:
   dialyzer --build_plt --apps erts kernel stdlib mnesia
Note that building a PLT such as the above may take 20 mins or so
```

```
If you later need information about other applications, say crypto,
you can extend the PLT by the command:
  dialyzer --add_to_plt --apps crypto
For applications that are not in Erlang/OTP use an absolute file name.
```

Awesome—you've convinced yourself that Dialyzer is installed. But what is this *PLT* that Dialyzer is searching for?

10.3.1 *The persistent lookup table*

Dialyzer uses a *persistent lookup table* (PLT) to store the result of its analysis. You can also use a previously constructed PLT that serves as a starting point for Dialyzer. This is important because any nontrivial Elixir application will probably involve OTP; if you run Dialyzer on such an application, the analysis will undoubtedly take a long time. Because the OTP libraries won't change, you can always build a base PLT and only run Dialyzer on your application, which by comparison will take much less time. But when you upgrade Erlang and/or Elixir, you must remember to rebuild the PLT.

10.3.2 *Dialyxir*

Traditionally, running Dialyzer involved quite a bit of typing. Fortunately, thanks to the laziness of programmers, there are libraries that contain `mix` tasks that will make your life easier. The one you'll use here is *Dialyxir*; it contains `mix` tasks that make Dialyzer a joy to use in Elixir projects.

Dialyxir can be either installed as a dependency (as you'll see later) or installed globally. You'll install Dialyxir globally first so that you can build the PLT. This isn't strictly necessary, but it's useful when you don't want to install Dialyxir as a project dependency:

```
% git clone https://github.com/jeremyjh/dialyxir
% cd dialyxir
% mix archive.build

% mix archive.install
```

Let's start using Dialyxir!

10.3.3 *Building a PLT*

As previously mentioned, you need to build a PLT first. Happily, Dialyxir has a `mix` task to do this:

```
% mix dialyzer.plt
```

Grab some coffee, because this will take a while:

```
Starting PLT Core Build ... this will take awhile
dialyzer --output_plt /Users/benjamintan/.dialyxir_core_18_1.2.0-rc.1.plt
--build_plt --apps erts kernel stdlib crypto public_key -r
/usr/local/Cellar/elixir/HEAD/bin/../lib/elixir/../eex/ebin
```

```
/usr/local/Cellar/elixir/HEAD/bin/../lib/elixir/../elixir/ebin
/usr/local/Cellar/elixir/HEAD/bin/../lib/elixir/../ex_unit/ebin
/usr/local/Cellar/elixir/HEAD/bin/../lib/elixir/../iex/ebin
/usr/local/Cellar/elixir/HEAD/bin/../lib/elixir/../mix/ebin
...
  cover:compile_beam_directory/1
  cover:modules/0
  cover:start/0
  fprof:analyse/1
  fprof:apply/3
  fprof:profile/1
  httpc:request/5
  httpc:set_options/2
  inets:start/2
  inets:stop/2
  leex:file/2
  yecc:file/2
Unknown types:
  compile:option/0
 done in 2m33.16s
done (passed successfully)
```

You don't have to worry about "Unknown types" and other warnings as long as the PLT was built successfully.

10.4 Software discrepancies that Dialyzer can detect

In this section, you'll create a project to play with. The example project is a simple currency converter that converts Singapore dollars to United States dollars. Create the project:

```
% mix new dialyzer_playground
```

Now, open mix.exs and add Dialyxir, as shown in the following listing.

Listing 10.1   Adding the `dialyxir` dependency (mix.exs)

```
defmodule DialyzerPlayground.Mixfile do
  # ...

  defp deps do
    [{:dialyxir, "~> 0.3", only: [:dev]}]
  end
end
```

As usual, remember to run `mix deps.get`. Now the fun begins!

10.4.1 Catching type errors

Let's begin with an example that demonstrates how Dialyzer can catch simple type errors. Create lib/bug_1.ex, as shown in the next listing.

Listing 10.2   `Cashy.Bug1`, which has a type error (lib/bug_1.ex)

```elixir
defmodule Cashy.Bug1 do

  def convert(:sgd, :usd, amount) do
    {:ok, amount * 0.70}
  end

  def run do
    convert(:sgd, :usd, :one_million_dollars)
  end

end
```

The `convert/3` function takes three arguments. The first two arguments must be the atoms `:sgd` and `:usd`, respectively. `amount` is assumed to be a number and is used to compute the exchange rate from Singapore dollars to United States dollars. Pretty straightforward stuff.

Now imagine the `run/1` function could live on another module. Someone might use this function incorrectly, such as by passing an atom as the last argument to `convert/3` instead of a number. The problem with the code only surfaces when `run/1` is executed; otherwise, the issue may not even be apparent. It's worthwhile to note that a statically typed language will never allow code like this. Fortunately, you have Dialyzer! Let's run Dialyzer and see what happens:

```
% mix dialyzer
```

Here's the output:

```
Compiled lib/bug_1.ex
Generated dialyzer_playground app
...
  Proceeding with analysis...
bug_1.ex:7: Function run/0 has no local return
bug_1.ex:8: The call
'Elixir.Cashy.Bug1':convert('sgd','usd','one_million_dollars') will never
return since it differs in the 3rd argument from the success typing
arguments: ('sgd','usd',number())
 done in 0m1.00s
done (warnings were emitted)
```

Dialyzer has found a problem: "no local return" in Dialyzer-speak means the function will definitely fail. This usually means Dialyzer has found a type error and has therefore determined that the function can never return. As it correctly points out, in this case `convert/3` will never return because the arguments you gave it will cause an `ArithmeticError`.

10.4.2 *Finding incorrect use of built-in functions*

Let's examine another case. Create lib/bug_2.ex, shown in the next listing.

Listing 10.3 `Cashy.Bug2`, which incorrectly uses a built-in function (lib/bug_2.ex)

```
defmodule Cashy.Bug2 do

  def convert(:sgd, :usd, amount) do
    {:ok, amount * 0.70}
  end

  def convert(_, _, _) do
    {:error, :invalid_amount}
  end

  def run(amount) do
    case convert(:sgd, :usd, amount) do
      {:ok, amount} ->
        IO.puts "converted amount is #{amount}"

      {:error, reason} ->
        IO.puts "whoops, #{String.to_atom(reason)}"
    end
  end

end
```

The first function clause is identical to the one in `Cashy.Bug1`. In addition, there's a catch-all clause that returns `{:error, :invalid_amount}`. Once again, imagine `run/1` is called by client code elsewhere. Can you spot the problem? Let's see what Dialyzer says:

```
% mix dialyzer
...
bug_2.ex:18: The call
erlang:binary_to_atom(reason@1::'invalid_amount','utf8') breaks the
contract (Binary,Encoding) -> atom() when is_subtype(Binary,binary()),
is_subtype(Encoding,'latin1' | 'unicode' | 'utf8')
 done in 0m1.02s
done (warnings were emitted)
```

Interesting! There seems to be a problem with

```
erlang:binary_to_atom(reason@1::'invalid_amount','utf8')
```

It's breaking some form of contract. On line 18, as Dialyzer points out, you're invoking `String.to_atom/1`, and this is causing the problem. The contract that `erlang:binary_to_atom/2` is looking for is

```
(Binary,Encoding) -> atom()
```

You're supplying `'invalid_amount'` and `'utf8'` as inputs, which work out to be `(Atom, Encoding)`. On closer inspection, you should call `Atom.to_string/1` instead of `String.to_atom/1`. Whoops.

10.4.3 *Locating redundant code*

Dead code impedes maintainability. In certain cases, Dialyzer can analyze code paths and discover redundant code. lib/bug_3.ex provides an example of this, as shown in the next listing.

Listing 10.4 `Cashy.Bug3`, which has a redundant code path (lib/bug_3.ex)

```
defmodule Cashy.Bug3 do

  def convert(:sgd, :usd, amount) when amount > 0 do
    {:ok, amount * 0.70}
  end

  def run(amount) do
    case convert(:sgd, :usd, amount) do
      amount when amount <= 0 ->
        IO.puts "whoops, should be more than zero"
      _ ->
        IO.puts "converted amount is #{amount}"
    end
  end

end
```

This time, you add a guard clause to `convert/2`, making sure the currency conversion takes place only when `amount` is larger than zero. Take a look at `run/1`: it has two clauses. One handles the case when `amount` is less than or equal to zero, and the second clause handles the case when `amount` is larger. What does Dialyzer say about this?

```
% mix dialyzer
...
bug_3.ex:9: Guard test amount@2::{'ok',float()} =< 0 can never succeed
 done in 0m0.97s
done (warnings were emitted)
```

Dialyzer has helpfully identified some redundant code! Because you have the guard clause in `convert/3`, you can be sure the `amount <= 0` case will never happen. Again, this is a trivial example. But it isn't hard to imagine that a programmer might not be aware of this behavior and therefore try to cover all the cases, when doing so is redundant.

10.4.4 *Finding type errors in guard clauses*

Type errors can occur when guard clauses are used. Guard clauses constrain the types of the arguments they wrap. In the next example, that argument is `amount`. Let's look at lib/bug_4.ex in the following listing—you may be able to spot the problem easily.

Listing 10.5 `Cashy.Bug4`, which has an error when `run/1` executes (lib/bug_4.ex)

```
defmodule Cashy.Bug4 do

  def convert(:sgd, :usd, amount) when is_float(amount) do
    {:ok, amount * 0.70}
  end
```

```
def run do
  convert(:sgd, :usd, 10)
end

end
```

Let Dialyzer do its thing:

```
% mix dialyzer
...
bug_4.ex:7: Function run/0 has no local return
bug_4.ex:8: The call 'Elixir.Cashy.Bug4':convert('sgd','usd',10) will never
return since it differs in the 3rd argument from the success typing
arguments: ('sgd','usd',float())
 done in 0m0.97s
done (warnings were emitted)
```

If you stare hard enough, you'll realize that 10 isn't of type float() and therefore fails the guard clause. An interesting thing about guard clauses is that they never throw exceptions, which is the point—you're specifically allowing only certain kinds of input. But this may sometimes lead to confusing bugs such as the one here, where it seems as though 10 should be allowed past the guard clause.

10.4.5 *Tripping up Dialyzer with indirection*

In this last example, let's look at a slightly modified version of Cashy.Bug1. Create lib/bug_5.ex, as shown in the following listing.

> **Listing 10.6 Cashy.Bug5: a bug that Dialyzer can't catch (lib/bug_5.ex)**

```
defmodule Cashy.Bug5 do

  def convert(:sgd, :usd, amount) do
    amount * 0.70
  end

  def amount({:value, value}) do
    value
  end

  def run do
    convert(:sgd, :usd, amount({:value, :one_million_dollars}))
  end

end
```

Here you add a layer of indirection by making amount/1 a function call that returns the actual value of the amount you want to convert. It seems obvious that Dialyzer will report the same bugs it did for Cashy.Bug1. Let's test this hypothesis:

```
% mix dialyzer
...
  Proceeding with analysis... done in 0m1.05s
done (passed successfully)
```

Wait, what? Unfortunately, in this instance, Dialyzer can't detect the discrepancy because of the indirection. This is a perfect segue into the next topic: type specifications. We'll come back to Cashy.Bug5 after that.

10.5   *Type specifications*

I've mentioned that Dialyzer can happily run without any help from you. And you've seen some examples of software discrepancies that Dialyzer can detect, from Cashy.Bug1 through Cashy.Bug4. But as Cashy.Bug5 shows, all isn't rainbows and unicorns. Although Dialyzer may report "passed successfully," that doesn't mean your code is free of bugs. There are some cases where Dialyzer can't detect problems entirely on its own.

With some effort, you can help Dialyzer reveal hard-to-detect bugs. You do this by adding *type specifications* (typespecs). The other advantage of adding type specifications to your code is that they serve as a form of documentation. Especially with dynamic languages, valid inputs and the type of the return value are sometimes not obvious. In this section, you'll learn to write your own typespecs, not only to write better documentation, but also to write more reliable code.

10.5.1   *Writing typespecs*

The best way to see how to work with typespecs is through a few examples. The format for defining a type specification is as follows:

```
@spec function_name(type1, type2) :: return_type
```

This format should be self-explanatory; I'll cover the valid type values later (type1, type2, and return_type). Table 10.1 lists some of the predefined types and type unions (they will make more sense when you work through the examples). This list isn't exhaustive, but rather is a good sampling of the available types.

Table 10.1   Some of the available types for use in typespecs

Type	Description
term	Defined as any. term. Represents any valid Elixir term, including functions with _ as the argument.
boolean	Union of both Boolean types: false | true.
char	Range of valid characters: 0..0x10ffff. Note that .. is the range operator.
number	Union of integers and floats: integer | float.
binary	Used for Elixir strings.
char_list	Used for Erlang strings. Defined as [char].
list	Defined as [any]. You can always constrain the type of the list. For example, [number].

Table 10.1 Some of the available types for use in typespecs *(continued)*

Type	Description
fun	`(... -> any)` represents any anonymous function. You may want to constrain this based on the function's arity and return type. For example, `(() -> integer)` is an arity-zero anonymous function that returns an integer, whereas `(integer, atom -> [boolean])` is an arity-two function that takes an integer and an atom, respectively, and returns a list of Booleans.
pid	Process id.
tuple	Any kind of tuple. Other valid options are `{}` and `{:ok, binary}`.
map	Any kind of map. Other valid options are `%{}` and `%{atom => binary}`.

EXAMPLE: ADDITION

Let's start with a simple `add` function that takes two numbers and returns another number. This is one possible type specification for `add/2`:

```
@spec add(integer, integer) :: integer
def add(x, y) do
  x + y
end
```

As it stands, `add/2` may be too restrictive: you may also want to include floats or integers. The way to write that would be as follows:

```
@spec add(integer | float, integer | float) :: integer | float
def add(x, y) do
  x + y
end
```

Fortunately, you can use the built-in shorthand type `number`, which is defined as `integer | float`. The `|` means `number` is a union type. As the name suggests, a *union type* is a type that's made up of two or more types. The union type can apply to both input types and the types of return values:

```
@spec add(number, number) :: number
def add(x, y) do
  x + y
end
```

You'll see more examples of union types when you learn to define your own types.

EXAMPLE: LIST.FOLD/3

Let's tackle something more challenging: `List.fold/3`. This function reduces the given list from the left, using a function. It also requires a starting value for the accumulator. Here's how the function works:

```
iex> List.foldl([1, 2, 3], 10, fn (x, acc) -> x + acc end)
```

As expected, this function will return 16. The first argument is the list, followed by the starting value of the accumulator. The last argument is the function that performs each step of the reduction. Here's the function signature (taken from the List source code):

```
def foldl(list, acc, function)
  when is_list(list) and is_function(function) do
    # the implementation is not important here
end
```

List.foldl/3 already constrains the type of list to be, well, a list, due to the is_list/1 guard clause. But the elements of the list can be any valid Elixir terms. The same goes for function, which needs to be an actual function. function must have an arity of two, where the first argument is the same type as elem and the second argument is the same type as acc. Finally, the return result of this function should be the same type as acc. Here's one possible (but not very helpful) way to specify the type specification of List.foldl/3:

```
@spec foldl([any], any, (any, any -> any)) :: any
def foldl(list, acc, function)
  when is_list(list) and is_function(function) do
    # the implementation is not important here
end
```

Although there's technically nothing wrong with this type specification as far as Dialyzer is concerned, it doesn't show the relation between the types of the input arguments and the return value. You can use type variables with no restriction, which are given as arguments to the function like so:

```
@spec function(arg) :: arg when arg: var
```

Note the use of var, which means any variable. Therefore, you can supply better variable names to the type specification as follows:

```
@spec foldl([elem], acc, (elem, acc -> acc)) :: acc when
  elem: var, acc: var
def foldl(list, acc, function)
  when is_list(list) and is_function(function) do
  # the implementation is not important here
end
```

EXAMPLE: MAP FUNCTION

You can also use guards to restrict type variables given as arguments to the function:

```
@spec function(arg) :: arg when arg: atom
```

In this example, you have your own implementation of Enum.map/2. Create lib/my _enum.ex, and notice the type specifications of the individual arguments and return result in the next listing.

Listing 10.7   Type specification for the `map` function (lib/my_enum.ex0

```
defmodule MyEnum do

  @spec map(f, list_1) :: list_2 when
    f: ((a) -> b),
    list_1: [a],
    list_2: [b],
    a: term,
    b: term
  def map(f, [h|t]), do: [f.(h) | map(f, t)]

  def map(f, []) when is_function(f, 1), do: []

end
```

From the type specification, you're declaring the following:

- `f` (the first argument to `map/2`) is a single-arity function that takes a term and returns another term.
- `list_1` (the second argument to `map/2`) and `list_2` (the return result of `map/2`) are lists of terms.

You also take pains to name the input and output types of `f`. This isn't strictly necessary; but explicitly putting a and b says that `f` operates on a type a and returns a type b, and that `map/2` takes as input a list of type a and outputs a list of type b. As you can see, type specifications can convey a lot of information.

10.6   *Writing your own types*

You can define your own types using `@type`. For example, let's come up with a custom type for RGB color codes in the next listing. Create lib/hexy.ex.

Listing 10.8   Using `@type` to define custom types (lib/hexy.ex)

```
defmodule Hexy do                                        │ Type alias for an
  @type rgb() :: {0..255, 0..255, 0..255}        ◁─┘ RGB color code
  @type hex() :: binary                          ◁─────── Type alias for a Hex color code

  @spec rgb_to_hex(rgb) :: hex                          ◁┐ Uses the custom type
  def rgb_to_hex({r, g, b}) do                           │ definitions in the specification
      [r, g, b]
      |> Enum.map(fn x -> Integer.to_string(x, 16) |> String.rjust(2, ?0)
    end)
    |> Enum.join
  end
end
```

You could specify `@spec rgb_to_hex(tuple) :: binary`, but that doesn't convey a lot of information; it also doesn't constrain the input arguments much, except to say that a tuple is expected. In this case, even an empty tuple is acceptable.

Instead, you specify a tuple with three elements, and you further specify that each element is an integer in the range from 0 to 255. Finally, you give the type a descriptive name like rgb. For hex, instead of calling it binary (a string in Elixir), you alias it to hex to be more descriptive.

10.6.1 *Multiple return types and bodiless function clauses*

It isn't uncommon to have functions that consist of multiple return types. In this case, you can use *bodiless function clauses* to group type annotations together. Consider the following listing.

> **Listing 10.9   Using a bodiless function clause and attaching the typespec (lib/hexy.ex)**

```
defmodule Hexy do
  @type rgb() :: {0..255, 0..255, 0..255}
  @type hex() :: binary

  @spec rgb_to_hex(rgb) :: hex | {:error, :invalid}
  def rgb_to_hex(rgb)                        ◁─────  Bodiless function clause

  def rgb_to_hex({r, g, b}) do
    [r, g, b]
    |> Enum.map(fn x -> Integer.to_string(x, 16) |> String.rjust(2, ?0)
  end)
    |> Enum.join
  end

  def rgb_to_hex(_) do
    {:error, :invalid}
  end
end
```

This time, rgb_to_hex/1 has two clauses. The second one is the fallback case, which will always return {:error, :invalid}. This means you have to update your typespec.

Instead of writing it above the first function clause, as you did in the previous example, you can create a bodiless function clause. One thing to note is how you define the clause. This will work:

```
def rgb_to_hex(rgb)
```

But this will not work:

```
def rgb_to_hex({r, g, b})
```

If you try to compile the file, you get an error message:

```
** (CompileError) lib/hexy.ex:7: can use only variables and \\ as
arguments of bodiless clause
```

Having a bodiless function clause is useful to group all the possible typespecs in one place, which saves you from sprinkling the typespecs on every function clause.

10.6.2 Back to bug #5

Before we end this chapter, let's go back to Cashy.Bug5 (listing 10.6), as promised. Without typespecs, Dialyzer couldn't find the obvious bug. Let's add the typespecs in the next listing.

> **Listing 10.10   Adding typespecs to Cashy.Bug5 (lib/bug_5.ex)**

```
defmodule Cashy.Bug5 do

  @type currency() :: :sgd | :usd

  @spec convert(currency, currency, number) :: number
  def convert(:sgd, :usd, amount) do
    amount * 0.70
  end

  @spec amount({:value, number}) :: number
  def amount({:value, value}) do
    value
  end

  def run do
    convert(:sgd, :usd, amount({:value, :one_million_dollars}))
  end

end
```

This time, when you run Dialyzer, it shows an error that you don't expect and one that you did expect but didn't get previously:

```
bug_5.ex:22: The specification for 'Elixir.Cashy.Bug5':convert/3 states
that the function might also return integer() but the inferred return is
float()

bug_5.ex:32: Function run/0 has no local return
bug_5.ex:33: The call
      'Elixir.Cashy.Bug5':amount({'value','one_million_dollars'}) breaks the
contract ({'value',number()}) -> number()
 done in 0m1.05s
done (warnings were emitted)
```

Let's deal with the second, more straightforward, error first. Because you're passing in an atom (:one_million_dollars) instead of a number, Dialyzer rightly complains.

What about the second error? It's saying your typespecs indicate that an integer could be returned, but Dialyzer has inferred that the function only returns float. When you inspect the body of the function, you see this:

```
amount * 0.70
```

Of course! Multiplying by a float always returns a float! That's why Dialyzer complains. This is nice because Dialyzer can check your typespecs in some cases for obvious errors.

10.7 Exercises

1   Play around with Cashy.Bug1 through Cashy.Bug5, and try to add erroneous typespecs. See if the error messages make sense to you. A harder exercise is to devise code that has an obvious error Dialyzer fails to catch. This is the case in Cashy.Bug5.

2   Imagine you're writing a card game. A card consists of a suit and a value. Come up with types for a card, a suit, and the card's value. This will get you started:

```
@type card :: {suit(), value()} @type suit :: <FILL THIS IN> @type value ::
<FILL THIS IN>
```

3   Try your hand at specifying the types for some built-in functions. A good place to start is the List and Enum modules. A good source of inspiration is the Erlang/OTP (yes, Erlang!) code base. The syntax is slightly different, but it shouldn't pose a major obstacle for you.

10.8 Summary

Dialyzer has been used in production to great effect. It has discovered software discrepancies in OTP, for example, that weren't found previously. It's no silver bullet, but Dialyzer provides some of the benefits of the static type-checkers that languages such as Haskell have.

Including types in your functions not only serves as documentation, but also allows Dialyzer to be more accurate in spotting discrepancies. As an added benefit, Dialyzer can point out whether you've made a mistake in the type specification.

In this chapter, you learned about the following:

- Success typings, the type inference mechanism that Dialyzer uses
- How to use Dialyzer and interpret its sometimes cryptic error messages
- How to increase the accuracy of Dialyzer by providing typespecs and guards like is_function(f, 1) and is_list(l)

In the next chapter, you'll look at testing tools written especially for the Erlang ecosystem. These aren't run-of-the-mill unit-testing tools; they're power tools that can generate test cases, based on general properties you define, and hunt down concurrency errors.

11

Property-based and concurrency testing

This chapter covers

- Property-based testing with QuickCheck
- Detecting concurrency errors with Concuerror

In this final chapter (hurray!), we'll continue our survey of some of the testing tools that are available. Chapter 10 introduced Dialyzer and type specifications. But the Erlang ecosystem has much more to offer, as the following sections will demonstrate.

First, there's QuickCheck, a property-based testing tool. Property-based testing turns unit testing on its head. Instead of writing *specific* test cases, as with traditional unit testing, property-based testing forces you to express test cases in terms of *general* specifications. Once you have these specifications in place, the tool can generate as many test cases as your heart desires.

Next, we'll look at Concuerror, which is a tool that systematically detects concurrency errors in programs. Concuerror can point out hard-to-detect and often surprising race conditions, deadlocks, and potential process crashes.

This chapter contains plenty of examples to try out, providing you with ample opportunity to get a feel for these tools. QuickCheck and Concuerror can give you an incredible amount of insight into your programs, especially when they start to grow in complexity. Let's begin upgrading your testing skills!

11.1 Introduction to property-based testing and QuickCheck

Face it—unit testing can be hard work. You often need to think of several scenarios and make sure you cover all the edge cases. You have to cater to cases like garbage data, extreme values, and lazy programmers who just want the test to pass in the dumbest way possible. What if I told you that instead of writing individual test cases by hand, you could instead *generate* test cases by writing a *specification?* That's exactly what property-based testing is about.

Here's a quick example. Say you're testing a sorting function. In unit-testing land, you'd come up with different examples of lists, like these:

- `[3, 2, 1, 5, 4]`
- `[3, 2, 4, 4, 1, 5, 4]` # With duplicates
- `[1, 2, 3, 4, 5]`   # Already sorted

Can you think of other cases I missed? Off the top of my head, I'm missing cases such as an empty list and a list that contains negative integers. Speaking of integers, what about other data types, like atoms and tuples? As you can see, the process becomes tedious, and the probability of missing an edge case is high.

With property-based testing, you can specify properties for your sorting function. For example, sorting a list once is the same as sorting the list twice. You can specify a property like so (don't worry about the syntax yet):

```
@tag numtests: 1000
property "sorting twice will yield the same result" do
  forall l <- list(int) do
    ensure l |> Enum.sort == l |> Enum.sort |> Enum.sort
  end
end
```

This property generates *1,000* different kinds of lists of integers and makes sure the properties hold for each list. If the property fails, the tool automatically shrinks the test case to find the smallest list that fails the same property.

QuickCheck is the property-based testing tool you'll use in this chapter. To be precise, you'll use Erlang QuickCheck, developed by Quviq. Although the full version of Erlang QuickCheck requires a commercial license, here you'll use a scaled-down version called Erlang QuickCheck *Mini.*

> **What's the difference between the paid and free versions of Quviq QuickCheck?**
>
> Both versions support property-based testing, which is the whole point. The paid version includes other niceties, such as testing with state machines, parallel execution of test cases to detect race conditions (you'll have Conqueror for that), and, of course, commercial support.

Be aware that in addition to Erlang QuickCheck, a couple of other flavors of similar property-based testing tools are available:

- Trifork QuickCheck or *Triq* (http://krestenkrab.github.io/triq)
- PropEr, a QuickCheck-inspired property-based testing tool for Erlang (https://github.com/manopapad/proper)

Quivq's version is arguably the most mature of the three. Although the free version is somewhat limited in features, it's more than adequate for our purposes. Once you've grasped the basics, you can easily move on to the other flavors of QuickCheck—the concepts are identical, and the syntax is similar. Let's get started by installing Quick-Check on your system.

11.1.1 *Installing QuickCheck*

Installing QuickCheck is slightly more involved than the usual Elixir dependency, but not difficult. First, head over to QuviQ (www.quviq.com/downloads), and download QuickCheck (Mini). Unless you have a valid license, you should download the free version; otherwise, you'll be prompted for a license. Here are the steps once you've downloaded the file:

1 Unzip the file and `cd` into the resulting folder.
2 Run `iex`.
3 Run `:eqc_install.install()`.

If everything went well, you'll see something like this:

```
iex(1)> :eqc_install.install
Installation program for "Quviq QuickCheck Mini" version 2.01.0.
Installing in directory /usr/local/Cellar/erlang/18.1/lib/erlang/lib.
Installing ["eqc-2.01.0"].
Quviq QuickCheck Mini is installed successfully.
Bookmark the documentation at
/usr/local/Cellar/erlang/18.1/lib/erlang/lib/eqc-2.01.0/doc/index.html.
:ok
```

It would be wise to heed the helpful prompt to bookmark the documentation.

11.1.2 *Using QuickCheck in Elixir*

Now that you have QuickCheck installed, you're back into familiar territory. Let's create a new project to play with QuickCheck:

```
% mix new quickcheck_playground
```

Open mix.ex, and add the following code.

Listing 11.1   Setting up a project to use QuickCheck

```
defmodule QuickcheckPlayground.Mixfile do
  use Mix.Project

  def project do
    [app: :quickcheck_playground,
     version: "0.0.1",
     elixir: "~> 1.2-rc",
     build_embedded: Mix.env == :prod,
     start_permanent: Mix.env == :prod,
     test_pattern: "*_{test,eqc}.exs",
     deps: deps]
  end

  def application do
    [applications: [:logger]]
  end

  defp deps do
    [{:eqc_ex, "~> 1.2.4"}]
  end
end
```

Specifies the test pattern for tests. Note the suffix "_eqc" for QuickCheck tests. ⟵

Adds the Elixir wrapper for Erlang QuickCheck ⟵

Do a `mix deps.get` to fetch the dependencies. Let's try an example next!

LIST REVERSING: THE "HELLO WORLD" OF QUICKCHECK

You'll make sure you have everything set up correctly by writing a simple property of list reversal. That is, reversing a list twice should yield back the same list:

```
defmodule ListsEQC do
  use ExUnit.Case
  use EQC.ExUnit

  property "reversing a list twice yields the original list" do
    forall l <- list(int) do
      ensure l |> Enum.reverse |> Enum.reverse == l
    end
  end

end
```

Never mind what all this means for now. To run this test, execute `mix test test/lists_eqc.exs`:

```
% mix test test/lists_eqc.exs
................................................................
.....................
OK, passed 100 tests
.

Finished in 0.06 seconds (0.05s on load, 0.01s on tests)
1 test, 0 failures

Randomized with seed 704750
```

Sweet! QuickCheck just ran *100* tests. That's the default number of tests QuickCheck generates. You can modify this number by annotating with @tag numtests: <N>, where <N> is a positive integer. Let's purposely introduce an error into the property in the next listing.

> **Listing 11.2   Erroneous list-reversing property**

```
defmodule ListsEQC do
  use ExUnit.Case
  use EQC.ExUnit

  property "reversing a list twice yields the original list" do
    forall l <- list(int) do
      # NOTE: THIS IS WRONG!
      ensure l |> Enum.reverse == l
    end
  end

end
```

ensure/2 checks whether the property is satisfied and prints out an error message if the property fails. Let's run mix test test/lists_eqc.exs again and see what happens:

```
% mix test test/lists_eqc.exs
...................Failed! After 20 tests.
[0,-2]
not ensured: [-2, 0] == [0, -2]
Shrinking xxxx..x(2 times)
[0,1]
not ensured: [1, 0] == [0, 1]

test Property reversing a list twice gives back the original list
(ListsEQC)
     test/lists_eqc.exs:5
     forall(l <- list(int)) do
       ensure(l |> Enum.reverse() == l)
     end
     Failed for [0, 1]

     stacktrace:
       test/lists_eqc.exs:5

Finished in 0.1 seconds (0.05s on load, 0.06s on tests)
1 test, 1 failure
```

After 20 tries, QuickCheck reports that the property failed, and even provides a *counter example* to back up its claim. Now that you're confident you have QuickCheck properly set up, you can get into the good stuff. But first, how do you go about designing your own properties?

11.1.3 *Patterns for designing properties*

Designing properties is by far the trickiest part of property-based testing. Fear not! Here are a couple of pointers that are helpful when devising your own properties. As you work through the examples, try to figure out which of these heuristics fits.

INVERSE FUNCTIONS

This is one of the easiest patterns to exploit. Some functions have an inverse counterpart, as illustrated in figure 11.1. The main idea is that the inverse function undoes the action of the original function. Therefore, executing the original function followed by executing the inverse function basically does nothing. You can use this property to test encoding and decoding of binaries using `Base.encode64/1` and `Base.decode64!` Here's an example:

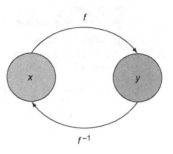

Figure 11.1   An inverse function

```
property "encoding is the reverse of decoding" do
  forall bin <- binary do
    ensure bin |> Base.encode64 |> Base.decode64! == bin
  end
end
```

If you try executing this property, unsurprisingly, all the tests should pass. Here are a few more examples of functions that have inverses:

- Encoding and decoding
- Serializing and deserializing
- Splitting and joining
- Setting and getting

EXPLOITING INVARIANTS

Another technique is to exploit invariants. An *invariant* is a property that remains unchanged when a specific transformation is applied. Here are two examples of invariants:

- A sort function always sorts elements in order.
- A monotonically increasing function is always such that the former element is less than or equal to the next element.

Say you wanted to test a sorting function. First, you create a helper function that checks whether a list is sorted in increasing order:

```
def is_sorted([]), do: true

def is_sorted(list) do
  list
  |> Enum.zip(tl(list))
  |> Enum.all?(fn {x, y} -> x <= y end)
end
```

You can then use the function in the property to check whether the sorting function does its job properly:

```
property "sorting works" do
  forall l <- list(int) do
    ensure l |> Enum.sort |> is_sorted == true
  end
end
```

When you execute this property, everything should pass.

USING AN EXISTING IMPLEMENTATION

Suppose you've developed a sorting algorithm that can perform sorting in constant time. One simple way to test your implementation is against an existing implementation that's known to work well. For example, you can test your custom implementation with one from Erlang:

```
property "List.super_sort/1" do
  forall l <- list(int) do
    ensure List.super_sort(l) == :lists.sort(l)
  end
end
```

USING A SIMPLER IMPLEMENTATION

This is a slight variation of the previous technique. Let's say you want to test an implementation of Map. One way is to use a previous implementation of a map. But that might be too cumbersome, and not every operation of your implementation might (pardon the pun) map to the implementation you want to test against.

There's another way! Instead of using a map, why not use something simpler, like a list? It may not be the most efficient data structure in the world, but it's simple, and you can easily create implementations of the map operations.

For example, let's test the Map.put/3 operation (see figure 11.2). When a value is added using an existing key, the old value will be replaced.

> **Listing 11.3 Using a simpler implementation to test a more complicated one**

```
property "storing keys and values" do
  forall {k, v, m} <- {key, val, map} do
    map_to_list = m |> Map.put(k, v) |> Map.to_list
    map_to_list == map_store(k, v, map_to_list)
  end
end

defp map_store(k, v, list) do
  case find_index_with_key(k, list) do
    {:match, index} ->
      List.replace_at(list, index, {k, v})
    _ ->
      [{k, v} | list]
  end
end
```

```
defp find_index_with_key(k, list) do
  case Enum.find_index(list, fn({x,_}) -> x == k end) do
    nil   -> :nomatch
    index -> {:match, index}
  end
end
```

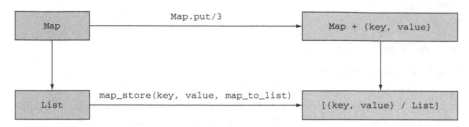

Figure 11.2   Using a simpler implementation to test against a tested implementation

The `map_store/3` helper function basically simulates the way `Map.put/3` would add a key/value pair. The list contains elements that are two-element tuples, and the tuple represents a key/value pair. When `map_store/3` finds a tuple that matches the key, it replaces the entire tuple with the same key but with the new value. Otherwise, the new key/value is inserted into the list.

Here, you're exploiting the fact that a map can be represented as a list, and also that the behavior of `Map.put/3` can be easily implemented using a list. Many operations can be represented (and therefore tested) using a similar technique.

PERFORMING OPERATIONS IN DIFFERENT ORDERS

For certain operations, the order doesn't matter. Here are three examples:

- Appending a list and reversing it is the same as prepending a list and reversing the list.
- Adding elements to a set in different orders shouldn't affect the resulting elements in the set.
- Adding an element and sorting it gives the same result as prepending an element and sorting.

For example:

```
property "appending an element and sorting it is the same as prepending an
    ➥element and sorting it" do
  forall {i, l} <- {int, list(int)}
    [i|l] |> Enum.sort == l ++ [i] |> Enum.sort
  end
end
```

When you execute this property, everything should pass.

IDEMPOTENT OPERATIONS

Calling an operation *idempotent*[1] is a fancy way of saying it will yield the same result when it's performed once or performed repeatedly. For example:

- Calling `Enum.filter/2` with the same predicate twice is the same as doing it once.
- Calling `Enum.sort/1` twice is the same as doing it once.
- Making multiple HTTP GET requests should have no other side effects.

Another example is `Enum.uniq/2`, where calling the function twice shouldn't have any additional effect:

```
property "calling Enum.uniq/1 twice has no effect" do
  forall l <- list(int) do
    ensure l |> Enum.uniq == l |> Enum.uniq |> Enum.uniq
  end
end
```

Running this property will pass all tests. Of course, these six cases aren't the only ones, but they're a good starting point. The next piece of the puzzle is generators. Let's get right to it.

11.1.4 Generators

Generators are used to generate random test data for QuickCheck properties. This data can consist of numbers (integers, floats, real numbers, and so on), strings, and even different kinds of data structures like lists, tuples, and maps.

In this section, we'll explore the generators that are available by default. Then, you'll learn how to create your own custom generators.

11.1.5 Built-in generators

QuickCheck ships with a bunch of generators/generator combinators. Table 11.1 lists some of the more common ones you'll encounter.

Table 11.1 Generators and generator combinators that come with QuickCheck

Generator / Combinator	Description
`binary/0`	Generates a binary of random size
`binary/1`	Generates a binary of a given size in bytes
`bool/0`	Generates a random Boolean
`char/0`	Generates a random character
`choose/2`	Generates a number in the range *M* to *N*
`elements/1`	Generates an element of the list argument

---

[1] This is an excellent word to use to impress your friends and annoy your coworkers.

Table 11.1 Generators and generator combinators that come with QuickCheck *(continued)*

Generator / Combinator	Description
frequency/1	Makes a weighted choice between the generators in its argument, such that the probability of choosing each generator is proportional to the weight paired with it
list/1	Generates a list of elements generated by its argument
map/2	Generates a map with keys generated by K and values generated by V
nat/0	Generates a small natural number (bounded by the generation size)
non_empty/1	Makes sure that the generated value isn't empty
oneof/1	Generates a value using a randomly chosen element from the list of generators
orderedlist/1	Generates an ordered list of elements generated by G
real/0	Generates a real number
sublist/1	Generate a random sublist of the given list
utf8/0	Generates a random UTF8 binary
vector/2	Generates a list of the given length, with elements generated by G

You've already seen generators in action in the previous examples. Let's look at some other examples of using generators.

EXAMPLE: SPECIFYING THE TAIL OF A LIST

How would you write a specification for getting the tail of a list? As a refresher, this is what tl/1 does:

```
iex> h tl

                          def tl(list)

Returns the tail of a list. Raises ArgumentError if the list is empty.

Examples

  iex> tl([1, 2, 3, :go])
  [2, 3, :go]
```

The representation of a non-empty list is [head|tail], where head is the first element of the list and tail is a smaller list, not including the head. With this definition in mind, you can define the property:

```
property "tail of list" do
  forall l <- list(int) do
    [_head|tail] = l
    ensure tl(l) == tail
  end
end
```

Let's try this and see what happens:

```
1) test Property tail of list (ListsEQC)
     test/lists_eqc.exs:11
     forall(l <- list(int)) do
       [_ | tail] = l
       ensure(tl(l) == tail)
     end
     Failed for []
```

Whoops! QuickCheck found a counterexample—the empty list! And that's spot on, because if you look back at the definition of tl/1, it raises `ArgumentError` if the list is empty. In order words, you should correct your property.

You can try using `implies/1` to add a precondition to the property. This precondition always makes sure the generated list is empty. Let's set the precondition that you only want *non-empty* lists:

```
property "tail of list" do
  forall l <- list(int) do
    implies l != [] do
      [_head|tail] = l
      ensure tl(l) == tail
    end
  end
end
```

This time, when you run the test, everything passes, but you see something slightly different:

```
xxxxxxxxxx.xxxxx.xx...x...x...xxx.xx..x....x.........x....x............x..
x......................(x10)...(x1)xxxxx
OK, passed 100 tests
```

The crosses (x) indicate that some tests were discarded because they failed the post-condition. Ideally, you don't want test cases to be discarded. You can instead express the assertion differently and make sure your generated list is always non-empty. In QuickCheck, you can easily add a generator combinator and therefore get rid of `implies/1`:

```
property "tail of list" do
  forall l <- non_empty(list(int)) do
    [_head|tail] = l
    ensure tl(l) == tail
  end
end
```

This time, none of the test cases are discarded:

```
...............................................................................
......................... OK, passed 100 tests
```

So far, you've used only one generator. Sometimes that isn't enough. Say you want to test `Enum.concat/2`. A straightforward way is to test `Enum.concat/2` against the built-in `++` operator that does the same thing. This requires two lists:

```
property "list concatenation" do
  forall {l1, l2} <- {list(int), list(int)} do
    ensure Enum.concat(l1, l2) == l1 ++ l2
  end
end
```

In the next section, you'll see how to define your own custom generators. You'll find that QuickCheck is expressive enough to produce any kind of data you need.

11.1.6 *Creating custom generators*

All the generators you've been using are built-in. But you can just as easily create your own generators. Why go through the trouble? Because sometimes you want the random data that QuickCheck generates to have certain characteristics.

Let's say you want to test `String.split/2`. This function takes a string and a delimiter and splits the string based on the delimiter. For example:

```
iex(1)> String.split("everything|is|awesome|!", "|")
["everything", "is", "awesome", "!"]
```

Step back and think for a moment how you might write a property for `String` `.split/2`. One way would be to test the *inverse* of a string. Given a function $f(x)$ and its inverse, $f^1(x)$, you can say the following:

$$f(f^{-1}x)) = x$$

This means when you apply a function to a value and then apply the inverse function to the resulting value, you get back the original value.

In this case, the inverse operation of splitting a string using a delimiter is *joining* the result of the split with that same delimiter. For this, you can write a quick helper function called `join` that takes the tokenized result from the split operation and the delimiter:

```
def join(parts, delimiter) do
  parts |> Enum.intersperse([delimiter]) |> Enum.join
end
```

Here's an example:

```
iex> join(["everything", "is", "awesome", "!"], [?|])
"everything|is|awesome|!"
```

With this, you can write a property for `String.split/2`:

```
defmodule StringEQC do
  use ExUnit.Case
  use EQC.ExUnit

  property "splitting a string with a delimiter and joining it again yields
      the same string" do
    forall s <- list(char) do
      s = to_string(s)
      ensure String.split(s, ",") |> join(",") == s
    end
  end

  defp join(parts, delimiter) do
    parts |> Enum.intersperse([delimiter]) |> Enum.join
  end

end
```

> ## to_string on character lists
> Notice the use of `to_string/1`. This function is used to convert an argument to a string according to the `String.Chars` *protocol*. Protocols aren't covered in this book, but the point is that you must massage the list of characters into a format that `String.split/2` can understand.

There's a tiny problem, though. What's the probability that QuickCheck generates a string that contains commas? Let's find out with `collect/2`:

```
property "splitting a string with a delimiter and joining it again yields
  ➥the same string" do
  forall s <- list(char) do
    s = to_string(s)
    collect string: s, in:                                 Reports statistics for
      ensure String.split(s, ",") |> join(",") == s        the generated data
  end
end
```

Here's a snippet of the output from `collect/2`:

```
1% <<"Ã,Â¡N?Ã,Â½W.E">>
1% <<121,6,53,194,189,5>>
1% <<"x2AÃ,Â¤">>
1% <<"q$">>
1% <<"g">>
1% <<102,7,112>>
1% <<"f">>
1% <<98,75,6,194,154>>
1% <<"\\Ã,Â¯\e">>
```

Even if you were to inspect the entire generated data set, you'd be hard-pressed to find anything with a comma. How hard-pressed, exactly? QuickCheck has `classify/3` for that:

```
property "splitting a string with a delimiter and joining it again yields
  ➥the same string" do
  forall s <- list(char) do
    s = to_string(s)
    :eqc.classify(String.contains?(s, ","),
                    :string_with_commas,
                    ensure String.split(s, ",") |> join(",") == s)
  end
end
```

classify/3 runs a Boolean function against the generated string input and property and displays the result. In this case, it reports the following:

```
................................................................................
........................
OK, passed 100 tests

1% string_with_commas
```

All the tests pass, but only a paltry 1% of the data includes commas. Because you have only 100 tests, only 1 string that was generated had one or more commas.

What you really want is to generate *more* strings that have *more* commas. Luckily, QuickCheck gives you the tools to do just that. The end result is that you can express the property this way, where string_with_commas is the custom generator you'll implement next:

```
property "splitting a string with a delimiter and joining it again yields
  ➥the same string" do
  forall s <- string_with_commas do
    s = to_string(s)
    ensure(String.split(s, ",") |> join(",") == s)
  end
end
```

EXAMPLE: GENERATING STRINGS WITH COMMAS

Let's come up with a few requirements for your list:

- It has to be 1–10 characters long.
- The string should contain lowercase letters.
- The string should contain commas.
- Commas should appear less frequently than letters.

Let's tackle the first thing on the list. When using the list/1 generator, you don't have control of the length of the list. For that, you have to use the vector/2 generator, which accepts a length and a generator.

Create a new file called eqc_gen.ex in lib. Let's start your first custom generator in the next listing.

Listing 11.4   `vector/2`: generates a list with a specified length

```
defmodule EQCGen do
  use EQC.ExUnit

  def string_with_fixed_length(len) do
    vector(len, char)
  end

end
```

Open an `iex` session with `iex -S mix`. You can get a sample of what QuickCheck might generate with `:eqc_gen.sample/1`:

```
iex> :eqc_gen.sample(EQCGen.string_with_fixed_length(5))
```

Here's some possible output:

```
[170,246,255,153,8]
"ñísɔ£"
"×¾sûÛ"
"ÈÚwä\t"
[85,183,155,222,83]
[158,49,169,40,2]
"¥Ùêr¿"
[58,51,129,71,177]
"æ¿q5°"
"C°{Sð"
```

> **NOTE**   Recall that internally, strings are lists of characters, and characters can be represented using integers.

Generating fixed-length strings is no fun. With `choose/2`, you can introduce some variation, as shown in the following listing.

Listing 11.5   `choose/2`: returns a random number you can use in `vector/2`

```
def string_with_variable_length do
  let len <- choose(1, 10) do
    vector(len, char)
  end
end
```

The use of `let/2` here is important. `let/2` binds the generated value for use with another generator. In other words, this won't work:

```
# NOTE: This doesn't work!
def string_with_variable_length do
  vector(choose(1, 10), char)
end
```

That's because the first argument of `vector/1` should be an integer, not a generator.

> ### You don't have to restart the iex session
> Instead of restarting the `iex` session, you can recompile and reload the specified module's source file. Therefore, after you've added the new generator, you can reload EQCGen directly from the session:
>
> ```
> iex(1)> r(EQCGen)
> lib/eqc_gen.ex:1: warning: redefining module EQCGen
> {:reloaded, EQCGen, [EQCGen]}
> ```

Try running `:eqc_gen.sample/1` against `string_with_variable_length`:

```
iex(1)> :eqc_gen.sample(EQCGen.string_with_variable_length)
"ß"
[188,220,86,82,6,14,230,136]
[150]
[65,136,250,131,106]
[4]
[205,6,254,43,64,115]
",ÄØ"
[184,203,190,93,158,29,250]
"vp\vwSçú"
[186,128,49]
[247,158,120,140,113,186]
```

It works! There are no empty lists, and the longer list has 10 elements. Now to tackle the second requirement: the generated string should only contain lowercase characters. The key here is to limit the values that are generated in the string. Currently, you allow any character (including UTF–8) to be part of the string:

```
vector(len, char)
```

To handle the second requirement, you can use the `oneof/1` generator that randomly picks an element from a list of generators. In this case, you only need to supply a single list containing lowercase letters. Note that you use the Erlang `:lists.seq/2` function to generate a sequence of lowercase letters:

```
vector(len, oneof(:lists.seq(?a, ?z)))
```

Reload the module and run `eqc_gen.sample/1` again:

```
iex> :eqc_gen.sample(EQCGen.string_with_variable_length)
```

Here's a taste of what QuickCheck might generate:

```
"kcra"
"iqtg"
"yqwmqusd"
"hoyacocy"
"jk"
```

```
"a"
"iekkoi"
"nugzrdgon"
"tcopskokv"
"wgddqmaq"
"lexsbkosce"
```

Nice! How do you include commas as part of the generated string? A naïve way would be to add the comma character as part of the generated string:

```
vector(len, oneof(:lists.seq(?a, ?z) ++ [?,]))
```

The problem with this approach is that you can't control how many times the comma appears. You can fix this using `frequency/1`. It's easier to show how `frequency/1` is used before explaining:

```
vector(len,frequency([{3, oneof(:lists.seq(?a, ?z))},
                      {1, ?,}]))
```

When you express it like that, a lowercase letter will be generated 75% of the time, and a comma will be generated 25% of the time. The next listing shows the final result.

> **Listing 11.6 Using `frequency/1` to increase the probability of commas in a string**

```
def string_with_commas do
  let len <- choose(1, 10) do
    vector(len, frequency([{3, one_of(:lists.seq(?a, ?z))},
                           {1, ?,}]))

    end
  end
end
```

Reload the module, and run `eqc_gen.sample/1`:

iex> **:eqc_gen.sample(EQCGen.string_with_commas)**

Here's a sample of the generated data:

```
"acrn"
",,"
"uandbz,afl"
"o,,z"
",,wwkr"
",lm"
",h,s,aej,"
",mpih,vjsq"
"swz"
"n,,yc,"
"jlvmh,g"
```

Much better! Now let's use your newly minted generator in the following listing.

Listing 11.7   Using a generator that generates strings with (more) commas

```
property "splitting a string with a delimiter and joining it again yields
  ➥the same string" do
  forall s <- EGCGen.string_with_commas do        ◁─┐ Uses your new
    s = to_string(s)                                 │ generator
    :eqc.classify(String.contains?(s, ","),
                  :string_with_commas,
                  ensure String.split(s, ",") |> join(",") == s)
  end
end
```

This time, the results are much better:

```
.........................................................................
.......................
OK, passed 100 tests

65% string_with_commas
```

Of course, if you're still not satisfied with the test data distribution, you have the power to tweak the values. It's always good practice to check the distribution of test data, especially when your data depends on certain characteristics such as including at least one comma. Here are a few example generators you can try implementing:

- A DNA sequence consisting of only *A*s, *T*s, *G*s, and *C*s. An example is ACGTGGTCTTAA.
- A hexadecimal sequence including only the numbers 0–9 and the letters *A–F*. Two examples are 0FF1CE and CAFEBEEF.
- A sorted and unique sequence of numbers, such as -4, 10, 12, 35, 100.

11.1.7 *Recursive generators*

Let's try something slightly more challenging. Suppose you need to generate *recursive* test data. An example is JSON, where the value of a JSON key can be yet another JSON structure. Another example is the tree data structure (which you'll see in the next section).

This is when you need *recursive* generators. As their name suggests, these are generators that call themselves. In this example, imagine that you're going to write a property for List.flatten/1, and you need to generate nested lists.

When solving problems with recursion, you must take care not to have infinite recursion. You can prevent that by having the input to the recursive calls be smaller at each invocation and reach a terminal condition somehow.

The standard way to handle recursive generators in QuickCheck is to use sized/2. sized/2 gives you access to the current size parameter of the test data being generated. You can use this parameter to control the size of the input of the recursive calls.

EXAMPLE: GENERATING ARBITRARILY NESTED LISTS (TESTING WITH LIST.FLATTEN/2)

An example is in order. First, create an entry point for your tests to use the nested-list generator, as shown in the next listing.

Listing 11.8 `sized/2`: gives you access to the data's `size` parameter

```
defmodule EQCGen do
  use EQC.ExUnit

    def nested_list(gen) do
    sized size do
      nested_list(size, gen)
    end
  end

  # nested_list/2 not implemented yet

end
```

`nested_list/1` accepts a generator as an argument and hands it to `nested_list/2`, which is wrapped in `sized/2`. `nested_list/2` takes two arguments: `size` is the size of the current test data to be generated by `gen`, and the second argument is the generator.

You now need to implement `nested_list/2`. For lists, there are two cases: either the list is empty or it isn't. An empty list should be returned if the size passed in is zero. See the next listing

Listing 11.9 Implementing the empty list case of `nested_list/2`

```
defmodule EQCGen do
  use EQC.ExUnit

  # nested/1 goes here

  defp nested_list(0, _gen) do
    []
  end

end
```

The second case, shown in the following listing, is where the recursion happens.

Listing 11.10 Implementing the non-empty list case of `nested_list/2`

```
defmodule EQCGen do
  use EQC.ExUnit

  # nested/1 goes here

  # nested/2 empty case goes here

  defp nested_list(n, gen) do
    oneof [[gen|nested_list(n-1, gen)],
           [nested_list(n-1, gen)]]
    end

end
```

Let's try it with this comment:

```
iex(1)> :eqc_gen.sample EQCGen.nested_list(:eqc_gen.int)
```

Here are the results:

```
[[-10,[-7,[9,[4,[[]]]]]]]]
[10,0,2,-3,[[-6,[[-2,-1]]]]]
[[8,[[11,[-7,-3,-9,10,-8,-10]]]]]
[5,8,[-10,-11,[7,[-4,-10,0,[5]]]]]
[[-8,-4,2,12,-6,9,1,[[[12,-4,[]]]]]]
[8,[4,12,[13,-12,[12,4,[15,14,[4]]]]]]
[[[[6,[-11,[[-6,[[[[[[-16]]]]]]]]]]]]]]
[-7,13,[15,-13,[-3,[5,0,[16,-17,[[[[]]]]]]]]]
[18,[[[[[-8,-8,[3,[-12,[18,[13,[[]]]]]]]]]]]]
[[-2,[[[-6,-17,3,[[-18,[[12,[[[13,1]]]]]]]]]]]]
[[[[-15,[-17,[[[-16,[[[20,[[[17,10,[]]]]]]]]]]]]]]]
:ok
```

Hurray! You managed to generate a bunch of nested lists of integers. But did you notice that the generation took a very long time? The problem lies with this line:

```
oneof [[gen|nested_list(n-1, gen)],
       [nested_list(n-1, gen)]]
```

What's happening internally is that you're saying to choose either `[gen|nested_list (n-1, gen)]` or `[nested_list(n-1, gen)]`, but both expressions are being evaluated, even though you only need one of them. You need to use *lazy evaluation*. Being lazy only evaluates the part of `oneof/1` that you need. Fortunately, all you have to do is wrap `lazy/1` around `oneof/1`:

```
lazy do
  oneof [[gen|nested_list(n-1, gen)],
         [nested_list(n-1, gen)]]
end
```

The next listing shows the final version.

> ### Listing 11.11   Final version of the nested-list generator

```
defmodule EQCGen do
  use EQC.ExUnit

  def nested_list(gen) do
    sized size do
      nested_list(size, gen)
    end
  end

  defp nested_list(0, _gen) do
    []
  end

  defp nested_list(n, gen) do
```

```
    lazy do
      oneof [[gen|nested_list(n-1, gen)],
             [nested_list(n-1, gen)]]
    end
  end
end
```

This time, the generation of the nested lists zips right along. In order to let the concepts sink in, let's work through another example.

EXAMPLE: GENERATING A BALANCED TREE

In this example, you'll learn to build a generator that spits out *balanced trees*. As a refresher, a balanced tree is one such that the following are true:

- The left and right subtrees' heights differ by at most one.
- The left and right subtree are both balanced.

As before, first create the entry point (note the use of `sized/2` again in the following listing).

Listing 11.12   Entry point to the balanced tree generator

```
defmodule EQCGen do
  use EQC.ExUnit

  def balanced_tree(gen) do
    sized size do
      balanced_tree(size, gen)
    end
  end

  # balanced_tree/2 not implemented yet
end
```

A terminal node of a tree is the *leaf node*. The next listing shows the base case of the tree construction.

Listing 11.13   Base case, where the size of the tree is zero

```
defmodule EQCGen do
  use EQC.ExUnit

  # balanced_tree/1 goes here

  def balanced_tree(0, gen) do
    {:leaf, gen}
  end
end
```

Notice that you tag the leaf node with the `:leaf` atom. Next you need to implement the case where the node isn't a leaf, as shown in the following listing.

Listing 11.14   Recursively calling generators in the non-base case of `balanced_tree/2`

```
defmodule EQCGen do
  use EQC.ExUnit

  # balanced_tree/1 goes here

  # balanced_tree/2 leaf node case here

  def balanced_tree(n, gen) do
    lazy do
      {:node,
        gen,
        balanced_tree(div(n, 2), gen),
        balanced_tree(div(n, 2), gen)}
    end
  end

end
```

> Each recursive call halves
> the size of the subtree.

For non-leaf nodes, you tag the tuple with `:node` followed by the value of the generator. Finally, you recursively call `balanced_tree/2` twice: once for the left subtree and once for the right subtree. Each recursive call halves the size of the generated subtree. This ensures that you eventually hit the base case and terminate.

Finally, you wrap recursive calls with `lazy/1` to make sure the recursive calls are invoked only when needed. The next listing shows the final version.

Listing 11.15   Final version of the balanced-tree generator

```
defmodule EQCGen do
  use EQC.ExUnit

  def balanced_tree(gen) do
    sized size do
      balanced_tree(size, gen)
    end
  end

  def balanced_tree(0, gen) do
    {:leaf, gen}
  end

  def balanced_tree(n, gen) do
    lazy do
      {:node,
        gen,
        balanced_tree(div(n, 2), gen),
        balanced_tree(div(n, 2), gen)}
    end
  end

end
```

You can generate a few balanced trees. The following uses an integer generator to supply the values for the nodes:

```
iex> :eqc_gen.sample EQCGen.balanced_tree(:eqc_gen.int)
```

This gives you output like the following:

```
{node,0,
     {node,8,
          {node,8,{node,8,{leaf,6},{leaf,-3}},{node,1,{leaf,5},
{leaf,-7}}},
          {node,1,{node,-4,{leaf,8},{leaf,3}},{node,1,
{leaf,-8},{leaf,7}}}},
     {node,-4,
          {node,6,{node,-1,{leaf,6},{leaf,10}},{node,5,{leaf,-6},
{leaf,-3}}},
          {node,-4,{node,6,{leaf,3},
{leaf,-1}},{node,2,{leaf,8},{leaf,8}}}}}}
```

Try your hand at generating these recursive structures:

- An unbalanced tree
- JSON

11.1.8 Summary of QuickCheck

The big idea of QuickCheck is to write properties for your code and leave the generation of test cases and verification of properties to the tool. Once you've come up with the properties, the tool handles the rest and can easily generate hundreds or thousands of test cases.

On the other hand, it isn't all rainbows and unicorns—you have to think of the properties yourself. Coming up with properties does involve a lot of thinking on your part, but the benefits are huge. Often the process of thinking through the properties leaves you with a much better understanding of your code.

We've covered enough of the basics so that you can write your own QuickCheck properties and generators. There are other (advanced) areas that we haven't explored, such as shrinking test data and verifying state machines; I'll point you to the resources at the end of this chapter. Now, let's look at concurrency testing with a tool that's ambitiously named Concuerror.

11.2 Concurrency testing with Concuerror

The Actor concurrency model in Elixir eliminates an entire class of concurrency errors, but it's by no means a silver bullet. It's still possible (and easy) to introduce concurrency bugs. In the examples that follow, I challenge you to figure out what the concurrency bugs are by eyeballing the code.

Exposing concurrency bugs via traditional unit-testing is also a difficult, if not woefully inadequate, endeavor. Concuerror is a tool that systematically weeds out concurrency errors. Although it can't find every single kind of concurrency bug, the bugs it can reveal are impressive.

You'll learn how to use Concuerror and use its capabilities to reveal hard-to-find concurrency bugs. I guarantee you'll be surprised by the results. First, you need to install Concuerror.

11.2.1 *Installing Concuerror*

Installing Concuerror is simple. Here are the steps required:

```
$ git clone https://github.com/parapluu/Concuerror.git
$ cd Concuerror
$ make
 MKDIR ebin
 GEN   src/concuerror_version.hrl
 DEPS src/concuerror_callback.erl
 ERLC src/concuerror_callback.erl
 ...
 GEN   concuerror
```

The last line of the output is the Concuerror program (an Erlang script) that, for convenience, you should include into your PATH. On Unix systems, this means adding a line like

```
export PATH=$PATH:"/path/to/Concuerror"
```

11.2.2 *Setting up the project*

Create a new project:

```
% mix new concuerror_playground
```

Next, open mix.exs, and add the lines in bold in the next listing.

Listing 11.16   Setting up to use Concuerror

```
defmodule ConcuerrorPlayground.Mixfile do
  use Mix.Project

  def project do
    [app: :concuerror_playground,
     version: "0.0.1",
     elixir: "~> 1.2-rc",
     build_embedded: Mix.env == :prod,
     start_permanent: Mix.env == :prod,
     elixir_paths: elixirc_paths(Mix.env),
     test_pattern: "*_test.ex*",
     warn_test_pattern: nil,
     deps: deps]
  end

  def application do
    [applications: [:logger]]
  end                                              Required so that
                                                   Concuerror tests
  defp deps do                                     are compiled
    []
  end

  defp elixirc_paths(:test), do: ["lib", "test/concurrency"]
  defp elixirc_paths(_),     do: ["lib"]
end
```

By default, Elixir tests end with .exs. This means they aren't compiled. Concuerror doesn't understand .exs files (or even .ex files, for that matter), so you need to tell Elixir to compile these files into .beam. For this to happen, you first modify the test pattern to accept .ex and .exs files. You also turn off the option for `warn_test _pattern`, which complains when there's an .ex file in the test directory.

Finally, you add two `elixirc_path/1` functions and the `elixir_paths` option. This explicitly tells the compiler that you want the files in both lib and test/concurrency to be compiled.

One last bit before we move on to the examples. Concuerror can display its output in a helpful diagram (you'll see a few examples later). The output is a Graphviz .dot file. Graphviz is open source graph-visualization software that's available for most package managers and can also be obtained at www.graphviz.org. Make sure Graphviz is properly installed:

```
% dot -V dot - graphviz version 2.38.0 (20140413.2041)
```

11.2.3 *Types of errors that Concuerror can detect*

How does Concuerror perform its magic? The tool instruments your code (usually in the form of a test), and it knows the points at which process-interleaving can happen. Armed with this knowledge, it systematically searches for and reports any errors it finds. Some of the concurrency-related errors it can detect are as follows:

- Deadlocks
- Race conditions
- Unexpected process crashes

In the examples that follow, you'll see the kinds of errors Concuerror can pick out.

11.2.4 *Deadlocks*

A *deadlock* happens when two actions are waiting for each other to finish and therefore neither can make progress. When Concuerror finds a program state where one or more processes are blocked on a `receive` and no other processes are available for scheduling, it considers that state to be deadlocked. Let's look at two examples.

EXAMPLE: PING PONG (COMMUNICATION DEADLOCK)

Let's start with something simple. Create ping_pong.ex in lib, as shown in the following listing.

Listing 11.17   Can you spot the deadlock?

```
defmodule PingPong do

  def ping do
    receive do
      :pong -> :ok
    end
  end
```

```
    def pong(ping_pid) do
      send(ping_pid, :pong)
      receive do
        :ping -> :ok
      end
    end

end
```

Create a corresponding test file in test/concurrency, and name it ping_pong_test.ex.
The test is as follows.

Listing 11.18   Implementing `test/0` so that Concuerror can test `PingPong`

```
Code.require_file "../test_helper.exs", __DIR__

defmodule PingPong.ConcurrencyTest do
  import PingPong

  def test do
    ping_pid = spawn(fn -> ping end)
    spawn(fn -> pong(ping_pid) end)
  end

end
```

The test itself is pretty simple. You spawn two processes, one running the ping/0 function and one running the pong/1 function. The pong function takes the pid of the
ping process.

There are a few slight differences compared to ExUnit tests. Notice once again
that unlike the usual test files, which end with .exs, concurrency tests via Concuerror
need to be compiled and therefore must end with .ex. In addition, the test function
itself is named test/0.

As you'll see later, Concuerror expects that test functions have *no arity* (no arguments). Additionally, if you don't explicitly supply the test function name, Concuerror
automatically looks for test/0.

Running the test is slightly involved. First you need to compile it:

```
% mix test
```

Next, you need to run Concuerror. You must explicitly tell Concuerror where to find
the compiled binaries for Elixir, ExUnit, and your project. You do that by specifying
the paths (--pa) and pointing to the respective ebin directory:

```
concuerror --pa /usr/local/Cellar/elixir/HEAD/lib/elixir/ebin/ \
           --pa /usr/local/Cellar/elixir/HEAD/lib/ex_unit/ebin \
           --pa _build/test/lib/concuerror_playground/ebin     \
           -m Elixir.PingPong.ConcurrencyTest \
           --graph ping_pong.dot \
           --show_races true
```

Then you need to tell Concuerror exactly which module, using the -m flag: say `Elixir.PingPong.ConcurrencyTest` instead of just `PingPong.ConcurrencyTest`. --graph tells Concuerror to generate a Graphviz visualization of the output, and --show_races true tells Concuerror to highlight race conditions.

There is also the -t option, which isn't shown here. This option, along with a value, tells Concuerror the test function to execute. As mentioned previously, it looks for test/0 by default. If you want to specify your own test function, you need to supply -t and the corresponding test function name.

Look at that! Concuerror found an error:

```
# ... output omitted
Error: Stop testing on first error. (Check '-h keep_going').

Done! (Exit status: warning)
  Summary: 1 errors, 1/1 interleaving explored
```

Here's the output from concuerror_report.txt:

```
Erroneous interleaving 1:
* Blocked at a 'receive' (when all other processes have exited):
    P.2 in ping_pong.ex line 11
--------------------------------------------------------------------------
-----

Interleaving info:
   1: P: P.1 = erlang:spawn(erlang, apply,
     [#Fun<'Elixir.PingPong.ConcurrencyTest'.'-test/0-fun-0-'.0>,[]])
    in erlang.erl line 2497
   2: P: P.2 = erlang:spawn(erlang, apply,
     [#Fun<'Elixir.PingPong.ConcurrencyTest'.'-test/0-fun-1-'.0>,[]])
    in erlang.erl line 2497
   3: P: exits normally
   4: P.2: pong = erlang:send(P.1, pong)
    in ping_pong.ex line 10
   5: Message (pong) from P.2 reaches P.1
   6: P.1: receives message (pong)
    in ping_pong.ex line 4
   7: P.1: exits normally

Done! (Exit status: warning)
  Summary: 1 errors, 1/1 interleaving explored
```

You may be wondering what P, P.1, and P.2 are. P is the parent process, P.1 is the first process spawned by the parent process, and P.2 is the second process spawned by the parent process.

Now let's tell Concuerror to generate a visualization of the interleaving:

```
% dot -Tpng ping_pong.dot > ping_pong.png
```

ping_pong.png looks like figure 11.3.

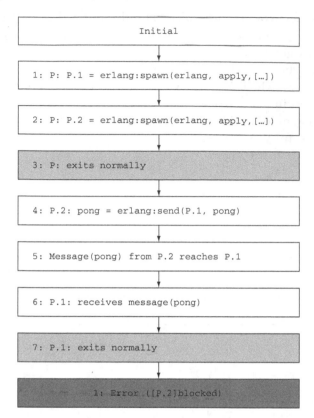

Figure 11.3 Concuerror
showing a blocked process

The numbered lines on the report correspond with the numbers on the image. It helps to view the image and the report side by side to figure out the events leading up to the problem. It's like playing detective and piecing together the clues of a crime scene! In the next example, the crime scene is a GenServer program.

EXAMPLE: GENSERVER DOING A SYNC CALL TO ITSELF IN ANOTHER SYNC CALL

OTP behaviors shield you from many potential concurrency bugs, but it's possible to shoot yourself in the foot. The example in the next listing showcases how to do exactly that. In other words, don't try this at home.

Listing 11.19   Complete implementation of a shady `Stacky` GenServer

```
defmodule Stacky do
  use GenServer
  require Integer

  @name __MODULE__

  def start_link do
    GenServer.start_link(__MODULE__, :ok, name: @name)
  end

  def add(item) do
```

```
    GenServer.call(@name, {:add, item})
  end

  def tag(item) do
    GenServer.call(@name, {:tag, item})
  end

  def stop do
    GenServer.call(@name, :stop)
  end

  def init(:ok) do
    {:ok, []}
  end

  def handle_call({:add, item}, _from, state) do
    new_state = [item|state]
    {:reply, {:ok, new_state}, new_state}
  end

  def handle_call({:tag, item}, _from, state) when Integer.is_even(item) do
    add({:even, item})
  end

  def handle_call({:tag, item}, _from, state) when Integer.is_odd(item) do
    add({:odd, item})
  end

  def handle_call(:stop, _from, state) do
    {:stop, :normal, state}
  end

end
```

Numbers are added to the Stacky GenServer. If the number is an even number, then a tagged tuple {:even, number} is added to the stack. If it's an odd number, then {:odd, number} is pushed into the stack instead. Here's the intended behavior (again, this doesn't work with the current implementation):

```
iex(1)> Stacky.start_link
{:ok, #PID<0.87.0>}

iex(2)> Stacky.add(1)
{:ok, [1]}

iex(3)> Stacky.add(2)
{:ok, [2, 1]}

iex(4)> Stacky.add(3)
{:ok, [3, 2, 1]}

iex(5)> Stacky.tag(4)
{:ok, [{:even, 4], 3, 2, 1]}

iex(6)> Stacky.tag(5)
{:ok, [{:odd, 5}, {:even, 4], 3, 2, 1]}
```

Unfortunately, when you try Stack.tag/1, you get a nasty error message:

```
16:44:26.939 [error] GenServer Stacky terminating
** (stop) exited in: GenServer.call(Stacky, {:add, {:even, 4}}, 5000)
    ** (EXIT) time out
    (elixir) lib/gen_server.ex:564: GenServer.call/3
    (stdlib) gen_server.erl:629: :gen_server.try_handle_call/4
    (stdlib) gen_server.erl:661: :gen_server.handle_msg/5
    (stdlib) proc_lib.erl:240: :proc_lib.init_p_do_apply/3
Last message: {:tag, 3}
State: [3, 2, 1]
```

Take a moment and see if you can spot the problem. While you're thinking, let Concuerror help you a little. Create stacky_test.ex in test/concurrency, as shown in the following listing. The test is simple.

Listing 11.20 Creating `test/0` to test with Concuerror

```
Code.require_file "../test_helper.exs", __DIR__

defmodule Stacky.ConcurrencyTest do

  def test do
    {:ok, _pid} = Stacky.start_link
    Stacky.tag(1)
    Stacky.stop
  end

end
```

Run `mix test`, then run Concuerror, and see what happens:

```
% concuerror --pa /usr/local/Cellar/elixir/HEAD/lib/elixir/ebin \
             --pa /usr/local/Cellar/elixir/HEAD/lib/ex_unit/ebin \
             --pa _build/test/lib/concuerror_playground/ebin     \
             -m Elixir.Stacky.ConcurrencyTest \
             --graph stacky.dot
```

Here's the output:

```
# output truncated ...
Tip: A process crashed with reason '{timeout, ...}'. This may happen when a
call to a gen_server (or similar) does not receive a reply within some
standard timeout. Use the '--after_timeout' option to treat after clauses
that exceed some threshold as 'impossible'.
Tip: An abnormal exit signal was sent to a process. This is probably the
worst thing that can happen race-wise, as any other side-effecting
operation races with the arrival of the signal. If the test produces too
many interleavings consider refactoring your code.
Info: You can see pairs of racing instructions (in the report and --graph)
with '--show_races true'
Error: Stop testing on first error. (Check '-h keep_going').

Done! (Exit status: warning)
  Summary: 1 errors, 1/2 interleavings explored
```

11.2.5 Reading Concuerror's output

It's essential to read what Concuerror tells you. Part of the reason is that Concuerror may need your help with its error detection. Watch for *tips*. Let's start with the first one:

```
Tip: A process crashed with reason '{timeout, ...}'. This may happen when a
call to a gen_server (or similar) does not receive a reply within some
standard timeout. Use the '--after_timeout' option to treat after clauses
that exceed some threshold as 'impossible'.
```

Concuerror always assumes that the `after` clause is possible to reach. Therefore, it searches the interleaving that will trigger the clause. But because adding to the stack is a trivial operation, you can explicitly tell Concuerror to say that the `after` clause will never be triggered with the `--after_timeout N` flag, where any value higher than `N` is taken as `:infinity`. Let's run Concuerror again with the `--after_timeout 1000` flag:

```
% concuerror --pa /usr/local/Cellar/elixir/HEAD/lib/elixir/ebin/ \
             --pa /usr/local/Cellar/elixir/HEAD/lib/ex_unit/ebin \
             --pa _build/test/lib/concuerror_playground/ebin     \
             -m Elixir.Stacky.ConcurrencyTest \
             --graph stacky.dot \
             --after_timeout 1000
```

Interesting! This time, no more tips are emitted. But as previously reported, Concuerror has found an error:

```
% concuerror --pa /usr/local/Cellar/elixir/HEAD/lib/elixir/ebin/ \
             --pa /usr/local/Cellar/elixir/HEAD/lib/ex_unit/ebin \
             --pa _build/test/lib/concuerror_playground/ebin     \
             -m Elixir.Stacky.ConcurrencyTest \
             --graph stacky.dot \
             --after_timeout 1000

# ... output truncated
Error: Stop testing on first error. (Check '-h keep_going').

Done! (Exit status: warning)
  Summary: 1 errors, 1/1 interleavings explored
# ... output truncated
Error: Stop testing on first error. (Check '-h keep_going').

Done! (Exit status: warning)
  Summary: 1 errors, 1/1 interleavings explored
```

The report reveals some details about the error it found:

```
Erroneous interleaving 1:
* Blocked at a 'receive' (when all other processes have exited):
    P in gen.erl line 168
    P.1 in gen.erl line 168
```

`Blocked at a 'receive'` is basically Concuerror telling you that a deadlock occurred. Next, it shows the details of how it discovered the error:

```
Interleaving info:
   1: P: undefined = erlang:whereis('Elixir.Stacky')
     in gen.erl line 298
   2: P: [] = erlang:process_info(P, registered_name)
     in proc_lib.erl line 678
   3: P: P.1 =
erlang:spawn_opt({proc_lib,init_p,[P,[],gen,init_it,[gen_server,P,P,{local,
'Elixir.Stacky'},'Elixir.Stacky',ok,[]]],[link]})
     in erlang.erl line 2673
   4: P.1: undefined = erlang:put('$ancestors', [P])
     in proc_lib.erl line 234
   5: P.1: undefined = erlang:put('$initial_call',
{'Elixir.Stacky',init,1})
     in proc_lib.erl line 235
   6: P.1: true = erlang:register('Elixir.Stacky', P.1)
     in gen.erl line 301
   7: P.1: {ack,P.1,{ok,P.1}} = P ! {ack,P.1,{ok,P.1}}
     in proc_lib.erl line 378
   8: Message ({ack,P.1,{ok,P.1}}) from P.1 reaches P
   9: P: receives message ({ack,P.1,{ok,P.1}})
     in proc_lib.erl line 334
  10: P: P.1 = erlang:whereis('Elixir.Stacky')
     in gen.erl line 256
  11: P: #Ref<0.0.1.188> = erlang:monitor(process, P.1)
     in gen.erl line 155
  12: P: {'$gen_call',{P,#Ref<0.0.1.188>},{tag,1}} = erlang:send(P.1,
{'$gen_call',{P,#Ref<0.0.1.188>},{tag,1}}, [noconnect])
     in gen.erl line 166
  13: Message ({'$gen_call',{P,#Ref<0.0.1.188>},{tag,1}}) from P reaches
P.1
  14: P.1: receives message ({'$gen_call',{P,#Ref<0.0.1.188>},{tag,1}})
     in gen_server.erl line 382
  15: P.1: P.1 = erlang:whereis('Elixir.Stacky')
     in gen.erl line 256
  16: P.1: #Ref<0.0.1.209> = erlang:monitor(process, P.1)
     in gen.erl line 155
  17: P.1: {'$gen_call',{P.1,#Ref<0.0.1.209>},{add,{odd,1}}} =
erlang:send(P.1, {'$gen_call',{P.1,#Ref<0.0.1.209>},{add,{odd,1}}},
[noconnect])
     in gen.erl line 166
```

The last line tells you the line that's causing the deadlock:

```
17: P.1: {'$gen_call',{P.1,#Ref<0.0.1.209>},{add,{odd,1}}} =
erlang:send(P.1, {'$gen_call',{P.1,#Ref<0.0.1.209>},{add,{odd,1}}},
[noconnect])
     in gen.erl line 166
```

The problem is that when two or more synchronous calls are mutually waiting for each other, you get a deadlock. In this example, the callback of the synchronous tag/1 function calls add/1, which itself is synchronous. tag/1 will return when add/1 returns, but add/1 is waiting for tag/1 to return, too. Therefore, both processes are deadlocked.

Because you know where the problem is, let's fix it. The only changes needed are in `tag/1` callback functions, shown in the following listing.

Listing 11.21 Fixing `Stacky` by avoiding synchronous calls in synchronous calls

```elixir
defmodule Stacky do

  # ...

  def handle_call({:tag, item}, _from, state) when Integer.is_even(item) do
    new_state = [{:even, item} |state]
    {:reply, {:ok, new_state}, new_state}
  end

  def handle_call({:tag, item}, _from, state) when Integer.is_odd(item) do
    new_state = [{:odd, item} |state]
    {:reply, {:ok, new_state}, new_state}
  end

  # ...
end
```

Remember to compile, and then run Concuerror again:

```
# ... output omitted
Tip: An abnormal exit signal was sent to a process. This is probably the
worst thing that can happen race-wise, as any other side-effecting
operation races with the arrival of the signal. If the test produces too
many interleavings consider refactoring your code.
Error: Stop testing on first error. (Check '-h keep_going').

Done! (Exit status: warning)
  Summary: 1 errors, 1/1 interleavings explored
```

Whoops! Concuerror reported another error. What went wrong? Let's crack open the report:

```
Erroneous interleaving 1:
* At step 30 process P exited abnormally
    Reason:
      {normal,{'Elixir.GenServer',call,['Elixir.Stacky',stop,5000]}}
    Stacktrace:
      [{'Elixir.GenServer',call,3,[{file,"lib/gen_server.ex"},{line,564}]},
        {'Elixir.Stacky.ConcurrencyTest',test,0,
          [{file,"test/concurrency/stacky_test.ex"},{line,8}]}]
```

The tip indicates an abnormal exit. But from the looks of it, your `GenServer` exited normally, and `Stacky.stop/0` was the cause. Because this is something Concuerror shouldn't worry about, you can safely tell it that processes that exit with `:normal` as a reason are fine. You do so using the `--treat_as_normal normal` option:

```
% concuerror --pa /usr/local/Cellar/elixir/HEAD/lib/elixir/ebin/ \
          --pa /usr/local/Cellar/elixir/HEAD/lib/ex_unit/ebin \
          --pa _build/test/lib/concuerror_playground/ebin      \
          -m Elixir.Stacky.ConcurrencyTest \
```

```
            --graph stacky.dot \
            --show_races true  \
--after_timeout 1000 \
--treat_as_normal normal

# ... some output omitted
Warning: Some abnormal exit reasons were treated as normal
(--treat_as_normal).
Tip: An abnormal exit signal was sent to a process. This is probably the
worst thing that can happen race-wise, as any other side-effecting
operation races with the arrival of the signal. If the test produces too
many interleavings consider refactoring your code.
Done! (Exit status: completed)
  Summary: 0 errors, 1/1 interleavings explored
```

Hurray! Everything is good now.

EXAMPLE: RACE CONDITION WITH PROCESS REGISTRATION

This example will demonstrate a race condition caused by process registration. If you recall, process registration basically means assigning a process a name. Create lib/spawn_reg.ex, look at the following implementation, and see if you can spot the race condition.

Listing 11.22 Full implementation of `SpawnReg`

```elixir
defmodule SpawnReg do

  @name __MODULE__

  def start do
    case Process.whereis(@name) do
      nil ->
        pid = spawn(fn -> loop end)
        Process.register(pid, @name)
        :ok
      _ ->
        :already_started
    end
  end

  def loop do
    receive do
      :stop ->
        :ok
      _ ->
        loop
    end
  end

end
```

This program looks innocent enough. The start/0 function creates a named process, but not before checking whether it has already been registered with the name. When spawned, the process terminates on receiving a :stop message; it continues blissfully otherwise. Can you figure out what's wrong with this program?

Create the test file test/concurrency_test/spawn_reg_test.ex. You spawn the SpawnReg process within another process, after which you tell the SpawnReg process to stop:

```
Code.require_file "../test_helper.exs", __DIR__

defmodule SpawnReg.ConcurrencyTest do

  def test do
    spawn(fn -> SpawnReg.start end)
    send(SpawnReg, :stop)
  end

end
```

Concuerror discovers a problem (remember to do a mix test first):

```
% concuerror --pa /usr/local/Cellar/elixir/HEAD/lib/elixir/ebin/ \
         --pa /usr/local/Cellar/elixir/HEAD/lib/ex_unit/ebin \
         --pa _build/test/lib/concuerror_playground/ebin     \
         -m Elixir.SpawnReg.ConcurrencyTest \
           --graph spawn_reg.dot

# ... output omitted
Info: You can see pairs of racing instructions (in the report and --graph)
with '--show_races true'
Error: Stop testing on first error. (Check '-h keep_going').

Done! (Exit status: warning)
  Summary: 1 errors, 1/2 interleavings explored
```

It also tells you about using --show_races true to reveal pairs of racing instructions. Let's do that:

```
% concuerror --pa /usr/local/Cellar/elixir/HEAD/lib/elixir/ebin/ \
         --pa /usr/local/Cellar/elixir/HEAD/lib/ex_unit/ebin \
         --pa _build/test/lib/concuerror_playground/ebin     \
         -m Elixir.SpawnReg.ConcurrencyTest \
         --graph spawn_reg.dot \
         --show_races true
```

Now examine the report for the erroneous interleaving:

```
Erroneous interleaving 1:
* At step 3 process P exited abnormally
    Reason:
      {badarg,[{erlang,send,
                    ['Elixir.SpawnReg',stop],
                    [9,{file,"test/concurrency/spawn_reg_test.ex"}]}]]}
    Stacktrace:
      [{erlang,send,
              ['Elixir.SpawnReg',stop],
              [9,{file,"test/concurrency/spawn_reg_test.ex"}]}]}]
* Blocked at a 'receive' (when all other processes have exited):
    P.1.1 in spawn_reg.ex line 17
```

The report tells you that at the third step, the SpawnReg.stop/0 call fails with a :badarg. The P.1.1 process is also deadlocked. In other words, it never received a message that it was waiting for. Which is the P.1.1 process? It's the first process spawned by the first process that was spawned by the parent process. Here it is in fewer words:

```
spawn(fn -> SpawnReg.start end)
```

Another reason Concuerror might say that is because you failed to tear down your processes. In general, for Concuerror tests, it's good practice to make your processes exit once you're done with them, such as by sending :stop messages. If you inspect the interleaving info, you get a better sense of the problem:

```
Interleaving info:
   1: P: P.1 = erlang:spawn(erlang, apply,
     [#Fun<'Elixir.SpawnReg.ConcurrencyTest'.'-test/0-fun-0-'.0>,[]])
     in erlang.erl line 2495
   2: P: Exception badarg raised by: erlang:send('Elixir.SpawnReg', stop)
     in spawn_reg_test.ex line 9
   3: P: exits abnormally
     ({badarg,[[erlang,send,['Elixir.SpawnReg',stop],[9,{file,[116,101,115,11
     6,
47,99,111,110|...]}]}]}]})
   4: P.1: undefined = erlang:whereis('Elixir.SpawnReg')
     in process.ex line 359
   5: P.1: P.1.1 = erlang:spawn(erlang, apply, [#Fun<'Elixir.SpawnReg'.'
-start/0-fun-0-'.0>,[]])
     in erlang.erl line 2495
   6: P.1: true = erlang:register('Elixir.SpawnReg', P.1.1)
     in process.ex line 338
   7: P.1: exits normally
--------------------------------------------------------------------------
-----

Pairs of racing instructions:
*    2: P: Exception badarg raised by: erlang:send('Elixir.SpawnReg', stop)
     6: P.1: true = erlang:register('Elixir.SpawnReg', P.1.1)
```

Concuerror has helpfully discovered a race condition! It even points out the pair of racing instructions that are the cause. You may find the image more helpful; see figure 11.4. You'll also notice that the image contains an error pointing to the pair or racing instructions. Very handy!

The race condition here happens because the process may not complete setting up the name. Therefore, send/2 may fail if :name isn't registered yet. Concuerror has identified that this is a *possible* interleaving—if you tried this in the console, you might not encounter the error.

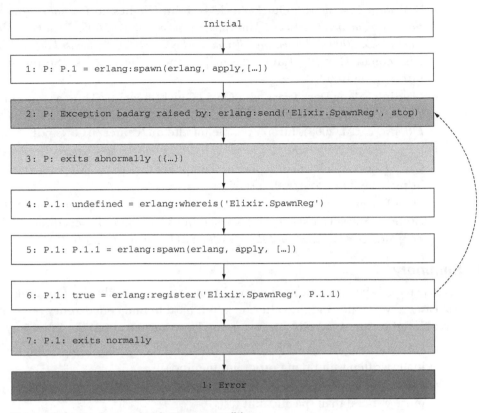

Figure 11.4 Concuerror showing a race condition

11.2.6 Concuerror summary

You've seen some of the concurrency bugs that Concuerror can pick out. Many of these bugs aren't obvious, and sometimes they're surprising. It's nearly impossible to use conventional unit-testing techniques and expose the concurrency bugs that Concuerror is able to identify relatively easily. Furthermore, unit-testing tools can't produce a process trace of the interleaving that led to the bug, whether it's a process deadlock, a crash, or a race condition. Concuerror is a tool I keep close by when I develop my Elixir programs.

11.3 Resources

Both QuickCheck and Concuerror were born out of research; therefore, you'll see more papers than books written about these tools. You're witnessing a humble attempt to contribute to the latter. Fortunately, in recent years, the creators of these two tools have been giving conference talks and workshops that are freely available online. Here's a list of resources you'll find useful if you want to dive deeper into QuickCheck and Concuerror:

- "Software Testing with QuickCheck" by John Hughes, in *Central European Functional Programming School: Third Summer School, CEFP 2009, Budapest, Hungary, May 21-23, 2009 and Komárno, Slovakia, May 25-30, 2009, Revised Selected Lectures,* eds. Zoltán Horváth, Rinus Plasmeijer, and Viktoria Zsók (Springer, 2011), http://mng.bz/6IgA.
- "Testing Erlang Data Types with Quviq QuickCheck" by Thomas Arts, Laura M. Castro, and John Hughes, *Proceedings of the 7th ACM SIGPLAN Workshop on ERLANG* (ACM, 2008), http://people.inf.elte.hu/center/p1-arts.pdf.
- Jesper Louis Anderson has a series of excellent posts where he develops a QuickCheck model to test the new implementation of Map in Erlang 18.0: https://medium.com/@jlouis666.
- "Test-Driven Development of Concurrent Programs Using Concuerror" by Alkis Gotovos, Maria Christakis, and Konstantinos Sangonas, Proceedings of the *10th ACM SIGPLAN Workshop on Erlang* (ACM, 2011), http://mng.bz/YU10.

11.4   *Summary*

In this chapter, you've seen two powerful tools. One is capable of generating as many test cases as you want, and the other seeks out hard-to-find concurrency bugs and may reveal insights into your code. To recap, you have learned about the following:

- How to use QuickCheck and Concuerror in Elixir (even though they were originally written with Erlang programs in mind)
- How to generate test cases with QuickCheck by specifying properties that are more general than specific unit tests
- A few pointers for coming up with own your properties
- Designing custom generators to produce exactly the kind of data you need
- Using Concuerror to detect various concurrency errors such as communication deadlocks, process deadlocks, and race conditions
- Examples of how concurrency bugs can occur

We haven't explored every feature there is, and some advanced but useful features have been left out. Thank goodness—otherwise, I would never be finished with this book! But this chapter should give you the fundamentals and tools needed to conduct your own exploration.

appendix
Installing Erlang and Elixir

This appendix explains how to set up Elixir on your system as quickly as possible. I'll cover Mac OS X, some Linux distributions, and MS Windows, in order of difficulty.

Getting Erlang

Before you install Elixir, you must install Erlang. At this time of writing, the minimum version of Erlang is 19.0. Elixir has so far been very good at keeping up with new Erlang releases.

Just as there are multiple ways to get Elixir, the same goes for Erlang. If you can get it via a package manager, do so. Otherwise, the least problematic approach (by far!) is to head over to the Erlang Solutions site (www.erlang-solutions.com /resources/download.html) and download a copy. It hosts Erlang packages for several Linux distributions (Ubuntu, CentOS, Debian, Fedora, and even Raspberry Pi), Mac OS X, and Windows.

Installing Elixir, method 1: package manager or prebuilt installer

If your operating system comes with it, you should always opt to install Elixir via a package manager. That usually will get you up to speed in the shortest time possible. The following sections outline the installation steps for some of the more popular operating systems. If your system isn't listed, don't fret; there are usually instructions floating around in cyberspace.

Mac OS X via Homebrew and MacPorts

Chances are, you have either the Homebrew or the MacPorts package manager installed. If so, you're only one step away from a shiny new Elixir (and Erlang) installation. For Homebrew, use this command:

```
% brew update && brew install elixir
```

For MacPorts, do the usual `port install`:

```
% sudo port install elixir
```

Notice that you aren't specifying version numbers. Installing via package manager usually installs the latest *stable* version. I'll cover how to build and install Elixir from source later.

Linux (Ubuntu and Fedora)

Because there are a billion Linux distributions out there, I'll limit this section to the more popular ones: Ubuntu and Fedora. If you have one of these, installing Elixir is a one-liner for you.

FEDORA 17 TO 22 (AND NEWER)

If you're on Fedora 17 and newer (and older than Fedora 21), use this command:

```
% yum install elixir
```

If you're on Fedora 22 and above, use this:

```
% dnf install elixir
```

UBUNTU

Ubuntu-flavored distributions require slightly more work. You first need to add the Erlang solutions repository:

```
% wget https://packages.erlang-solutions.com/erlang-solutions_1.0_all.deb
[CA]&& sudo dpkg -i erlang-solutions_1.0_all.deb
```

Next, as all Ubuntu users already know, do this:

```
% sudo apt-get update
```

Next, you need to get Erlang (and a bunch of Erlang-related applications):

```
% sudo apt-get install esl-erlang
```

Finally, you can grab Elixir:

```
% sudo apt-get install elixir
```

MS Windows

Getting Elixir on Windows couldn't be easier. All you need to do is install the Elixir web installer from https://repo.hex.pm/elixir-websetup.exe, and you should be set.

Installing Elixir, method 2:
compiling from scratch (Linux/Unix only)

So, you're feeling lucky, eh? Sometimes there's an awesome feature you can't wait to play with. Other times, you want to experiment with Elixir directly and maybe fix a bug or implement a new feature. If so, this is the route you should take.

Fortunately, the only thing Elixir has a dependency on is Erlang. If you've installed Erlang properly, compiling Elixir from source usually isn't a dramatic process.

In this section, I assume you're using a Unix/Linux system and have all the necessary build tools installed, such as `make`. First you need to clone Elixir from the official repository:

```
% git clone https://github.com/elixir-lang/elixir.git
```

Next, change into the newly created directory:

```
% cd elixir
```

Finally, you can start building the sources:

```
% make clean test
```

It's fascinating to see all the messages go by—it never gets old. When the build is finished, there's an additional step: you need to add the elixir directory to your `PATH` so that you can access commands like `elixir` and `iex`.

Depending on your shell, you can append the elixir directory to your `PATH`. For example, if you were using zsh, you'd locate ~/.zshrc and append the directory like this:

```
export PATH= ... # other PATH goes there export PATH=$PATH:"~/elixir"
```

Here, you're specifying that one of the `PATH`s containing the elixir directory is located directly under the home directory.

Verifying your Elixir installation

The last thing to do is to check that Elixir has been installed correctly:

```
% elixir -v
```

If all goes well, you'll be greeted by the Erlang/OTP version and the Elixir version:

```
Erlang/OTP 18 [erts-7.2] [source] [64-bit] [smp:4:4] [async-threads:10]
[hipe] [kernel-poll:false] [dtrace]  Elixir 1.3.2
```

What are you waiting for? On to chapter 1!

index